A BIBLIOGRAPHY OF PINDAR
1513–1966

PHILOLOGICAL MONOGRAPHS
OF THE
AMERICAN PHILOLOGICAL ASSOCIATION

NUMBER 28

Accepted for publication by the Committee on the Publication of Monographs
of the American Philological Association

Edited by John Arthur Hanson, Princeton University

A BIBLIOGRAPHY OF PINDAR

1513–1966

By
DOUGLAS E. GERBER
University of Western Ontario

PUBLISHED FOR
THE AMERICAN PHILOLOGICAL ASSOCIATION

BY THE PRESS OF
CASE WESTERN RESERVE UNIVERSITY
1969

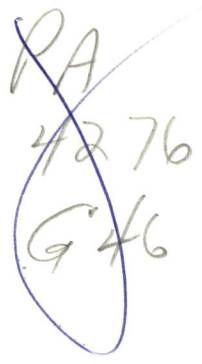

© The American Philological Association 1969

Library of Congress Catalog Number: 68–8750

Composed by William Clowes and Sons Ltd
London and Beccles, England

Photolithographed by Cushing-Malloy, Inc.
Ann Arbor, Michigan, U.S.A.

LEONARD WOODBURY

τροφεῖα

PREFACE

When I began as a graduate student to collect material for a dissertation on Pindar, I realized rather painfully that the length of my research would be reduced considerably if I did not have to work my way through the many bibliographical sources. It was then that the idea formed of compiling a list of material which would be of service to future students of Pindar. Over the years I kept adding to the bibliography begun in graduate school until finally I felt that my list was reasonably complete. It is my sincere hope that this compilation will save all those who are interested in Pindar from much of the bibliographical drudgery which has hitherto been necessary.

As a glance at the table of contents will indicate, the first part of the bibliography contains a list of texts, translations, commentaries, and publications pertaining to specific odes and fragments or to specific verses. The enumeration assigned by Bruno Snell in the third edition of his Teubner text has been adopted throughout. Scholia are listed according to Drachmann. If a work is devoted to a specific ode or verse the reference will be found there. For example, an article on the metre of *Olympian One* would be listed under that ode, not under Metre. Whenever it might be uncertain what areas are included, explanatory notes are added after the chapter heading. An asterisk signifies that I have not been able to examine the work concerned and cannot therefore vouch for the appropriateness of the heading to which it is assigned or for the bibliographical data. The second part contains all other publications on Pindar. It has sometimes proved difficult to assign certain works to a specific heading and I have either listed such publications under more than one heading or relegated them to the last category. In the case of books I have generally made only one or two entries, but I have added the table of contents after the title whenever this would be of use. It would obviously be pointless to subdivide works such as Norwood's *Pindar* or Wilamowitz' *Pindaros*. Numbers in parentheses indicate that only those pages apply to a given entry. Reviews are inserted within square brackets. I have tried to retain the exact form of the titles of articles or books, even though there is much divergence in the use of punctuation and capital letters, but I have not made any use of italics. In addition to including works devoted exclusively or almost exclusively to Pindar, I have also attempted to include references to essentially non-Pindaric studies whenever these seemed sufficiently relevant to warrant insertion. Histories of literature, however, anthologies, and general books on metre are omitted. I had at one time thought of including unpublished dissertations, but since it would be virtually impossible to compile a complete list I have disregarded them. With a few exceptions I have not been able to insert publications which appeared later than March of 1967.

Some will no doubt feel that the value of this bibliography would have been enhanced by the insertion of comments on the material listed. For various reasons, however, I have generally not done so. Summaries of many works are impossible to make, except in very general terms which are of little or no assistance. Emendations could have been inserted, but these are so numerous that they deserve a separate monograph, one which I may some day attempt to compile. Value judgements would be invidious without a detailed examination of the arguments involved, and that would either result in a work of unwieldy size or require a second monograph. It has not been my intention to write a history of Pindaric criticism and I have preferred to let the individual scholar consult the works listed and pass his own judgement on their merits.

I now have the pleasant task of recording my gratitude to Mrs. Eileen Duffin who so conscientiously typed my manuscript, to Ivars Avotins who was of immeasurable assistance to me while I was working at Harvard University and made my stay in Cambridge so pleasant, to my colleague, Donald Hill, who searched on my behalf in several European libraries, and finally to Leonard Woodbury who has taught me so much about Greek poetry. To him with deepest affection and regard this book is dedicated.

CONTENTS

	Preface	vii
	List of Abbreviations	xi
1.	Texts	1
2.	Text and Commentary	4
3.	Text, Translation, and Commentary	5
4.	Translations	6
5.	Notes and Commentaries	9
6.	Selected Odes	11
7.	Olympian Odes	13
8.	Pythian Odes	42
9.	Nemean Odes	67
10.	Isthmian Odes	83
11.	Fragments	91
12.	Manuscripts	111
13.	Scholia	113
14.	Syntax	116
15.	Dialect	118
16.	Specific Words	119
17.	Style and Imagery	122
18.	Structure and Unity	126
19.	Metre	128
20.	Concept of Poetry	131
21.	Classification	132
22.	Religion and Myth	133
23.	Thought	138
24.	History and Politics	140
25.	Chronology	142
26.	Games	143
27.	Relationship to Other Writers	145
28.	Lexica	150
29.	Bibliography	151
30.	General and Miscellaneous	152

LIST OF ABBREVIATIONS

AA	Archäologischer Anzeiger
AAHG	Anzeiger für die Altertumswissenschaft
AAN	Atti della R. Accademia di Archeologia, Lettere e Belle Arti di Napoli
AAntHung	Acta Antiqua Academiae Scientiarum Hungaricae
AAT	Atti della R. Accademia delle Scienze di Torino
ABSA	Annual of the British School at Athens
AC	L'Antiquité Classique
AFC	Anales de Filologia Clásica
AIPhO	Annuaire de l'Institut de Philologie et d'Histoire Orientales et Slaves de l'Université Libre de Bruxelles
AIV	Atti del R. Istituto Veneto di Scienze, Lettere ed Arti
AJA	American Journal of Archaeology
AJP	American Journal of Philology
AK	Antike Kunst
APF	Archiv für Papyrusforschung
ARW	Archiv für Religionswissenschaft
ASNP	Annali della Scuola Normale Superiore di Pisa
ASS	Archivio Storico Siciliano
ASSO	Archivio Storico per la Sicilia Orientale
AUMLA	Journal of the Australasian Universities Language and Literature Association
A&A	Antike und Abendland
A&R	Atene e Roma
BAClLg	Bulletin semestriel de l'Association des Classiques de l'Université de Liège
BAGB	Bulletin de l'Association G. Budé
BAGB(SC)	Bulletin de l'Association G. Budé (Supplément critique)
BAPC	Bulletin international de l'Académie Polonaise des Sciences et des Lettres de Cracovie
BBG	Blätter für das Bayerische Gymnasialwesen
BCLF	Bulletin Critique du Livre Français
BCO	Bibliotheca Classica Orientalis
BELL	Études de Lettres. Bulletin de la Société des Études de Lettres, Université de Lausanne
BF	Boletim de Filologia
BFC	Bollettino di Filologia Classica
BIBR	Bulletin de l'Institut Historique Belge de Rome
BICS	Bulletin of the Institute of Classical Studies of the University of London
BKIS	Beiträge zur Kunde der Indogermanischen Sprachen

BLK	Bibliothek der alten Litteratur und Kunst
BMB	Bulletin Bibliographique et Pédagogique du Musée Belge
BO	Bibliotheca Orientalis
BPW	Berliner Philologische Wochenschrift
BQR	Bodleian Quarterly Record
BSG	Berichte über die Verhandlungen der kgl. Sächsischen Gesellschaft der Wissenschaften zu Leipzig
BSI	La Biblioteca delle Scuole Italiane
BSL	Bulletin de la Société de Linguistique de Paris
ByzZ	Byzantinische Zeitschrift
CB	Classical Bulletin
CP	Classical Philology
CQ	Classical Quarterly
CR	Classical Review
CRAI	Comptes Rendus de l'Académie des Inscriptions et Belles-Lettres
CS	Critica Storica
CW	Classical World (formerly Classical Weekly)
DLZ	Deutsche Literatur-Zeitung
EA	Ἐφημερὶς Ἀρχαιολογική
EBS	Ἐπετηρὶς Ἑταιρείας Βυζαντινῶν Σπουδῶν
EClás	Estudios Clásicos
EEAth	Ἐπιστημονικὴ Ἐπετηρὶς τῆς φιλοσοφικῆς Σχολῆς τοῦ Πανεπιστημίου Ἀθηνῶν
EO	Échos d'Orient
EPh	Ἐφημερὶς τῶν Φιλομαθῶν
EPK	Egyetemes Philologiai Közlöny
Eos(S)	Eos: Süddeutsche Zeitschrift für Philologie und Gymnasialwesen
FL	Forum der Letteren
GGA	Göttingische Gelehrte Anzeigen
GIF	Giornale Italiano di Filologia
GRBS	Greek, Roman and Byzantine Studies
G&R	Greece and Rome
HJ	Historisches Jahrbuch
HSCP	Harvard Studies in Classical Philology
HTR	Harvard Theological Review
Hum(RES)	Humanités: Revue d'Enseignement Secondaire et d'Éducation
ICS	L'Italia Che Scrive
IL	L'Information Littéraire
JAI	Jahrbücher des Deutschen Archäologischen Instituts
JAW	Jahresbericht über die Fortschritte der Klassischen Altertumswissenschaft
JCS	Journal of Classical Studies: The Journal of the Classical Society of Japan
JCSP	Journal of Classical and Sacred Philology

JHS	Journal of Hellenic Studies
JMI	Journal du Ministre de l'Instruction Publique en Russie, Philologie Classique
JOEAI	Jahreshefte des Oesterreichischen Archäologischen Instituts
JP	Journal of Philology
JPh	Jahrbücher für Classische Philologie
JPhV	Jahresbericht des Philologischen Vereins zu Berlin (Supp. to ZG)
JPP	Jahrbücher für Philologie und Paedagogik
JPP(S)	Jahrbücher für Philologie und Paedagogik: Supplementband
JS	Journal des Savants
KK	Kwartalnik Klaszczny
LEC	Les Études Classiques
LF	Listy Filologické
LSCP	Leipziger Studien zur Classischen Philologie
LZB	Literarisches Zentralblatt für Deutschland
MB	Musée Belge
MC	Il Mondo Classico
MH	Museum Helveticum
MMAI	Monuments et Mémoires publiés par l'Académie des Inscriptions et Belles-Lettres (Fondation Piot)
MPh	Museum: Tijdschrift voor Philologie en Geschiedenis
MUB	Mélanges de l'Université Saint Joseph
Mnem	Mnemosyne
NJA	Neue Jahrbücher für das Klassische Altertum
NPR	Neue Philologische Rundschau
NRTh	Nouvelle Revue Théologique
NSM	Neues Schweizer Museum
NTF	Nordisk Tidsskrift for Filologi
PA	Philologischer Anzeiger
PAA	Πρακτικὰ τῆς ᾽Ακαδημίας ᾽Αθηνῶν
PACA	Proceedings of the African Classical Association
PCA	Proceedings of the Classical Association
PCPS	Proceedings of the Cambridge Philological Society
PhS	Philologische Studien
PhW	Philologische Wochenschrift
PP	La Parola del Passato
PU	Philologische Untersuchungen
P&I	Le Parole e le Idee
RA	Revue Archéologique
RAAN	Rendiconti della Accademia di Archeologia, Lettere e Belle Arti di Napoli
RAL	Rendiconti della R. Accademia dei Lincei
RB	Revue Bénédictine
RBPh	Revue Belge de Philologie et d'Histoire

RC	Revue Critique d'Histoire et de Littérature
RCC	Revue des Cours et Conférences
RCCM	Rivista di Cultura Classica e Medioevale
RCl	Rivista Clasica
RDM	Revue des Deux Mondes
REA	Revue des Études Anciennes
REByz	Revue des Études Byzantines
REur	Rivista Europea
REC	Revista de Estudios Clásicos
REG	Revue des Études Grecques
REL	Revue des Études Latines
RFC	Rivista di Filologia Classica
RFIC	Rivista di Filologia e di Istruzione Classica
RHR	Revue de l'Histoire des Religions
RI	Rivista d'Italia
RIB	Revue de l'Instruction Publique en Belgique
RIGI	Rivista Indo-Greca-Italica di Filologia, Lingua, Antichità
RIL	Rendiconti dell' Istituto Lombardo, Classe di Lettere, Scienze Morali e Storiche
RLC	Rassegna Italiana di Lingue e Letterature Classiche
RPAA	Rendiconti della Pontificia Accademia di Archeologia
RPh	Revue de Philologie
RPhilos	Revue Philosophique de la France et de l'Étranger
RSA	Rivista di Storia Antica e Scienze Affini
RSC	Rivista di Studi Classici
RSF	Rivista Critica di Storia della Filosofia
RUB	Revue de l'Université de Bruxelles
RécSR	Recherches de Science Religieuse
RhM	Rheinisches Museum für Philologie
SAWM	Sitzungsberichte der Akademie der Wissenschaften zu München
SAWW	Sitzungsberichte der Akademie der Wissenschaften in Wien
SIFC	Studi Italiani di Filologia Classica
SMSR	Studi e Materiali di Storia delle Religioni
SO	Symbolae Osloenses
SPAW	Sitzungsberichte der Preussischen Akademie der Wissenschaften zu Berlin
SicGymn	Siculorum Gymnasium
Sok	Sokrates (cf. ZG)
StudClas	Studii Clasice
StudUrb	Studi Urbinati di Storia, Filosofia e Letteratura
Syll	Ὁ ἐν Κωνσταντινουπόλει Ἑλληνικὸς Φιλολογικὸς Σύλλογος
TAPA	Transactions of the American Philological Association
TCPS	Transactions of the Cambridge Philological Society
TLS	Times Literary Supplement

TOPS	Transactions of the Oxford Philological Society
TPS	Transactions of the Philological Society
UR	Ungarische Rundschau
WKPh	Wochenschrift für Klassische Philologie
WS	Wiener Studien
YCS	Yale Classical Studies
ZA	Zeitschrift für die Altertumswissenschaft
ZAnt	Živa Antika
ZG	Zeitschrift für das Gymnasialwesen (=Sokrates from 1913)
ZOEG	Zeitschrift für die Österreichischen Gymnasien
ZPhF	Zeitschrift für Philosophische Forschung
ZVS	Zeitschrift für Vergleichende Sprachforschung auf dem Gebiete der Indogermanischen Sprachen

1. TEXTS

Editions containing brief notes are included here rather than under the following section.

AHLWARDT, C. W. *Pindari carmina*. Editio minor (Leipzig 1820).
BECK, C. D. *Pindari carmina et fragmenta Graece, Cum scholiis integris*. 2 vols. (Leipzig 1792–95).
BERGK, T. *Pindari carmina* (=Part 1 of *Poetae Lyrici Graeci*) Leipzig 1843, 1853², 1866³, 1878⁴. See also his *Addenda et Corrigenda* (Halle 1867) to his 3rd edition.

[E. J. Kiehl, *Mnem* 2 (1853) 257–64; F. W. Schneidewin, *Beiträge zur Kritik der Poetae Lyrici Graeci edidit Theodorus Bergk* (Göttingen 1844); W. Christ, "Randbemerkungen zu Th. Bergks neuester Bearbeitung des Pindaros," *JPh* 119 (1879) 1–14; R. Rauchenstein, *JPh* 77 (1858) 248–58.]

BOECKH, A. *Pindari carmina quae supersunt, cum deperditorum fragmentis selectis*. Editio secunda correctior. Addita sunt metrorum notatio, index carminum et temporum ac varietas lectionis Heynianae (Leipzig 1825).
BOISSONADE, J. F. *Pindarus* (Paris 1825).
BOWRA, C. M. *Pindari Carmina cum fragmentis* (Oxford 1935, 1947²).

[T. S. Duncan, *CJ* 34 (1939) 244–5; P. Chantraine, *RPh* 3rd S., 11 (1937) 157–9; J. T. Allen, *AJP* 58 (1937) 230–1; La Rue Van Hook, *CW* 30 (1937) 274; D. M. Robinson, *CP* 32 (1937) 280–3; H. J. Rose, *CR* 50 (1936) 14–16; A. Turyn, *Gnomon* 12 (1936) 360–7.]

CALLIERGES, Z. Πινδάρου, Ὀλύμπια. Πύθια. Νέμεα. Ἴσθμια. Μετὰ ἐξηγήσεως παλαιᾶς πάνυ ὠφελίμου καὶ σχολίων ὁμοίων (Rome 1515). An edition based on this "hinc inde a viro quodam docto correcta et depravata" (Fabricius) was published in Frankfurt, 1542.
*CEPORINUS, J. *Pindari Olympia, Pythia, Nemea, Isthmia* (Basel 1526, repr. 1556). Introduction by U. Zwingli.
CHRIST, W. *Pindari carmina cum deperditorum fragmentis selectis* (Leipzig 1869, repr. 1891, 1897²).

[A. B. Drachmann, *PhW* 18 (1898) 289–91; T. Reinach, *REG* 11 (1898) 234–5; *PA* 2 (1870) 321–3.]

*JANZON, J. P. *Pindari carmina quae supersunt edenda strophasque carminum in cola et semicola secundum rhythmum dispartiendas* (Lund 1841).
*MANUTIUS, A. Πινδάρου Ὀλύμπια, Πύθια, Νέμεα, Ἴσθμια. Καλλιμάχου ὕμνοι οἱ εὑρισκόμενοι. Διονυσίου Περιήγησις. Λυκόφρονος Ἀλεξάνδρα, τὸ σκοτεινὸν ποίημα (Venice 1513).
MOMMSEN, C. J. T. *Pindari carmina* (Berlin 1864).

[C. F. Schnitzer, *Eos(S)* 2 (1866) 269–93.]

*MOREL, W. *Pindari Olympia, Pythia, Nemea, Isthmia* (Paris 1558). The editor is uncertain, but according to Fabricius is probably Morel.

NEGRIS, A. *The Works of Pindar*; with various Readings, Notes, and Emendations (Edinburgh 1835).
*RAPHELENGIUS, F. *Pindari Olympia, Pythia, Nemea, Isthmia* (Leiden 1590).
SCHNEIDEWIN, F. G. *Pindari carmina cum deperditorum fragmentis selectis* (Leipzig 1850; rev. ed. 1865).
   [R. Rauchenstein, *JPh* 77 (1858) 405–6.]
SCHROEDER, O. *Pindari carmina* (=vol. 1, part 1 of the 5th ed. of T. Bergk, *Poetae Lyrici Graeci*, Leipzig 1900).
   [A. B. Drachmann, *PhW* 21 (1901) 641–7; A. Körte, *GGA* 163 (1901) 960–72.]
SCHROEDER, O. *Pindari carmina cum fragmentis selectis* (Leipzig 1908, 1914², 1930³).
   [E. B. Clapp, *CP* 4 (1909) 463–5; P. Maas, *DLZ* 30 (1909) 411–15; G. Fraccaroli, *RFIC* 37 (1909) 420–9; H. Alline, *RPh* NS 36 (1912) 323; My., *RC* 2 (1914) 103; G. Fraccaroli, *RFIC* 42 (1914) 506–8; H. Jurenka, *ZOEG* 65 (1914) 712–14; J. Sitzler, *BPW* 35 (1915) 609–11; K. Kuiper, *MPh* 22 (1915) 322–3; P. Shorey, *CP* 26 (1931) 454; *BAGB(SC)* 3 (1931) 66; D. S. Robertson, *CR* 45 (1931) 195–6; E. Kalinka, *PhW* 51 (1931) 897–8; A. Puech, *RPh* 3rd S., 6 (1932) 192; B. Snell, *Gnomon* 8 (1932) 329–30.]
SNELL, B. *Pindari carmina cum fragmentis* (Leipzig 1953, 1955², 1959³ (pars prior: Epinicia), 1964³ (pars altera: Fragmenta), 1964⁴ (pars prior: Epinicia).
   [J. C. Kamerbeek, *MPh* 59 (1954) 151–3; É. des Places, *RecSR* 42 (1954) 405; C. Gallavotti, *GIF* 7 (1954) 363–4; G. M. Kirkwood, *CW* 47 (1954) 189–90; R. Ruelle, *LEC* 22 (1954) 117; É. des Places, *AC* 23 (1954) 193–4; A. Colonna, *RFIC* 83 (1955) 74–9; D. S. Robertson, *CR* NS 5 (1955) 31–3; J. Irigoin, *RPh* 3rd S., 29 (1955) 76–8; Q. Cataudella, *SicGymn* 9 (1956) 122–4; E. Thummer, *AAHG* 9 (1956) 73–4; J. Irigoin, *REG* 69 (1956) 473–4; R. Ruelle, *LEC* 24 (1956) 299; W. Kullmann, *Gymnasium* 67 (1960) 246; A. Barigazzi, *Athenaeum* NS 34 (1956) 367–8; G. Rochefort, *BAGB* 4th S., No. 3 (1956) 116; E. Janssens, *RUB* 9 (1956–57) 112–113; B. A. van Groningen, *Mnem* 4th S., 10 (1957) 71; E. V. Marmorale, *GIF* 10 (1957) 69–70; D. S. Robertson, *CR* NS 7 (1957) 159; É. des Places, *AC* 26 (1957) 187; M. H. da Rocha Pereira, *Humanitas* NS 4–5 (1955–56) XLV–VII; P. Chantraine, *RPh* 3rd S., 31 (1957) 108; A. Garzya, *P&I* 1 (1959) 246; D. S. Robertson, *CR* NS 10 (1960) 254; R. Loriaux, *LEC* 28 (1960) 101; F. Lasserre, *AC* 29 (1960) 444–5; M. H. da Rocha Pereira, *Humanitas* NS 8–9 (1959–60) XI–XII; M. F. Galiano, *Emerita* 28 (1960) 332–3; J. Irigoin, *REG* 73 (1960) 275–6; E. Thummer, *AAHG* 16 (1963) 221; H. A. Pohlsander, *CW* 58 (1964–65) 220; J. A. Davison, *JHS* 85 (1965) 174; A. Garzya, *P&I* 6 (1964) 309; C. Gallavotti, *Gnomon* 37 (1965) 445–8; H. A. Pohlsander, *CW* 59 (1965–66) 52; P. Chantraine, *RPh* 3rd S., 39 (1965) 123.]
TURYN, A. *Pindari carmina cum fragmentis* (New York 1944 [Epinicia only], Cracow 1948, Oxford 1952²).

[R. Lattimore, *AJA* 48 (1944) 398–9; E. A. Robinson, *Traditio* 2 (1944) 513–9; E. S. Forster, *JHS* 64 (1944) 121; A. Severyns, *AC* 14 (1945) 179–80; M. F. Galiano, *Emerita* 13 (1945) 319–34; G. Norwood, *CP* 41 (1946) 172–4; P. Maas, *CR* 60 (1946) 24; C. Gallavotti, *RFIC* 74 (1946) 173–5; W. B. Stanford, *Hermathena* 68 (1946) 91–2; P. Chantraine, *RPh* 3rd S., 20 (1946) 161–2; E. Vanderborght, *RBPh* 25 (1946–47) 166–8; D. M. Robinson, *CJ* 42 (1947) 246–7; P. Friedländer, *AJP* 69 (1948) 214–17; E. Malcovati, *Athenaeum* NS 27 (1949) 307–10; A. Severyns, *AC* 18 (1949) 432–3; C. Gallavotti, *PP* 4 (1949) 284–5; W. Steffen, *Eos* 43 (1948–49) 127–8; W. Theiler, *MH* 6 (1949) 230–1; T. Sinko, *Bulletin du centre polonais de recherches scientifiques de Paris* 4 (1949) 30–3; M. Untersteiner, *Paideia* 5 (1950) 134–9; J. Němec, *LF* 74 (1950) 129–31; G. M. Kirkwood, *CW* 44 (1950) 57–8; D. S. Robertson, *CR* 64 (1950) 16; H. Lloyd-Jones, *JHS* 71 (1951) 267–8; Q. Cataudella, *SicGymn* 4 (1951) 145–6; J. Irigoin, *RPh* 3rd S., 25 (1951) 236–43; E. Wyckoff, *CP* 46 (1951) 39–42; R. Ruelle, *LEC* 21 (1953) 257–8; W. C. Korfmacher, *CB* 30 (1954) 59.]

WEISE, C. H. *Pindari epinicia*. Adiectis metrorum schematibus notisque criticis (Leipzig 1810; nova editio 1845).

2. TEXT AND COMMENTARY

CHRIST, W. *Pindari carmina prolegomenis et commentariis instructa* (Leipzig 1896).

    [A. B. Drachmann, *BPW* 17 (1897) 228–35; R. Y. Tyrrell, *CR* 11 (1897) 59–61; B. L. Gildersleeve, *AJP* 17 (1896) 517–18; T. Reinach, *REG* 11 (1898) 234–5; C. O. Zuretti, *BFC* 3 (1897) 132–4; G. Fraccaroli, *RFIC* 25 (1897) 108–18; W. Jaspar, *MB* 2 (1898) 237–40.]

COOKESLEY, W. G. *Pindari carmina*, ad fidem textus Böckhiani, cum fragmentis et indice, 2 vols. (Eton 1849–51).

DISSEN, L. *Pindari carmina quae supersunt cum deperditorum fragmentis selectis ex recensione Boeckhii*, 2 vols. (Gotha 1830). 2nd ed. enlarged and revised by F. G. Schneidewin (Gotha 1843 and 1847). The commentary applies only to the *Olympian* and *Pythian* odes.

    [G. Hermann, *JPP* 1 (1831) 44–91; F. G. Welcker, *RhM* 1 (1833) 461–85 (also in *Kleine Schriften* 2, Bonn 1845, 169–90); A. Boeckh, *Gesammelte Kleine Schriften* 7 (Leipzig 1872) 369–403.]

DONALDSON, J. W. *Pindar's Epinician or Triumphal Odes, in four books; together with the Fragments of his Lost Compositions: revised and explained* (London 1841; new ed. 1868).

FENNELL, C. A. M. *Pindar: The Olympian and Pythian Odes*, with notes explanatory and critical, introductions, and introductory essays (Cambridge 1879, new ed. 1893).

    [W. R. Hardie, *CR* 8 (1894) 49–50; B. L. Gildersleeve, *AJP* 14 (1893) 498–501; J. Sitzler, *NPR* (1894) 354–7.]

FENNELL, C. A. M. *Pindar: The Nemean and Isthmian Odes*, with notes explanatory and critical, introductions, and introductory essays (Cambridge 1883; new ed. 1899).

    [G. Davies, *CR* 14 (1900) 64–5.]

*HÓMANN, O. *Versezetei kritikai es Magyarázó jegyzetekkel kiadta* (Leipzig 1876).

3. TEXT, TRANSLATION, AND COMMENTARY

BENEDICTUS, J. Πινδάρου Περίοδος. *Pindari Olympia, Pythia, Nemea, Isthmia* (Saumur 1620).

BOECKH, A. *Pindari opera quae supersunt.* 2 vols., each in 2 parts (Leipzig 1811–21, vol. 2, 2 repr. Hildesheim 1963). 1, 1: text. 1, 2: metrical commentary and critical notes on the odes. 2, 1: scholia. 2, 2: Latin translation and commentary, fragments, indexes. The commentary on the *Nemean* and *Isthmian* odes is by L. Dissen.

CERRATO, L. *Pindaro, Le Odi. Testo, note e appendice con versione italiana* (Turin 1915, rev. ed. 1934).
  [A. Taccone, *MC* 5 (1935) 254–5; M. Valgimigli, *Leonardo* 7 (1936) 301.]

*DOUKAS, N. Πίνδαρος, παραφρασθείς, σχολιασθείς τε καὶ ἐκδοθείς, 3 vols. (Athens 1842).

FARNELL, L. R. *The Works of Pindar.* I: Translation in rhythmical prose with literary comments. II: Critical commentary. III: Text (London 1930–32, commentary repr. Amsterdam 1961 and 1965).
  [O. Schroeder, *PhW* 51 (1931) 529–31 (vol. 1); D. S. Robertson, *CR* 45 (1931) 136–7 (vol. 1); *JHS* 51 (1931) 136–7 (vol. 1); A. Puech, *REG* 44 (1931) 463 (vol. 1); A. Puech, *REG* 46 (1933) 360 (vols. 2–3); O. Schroeder, *PhW* 53 (1933) 113–18 (vols. 2–3); D. S. Robertson, *CR* 46 (1932) 205–8 (vols. 2–3). See also L. R. Farnell, "Pindar: a Reply," *CR* 47 (1933) 9–11 and D. S. Robertson, "Pindar: a Rejoinder," *CR* 47 (1933) 61–2; H. J. Rose, *JHS* 52 (1932) 321–3 (vols. 1–3); G. Coppola, *BFC* 39 (1933) 261–4 (vols. 1–3); M. Untersteiner, *MC* 3 (1933) 453–61 (vols. 1–3).]

*FRESSE-MONTVAL, A. *Pindare.* Oeuvres complètes traduites en vers accompagnées de la vie de ce poète, de prolégomènes et de notes historiques, littéraires, philosophiques et critiques (Paris 1854).

HARTUNG, J. A. *Pindar's Werke.* Griechisch mit metrischer Uebersetzung und prüfenden und erklärenden Anmerkungen, 4 vols. (Leipzig 1855–56).
  [R. Rauchenstein, *JPh* 77 (1858) 385–405.]

HEYNE, C. G. *Pindari carmina et fragmenta*; cum lectionis varietate et annotationibus, 3 vols. (Göttingen 1773; enlarged ed. 1797–99, repr. Oxford 1807–09; revised and enlarged ed. by G. H. Schaefer, Leipzig 1817, repr. London 1824).

KLEANTHES, K. Πινδάρου τὰ σωζόμενα μετὰ μεταφράσεων σημειώσεων καὶ πίνακος τῶν λέξεων, 5 vols. (Trieste 1886–87).
  [B. L. Gildersleeve, *AJP* 11 (1890) 529.]

LEKATSAS, P. G. Πίνδαρος. εἰσαγωγή. ἔμμετρη μετάφραση. ἑρμηνευτικά (Athens 1938).
  [B. Lavagnini, *RFIC* 68 (1941) 145.]

SCHMID, E. Πινδάρου Περίοδος hoc est Pindari lyricorum principis, plus quam sexcentis in locis emaculati, ut iam legi et intelligi possit, Ὀλυμπιονῖκαι. Πυθιονῖκαι. Νεμεονῖκαι. Ἰσθμιονῖκαι. illustrati (Wittenberg 1616).

4. TRANSLATIONS

Editions containing a text as well as a translation are included here.

*Acaico, I. *Odas de Píndaro traducidas en verso castellano*, con notas (Mexico 1882).

*Adimari, A. *Ode di Pindaro tradotte e dichiarate, con osservazioni e confronti di alcuni luoghi immitati o tocchi da Orazio Flacco* (Pisa 1631).

*Balbes, S. D. Πινδάρου 'Επίνικοι. Μεταγραφέντες ἐμμέτρως εἰς τὴν νέαν ἑλληνίδα φωνὴν χάριν τῶν πολλῶν (Athens 1904).

*Baring, T. C. *Pindar in English rhyme*, being an attempt to render the Epinikian Odes with the principal remaining fragments of Pindar into English rhymed verse (London 1875).

*Billson, C. J. Πινδάρου 'Επινίκια: *Pindar's Odes of Victory*. The Olympian and Pythian Odes, with an Introduction and a Translation into English Verse (Oxford 1928).
 [D. S. Robertson, *CR* 43 (1929) 174–5; *JHS* 49 (1929) 136.]

*Billson, C. J. Πινδάρου 'Επινίκια: *Pindar's Odes of Victory*. The Nemean and Isthmian Odes, with an Introduction and a Translation into English Verse (Oxford 1930).
 [D. S. Robertson, *CR* 44 (1930) 197.]

*Boethke, K. A. *Pindar, Siegeslieder* (Jena 1912).
 [F. Friedersdorff, *Sok* 1 (1913) 335–8; W. Nestle, *BPW* 34 (1914) 257–9; F. Dornseiff, *WKPh* 31 (1914) 65–7.]

*Boissonade, J. F. *Pindare Odes*. Traduction nouvelle, complétée et publiée par E. Egger (Grenoble and Paris 1867).

*Borghi, G. *Le odi di Pindaro* (Milan 1825)

*Colin, F. *Pindare, traduction complète. Olympiques, Pythiques, Neméennes, Isthmiques, Fragments avec discours préliminaire, arguments et notes* (Strasbourg 1841).

*Csengery, J. *Pindaros* (Budapest 1929).

*Damm, C. T. *Versuch einer prosaischen Uebersetzung der griechischen Lieder des Pindars*, 4 pts. in 1 vol. (Berlin and Leipzig 1770–71).

*Donner, J. J. C. *Pindars Siegesgesänge*. Deutsch in den Versmassen der Urschrift (Leipzig 1860).

Dornseiff, F. *Pindar*, übersetzt und erläutert (Leipzig 1921).
 [H. Fränkel, *GGA* 184 (1922) 199; E. von Prittwitz-Gaffron, *LZB* 72 (1921) 745; E. Bethe, *NJA* 49 (1922) 81–2; G. Calògero, *RFIC* 51 (1923) 354–60; O. Schroeder, *PhW* 42 (1922) 937–9.]

Fabricius, J. A. *Omnia Pindari quae exstant Olympia Pythia Nemeahmia Istcum interpretatione latina*, 2 vols. (Venice 1762).

*Faehse, G. *Pindars Siegeshymnen*, metrisch übersetzt, 2 vols. (Leipzig 1804–06, 1824²).

Fraccaroli, G. See under "Notes and Commentaries."

*Ganter, F. *Pindars Siegesklänge aus der griechischen Urschrift verdeutscht* (Donaueschingen 1844).

*DE LA GAUSIE, P. *Pindare* (Paris 1626).
*GEILINGER, M. *Altgriechische Lyrik. Bakchylides und Pindar auf Grund von Uebersetzungen in zeitgemässer Kürzung* (Glarus 1937).
HEYNE, C. G. *Pindari carmina. Accedit versio latina*, 2 vols. (London 1823).
HÖLSCHER, U. (ED.) *Pindar, Siegeslieder. Deutsche Übertragungen.* Nachwort von B. Snell (Frankfurt 1962).
LATTIMORE, R. *The Odes of Pindar* (Chicago 1947).
    [R. A. Swanson, *CJ* 57 (1961) 84–5; *G&R* 17 (1948) 137–8; J. A. Davison, *JHS* 67 (1947) 138–9; W. B. Stanford, *Hermathena* 72 (1948) 138–9; E. S. Forster, *CR* 63 (1949) 33; H. N. Couch, *CW* 41 (1947–48) 221–2; G. Norwood, *CP* 43 (1948) 60–1.]
LAURENT, P. E. *The Odes of Pindar in English Prose*, with Explanatory Notes: to which is added West's Dissertation on the Olympic Games, 2 vols. (Oxford 1824).
*LECTIUS, J. *Pindarus graece et latine.* Vol. 2 of *Corpus Poetarum Graecorum* (Geneva 1614).
LONICER, J. *Pindari poetae vetustissimi, lyricorum facile principis, Olympia Pythia Nemea Isthmia per Ioan. Lonicerum latinitate donata: adhibitis enarrationibus, e Graecis Scholiis, et doctissimis utriusque linguae autoribus desumptis* (Basel 1535, repr. 1543, 1560). This is a revised and expanded version of his edition of 1528.
*LUDWIG, G. *Pindars Siegesgesänge*, metrisch übersetzt, 3 vols. (Stuttgart 1856).
*MARINI, F. *Pindare* (Paris 1607, repr. 1617, 1677).
*MELANCHTHON, P. *Pindari Olympia, Pythia, Nemea, Isthmia, per Philippum Melanchthonem latinitate donata* (Basel 1558).
*MENCARINI, A. *Odas de Píndaro traducidas en verso* (Barcelona 1888).
*MERELLO, M. *Pindaro, Le Odi* (Genoa 1933).
*MITTLER, A. & BOGNER, H. *Pindar, Siegesgesänge* (Berlin 1923).
    [O. Schroeder, *PhW* 44 (1924) 511–12.]
*MOBERLY, G. *The Odes of Pindar translated into English Metre* (Winchester 1876).
*MONTES DE OCA, I. *Odas de Píndaro*, traducidas en verso castellano con carta, prólogo y notas (Madrid 1883).
MOMMSEN, J. T. *Des Pindaros Werke in die Versmaasse des Originals uebersetzt* (Leipzig 1846, 1852²).
*MURISON, A. F. *The Odes of Pindar rendered in English Verse* (London 1933).
    [E. S. Forster, *CR* 47 (1933) 125–6.]
MYERS, E. *The Extant Odes of Pindar*, translated into English with an introduction and short notes (London 1874, 1884²).
    [T. Maguire, "Myers' Pindar," *Hermathena* 4 (1883) 121–32.]
PALEY, F. A. *The Odes of Pindar.* Translated into English prose, with brief explanatory notes and a preface (London 1868).
*POYARD, C. *Pindare, Oeuvres complètes.* Nouvelle édition, complètement refondue, augmentée d'Anacréon, de Sappho et d'Erinna (Paris 1853, nouv. ed. 1881).

PUECH, A. *Pindare. Olympiques, Pythiques, Néméennes, Isthmiques et Fragments*, 4 vols. (Paris 1922–23, repr. several times).
 [A. Delatte, *BMB* 28 (1924) 145–6; O. Schroeder, *PhW* 44 (1924) 512–13; C. del Grande, *RIGI* 8 (1924) 296–7; S. Reinach, *RA* 18 (1923) 372.]

SANDYS, J. *The Odes of Pindar* (London 1915, repr. many times).
 [B. L. Gildersleeve, *AJP* 37 (1916) 88–92; G. C. Scoggin, *CJ* 13 (1917) 141–3; W. M. L. Hutchinson, *CR* 31 (1917) 98–100; *JHS* 36 (1916) 121; O. Schroeder, *PhW* 42 (1922) 937–9.]

*SCHNITZER, C. F. *Pindars Siegesgesänge*. Metrisch verdeutscht, 9 parts (Stuttgart and Berlin 1860–66).

STEPHANUS, H. *Pindari Olympia, Pythia, Nemea, Isthmia, Caeterorum octo-lyricorum carmina, Alcaei, Sapphus, Stesichori, Ibyci, Anacreontis, Bacchylidis, Simonidis, Alcmanis, nonnulla etiam aliorum* (Paris 1560, 2nd ed. rev. 1566, 3rd ed. with notes by I. Casaubon 1586, 1600 [4], 1612 [5], 1624 [6]). Fabricius also records a "mera repetitio primae Stephanianae" by A. Portus with brief notes (Heidelberg 1598).

*STEPHANUS, P. *Pindari opera omnia cum scholiis graecis et interpretatione latina ad verbum* (Geneva 1599).

*SUDORIUS, N. *Pindari opera omnia latino carmine reddita per Nic. Sudorium et eiusdem commentarius in Nemea* (Paris 1575).

THIERSCH, F. *Pindarus Werke, Urschrift, Uebersetzung in den pindarischen Versmaassen und Erläuterungen*, 2 pts. (Leipzig 1820).

TRAVERSO, L. & GRASSI, E. *Pindaro, Odi e frammenti* (Florence 1956).
 [Q. Cataudella, *SicGymn* 11 (1958) 129.]

*TREMENHEERE, H. S. *Translations from Pindar into English blank verse* (London 1866).

TURNER, D. W. *The Odes of Pindar*, literally translated into English prose. To which is adjoined A Metrical Version by Abraham Moore (London 1852).

WAY, A. S. *Pindar in English Verse* (London 1922).
 [A. D. Godley, *CR* 37 (1923) 167–8.]

WEST, G., GREENE, R. B., PYE, H. J. *Odes of Pindar, translated from the Greek, with Notes and Illustrations: to which is prefixed, A Dissertation on the Olympic Games*, 2 vols. (London 1810).

WEST, R. & WELSTED, R. (EDD.) *Pindari Olympia, Pythia, Nemea, Isthmia. Una cum latina omnium versione carmine lyrico per Nicolaum Sudorium* (Oxford 1697). This edition also contains the metaphrasis of E. Schmid and the paraphrasis and argumenta of J. Benedictus.

WOLDE, L. *Pindar, Die Dichtungen und Fragmente*, verdeutscht und erläutert (Leipzig 1942, repr. Wiesbaden 1958).
 [E. Kalinka, *PhW* 63 (1943) 265–6; F. Dirlmeier, *DLZ* 64 (1943) 8–10.]

5. NOTES AND COMMENTARIES

This section contains textual studies which discuss too many passages for them to be given separate entries under the appropriate verses, as well as commentaries of a more general nature.

ARETIUS, B. *Commentarii absolutissimi in Pindari Olympia Pythia Nemea Isthmia* (Geneva 1587).

*BERGK, T. *Observationes in Pindarum et alios lyricos graecos*, 3 pts. (Progr. Halle 1867–68).

BLAYDES, F. H. M. *Adversaria in varios poetas graecos ac latinos* (Halle 1898) 53–9.

BOECKH, A. *Specimen emendationum in Pindari carmina* (Heidelberg 1810).

CIOFI, A. *Ad Pindari carmina observationes* (Viterbo 1875).

DOBREE, P. P. "In Pindarum," *Adversaria* vol. 4 (Berlin 1874) 5–6.

FRACCAROLI, G. *Le odi di Pindaro dichiarate e tradotte* (Verona 1894).
   [R. Y. Tyrrell, *CR* 8 (1894) 207–9; B. L. Gildersleeve, *AJP* 15 (1894) 501–7; L. Levi, *RFIC* 24 (1896) 549–58; J. Sitzler, *NPR* (1896) 97–9; E. Ferrai, "D'un nuovo interprete ed espositore degli Epinicii di Pindaro," *AIV* 7th S., 5 (1893–94) 1250–68; F. Flamini, "Una nuova traduzione di Pindaro," *Spigolature di erudizione e di critica* (Pisa 1895) 202–13.]

FRACCAROLI, G. *Pindaro, Le odi e i frammenti*. Traduzione con prolegomeni e commento, 2 vols. (Milan 1914).
   [D. Bassi, *RFIC* 43 (1915) 370–6.]

HEIMSOETH, F. *Addenda et corrigenda in commentariis Pindari* (Bonn 1840).

VAN HERWERDEN, H. *Pindarica* (Leipzig 1882). Also in *JPh* Suppl. 13 (1884) 1–32.
   [L. Bornemann, *PA* 13 (1889) 293–9.]

VAN HERWERDEN, H. *Studia critica et epicritica in Pindarum* (Traiecti ad Rhenum 1884).

HEYNE, C. G. *Additamenta ad lectionis varietatem in Pindari carminum editione Gottingensi 1773 notatam* (Göttingen 1791).

KAYSER, C. L. *Lectiones Pindaricae* (Heidelberg 1840).

LINDAU, A. F. Εἰς Πίνδαρον, *JPP(S)* 13 (1847) 176–7.

*LÖSCHHORN, K. *Kleine kritische Bemerkungen zu Aristophanes und Pindar* (Magdeburg 1916).
   [E.? Steinborn, *LZB* 68 (1917) 239; R. Wagner, *WKPh* 34 (1917) 889–90.]

MÉAUTIS, G. *Pindare le Dorien* (Neuchâtel 1962).
   [J. Malye, *BAGB* 4th S. (1962) 354–5; A. Garzya, *P&I* 4 (1962) 327; J. Defradas, *REG* 76 (1963) 193–7; F. Chamoux, *RPh* 3rd S., 37 (1963) 293–4; C. Picard, *RA* (1963) 231–5; J. Duchemin, *REA* 65 (1963) 416–9; É. des Places, *RecSR* 52 (1964) 458; P. Chantraine, *CRAI* 8 (1963) 124–5; L. W. Daly, *AJP* 86 (1965) 106–8.]

MEZGER, F. *Pindars Siegeslieder* (Leipzig 1880).
    [B. L. Gildersleeve, *AJP* 2 (1881) 497–501.]
*MINGARELLI, D. I. A. *Coniecturae de Pindari odis* (Bonn 1772). Fabricius states that these conjectures are recorded in *Bibliotheca Philologica* 2, pt. 8 (Göttingen 1774) 645–73.
DE PAUW, J. C. *Notae in Pindari Olympia, Pythia, Nemea, Isthmia* (Traiecti ad Rhenum 1747).
PORTUS, F. *Commentarii in Pindari Olympia, Pythia, Nemea, Isthmia* (Geneva 1583).
RAUCHENSTEIN, R. *Commentationum Pindaricarum particula prima* (Aarau 1844).
    [T. Mommsen, *RhM* 4 (1846) 539–66.]
SCHMIDT, M. See under "Olympian Odes General" (XCV–CXLVI).
SCHNITZER, C. F. "Handschriftliche Anmerkungen des Martin Crusius zu Pindar nebst einer Probe daraus," *Eos(S)* 2 (1866) 334–8.
SCHNITZER, C. F. *De Pindaro nuperrime emendato* (Ellwangen 1867).
    [*PA* 1 (1869) 39–42.]
SCHWICKERT, J. J. See under "Olympian Odes General" (43–51).
THIERSCH, F. "De copiis Victorianis in Homerum, Hesiodum, Pindarum et Tragicos," *Acta philologorum Monacensium* 1 (Monachii 1812) 307–37 (310–16).
THIERSCH, F. "Additamenta ad Hermanni editionem secundam Vigeri, necnon ad Boeckhii notas criticas in Pindarum," *Acta philologorum Monacensium* 2 (Monachii 1815–16) 261–90.
VON WILAMOWITZ-MOELLENDORFF, U. *Pindaros* (Berlin 1922, repr. 1966).
    [P. Kretschmer, *Glotta* 14 (1925) 199–200; C. del Grande, *RIGI* 8 (1924) 295–6; N. Terzaghi, *BFC* 29 (1923) 173–5; A. B. Drachmann, *DLZ* 43 (1922) 1101–7; A. Körte, *LZB* 74 (1923) 284–6; E. Bethe, *NJA* 51 (1923) 248–9; J. Vürtheim, *MPh* 30 (1923) 281–3; O. Schroeder, *PhW* 43 (1923) 49–55; Istvan Lajti, *EPK* 47 (1923) 98–100.]

6. SELECTED ODES

BOEHMER, E. *Pindars sicilische Oden nebst den epizephyrischen.* Mit Prosaübersetzung und Erläuterungen (Bonn 1891).
    [J. B. Bury, *CR* 7 (1893) 206–8.]

*BORGEAUD, W. *Pindare, Dix odes,* mises en français avec commentaire (Lausanne 1951).
    [A. Rivier, *BELL* 24 No. 4 (1952) 1–16.]

*DEUBER, F. A. *Duodena Pindari carmina graeco-latina* (Freiburg 1819; Editio altera imitationibus adaucta, Heidelberg 1820). *O.* 1, 4, 5, 11, 12, *P.* 6–8, 10, *N.* 2, 9, *I.* 3.

*DEUBER, F. A. *Pindari odae Olympicae et aliae novem selectae ex Graeco textu, qui cum metris additus est, in Latinas mutatae* (Freiburg 1832, repr. 1833). *O.* 1–14, *P.* 1, 6–8, 10, 12, *N.* 2, 9, *I.* 3.

GEDIKE, F. *Pindari carmina selecta.* Cum scholiis selectis suisque notis (Berlin 1786). *O.* 1, 2, 4, 5, 9, 11, 12, 14, *P.* 1, 6, 7, 9, 11, *N.* 1, 11, *I.* 3, 7.

GENTILI, B. *Lirica corale greca. Pindaro Bacchilide Simonide.* Con testo a fronte, versioni, introduzione e note (Parma 1965).

*HEZEL, W. F. *Erklärung einiger pindarischen Oden für Anfänger.* Mit beigefügtem griech. Text der erläuterten Oden (Riga 1805). *O.* 1, 2, 4, 5, 9, 11, 12, 14, *P.* 1.

LATTIMORE, R. *Some Odes of Pindar in New English Versions* (Norfolk 1942). *P.* 1, 3, 4, 8, 10.
    [D. Grene, *CP* 39 (1944) 264–5; D. S. Robertson, *CR* 58 (1944) 32.]

*LENZONI, C. *La Parafrasi di alcune Ode di Pindaro* (Florence 1631).

LYDE, L. W. *A Patchwork from Pindar* (Oxford 1932).
    [D. S. Robertson, *CR* 47 (1933) 36; *G&R* 2 (1932–33) 128.]

*MAZARI, G. *Odi scelte di Pindaro* (Sassari 1776).

*NEANDER, M. *Aristologia Pindarica graeco-latina, sive sententiae et loca selecta cum notis et uberioribus excerptis ex aliis graecis auctoribus ad sensum locorum Pindaricorum historicum facientibus* (Basel 1556).

*RÖHRER, J. G. *Versuch einer gebundenen Uebersetzung einiger Olympischen und Pythischen Hymnen.* Mit Anmerkungen, 3 vols. (Leipzig 1815–16).

SEYMOUR, T. D. *Selected Odes of Pindar,* with notes and an introduction (Boston 1882). *O.* 1, 2, 6, 7, 11, 12, 14, *P.* 1, 2, 4, *N.* 1, 2, *I.* 1, 5, 8.

*TUROLLA, E. *Inni siciliani di vittoria* (Venice 1945).

*VAUVILLIERS, J. F. *Essai sur Pindare. Contenant une traduction de quelque odes—avec une analyse raisonnée et des notes historiques, poétiques et grammaticales. Le tout précédé d'un discours sur Pindare et sur la vraie manière de le traduire* (Paris 1772).

*VAUVILLIERS, J. F. *Pindare. Traduction poétique des odes les plus remarquables, avec des analyses raisonnées et des notes historiques et grammaticales, précédée d'un discours sur ce poète et sur la vraie manière de le traduire* (Paris 1859).

*Veverka, V. *Z viteznych zpevu Pindarovych* (Prague 1901).

West, G. *Odes of Pindar*, with several other pieces in prose and verse, translated from the Greek. To which is prefixed a Dissertation on the Olympick Games (London 1749). *O.* 1–3, 5, 7, 11, 12, 14, *P.* 1, *N.* 1, 11, *I.* 2.

*Wiernikowski, J. *Pindari nonnullae odae, graece et polonice* (Wilnae 1824).

*Wirth, G. (ed.) *Griechische Lyrik, von den Anfängen bis zu Pindar (Griechisch und Deutsch)* (Munich 1963). *O.* 1, 5, 6, 12, *P.* 1, 3, *N.* 3, 6, Frr. 110–19, 129–33.

7. OLYMPIAN ODES

General

*Bothe, E. H. *Pindars Olympische Oden in ihrem Sylbenmaasse übersetzt und mit einer kurzen Biographie dieses Dichters, nebst Bemerkungen über die Werke desselben*, 2 vols. (Berlin 1808).

*Cerrato, L. *Le Odi di Pindaro. Testo, versione e commento. Parte I: Olimpiche* (Sestri Ponente 1915).

[A. Beltrami, *Athenaeum* 5 (1917) 181–6; C. Cessi, *BFC* 24 (1918) 63–5; D. Bassi, *RFIC* 44 (1916) 341–2; C. Cessi, *RLC* 1 (1918) 88–93; B. L. Gildersleeve, *AJP* 37 (1916) 242–3; N. Terzaghi, *RIGI* 2 (1918) 183–4.]

*Chistoni, P. *Pindaro, Le odi Olimpiche*, con introduzione, proemi e note (Rome & Milan 1910).

[V. Brugnola, *BFC* 17 (1911) 194–6; N. Terzaghi, *A&R* 13 (1910) 377–8. See also P. Chistoni "Per una recensione," *A&R* 14 (1911) 150–1 and N. Terzaghi, "Replica," *A&R* 14 (1911) 185–7.]

*Costa, Giovanni & Costa, Giuseppe. *Pindaro, Odi Olimpiche* (Padua 1933).

[A. Taccone, *MC* 4 (1934) 205–6; C. Cessi, *Aevum* 8 (1934) 203–5.]

Dornseiff, F. *Pindars Olympische Hymnen* (Leipzig 1937, rev. ed. Wiesbaden 1960).

[E. Kalinka, *PhW* 59 (1939) 337.]

*Flores, F. *Odi olimpiachi di Pindaro volgarizzate* (Vercelli 1866).

Galiano, M. F. *Pindaro, Olimpicas*. Texto, Introducción y notas (Madrid 1944, 2nd ed. rev. 1956).

[M. Dolç, *EClás* 5 (1959) 143–4; R. Weil, *REG* 70 (1957) 536–7; P. Chantraine, *RPh* 3rd S., 32 (1958) 310–11; A. Barigazzi, *Athenaeum* NS 36 (1958) 282; M. H. da Rocha Pereira, *Humanitas* NS 6–7 (1957–58) lxxxiii–v; É. des Places, *AC* 26 (1957) 187–8; D. S. Robertson, *CR* NS 7 (1957) 201–3; A. Setti, *A&R* NS 2 (1957) 113–7; J. Alsina Clota, *Helmantica* 8 (1957) 143–4; F. Charlier, *LEC* 25 (1957) 483; F. J. Sanmarti, *Arbor* 36 (1957) 130–1; J. Duchemin, *REA* 59 (1957) 415–6.]

Gautier, G. 'Ολυμπιονῖκαι. *I vincitori olimpici di Pindaro*. Tradotti in Italiane canzoni ed illustrati con postille (Rome 1762).

*Gedicke, F. *Pindars Olympische Siegshymnen* (Berlin & Leipzig 1777).

Gildersleeve, B. L. *Pindar. The Olympian and Pythian Odes*, with an introductory essay, notes, and indexes (New York 1885, 1890², repr. Amsterdam 1966). For errata see *AJP* 15 (1894) 399.

*Guichemerre, J. *Pindare Olympiques*, traduites en vers français avec analyses littéraires et notes (Paris 1845).

Gurlitt, J. *Pindars Olympische Siegesgesänge*, übersetzt mit Anmerkungen (Hamburg & Leipzig 1810).

Houghton, H. P. *The Olympian Odes of Pindar* (Northfield 1949). Translation.

de Jongh, A. *Pindari carmina Olympia*. Cum annotatione critica, interpretatione Latina et commentario (Traiecti ad Rhenum 1865).

*Lekatsas, P. Πινδάρου, Α΄. Ὀλυμπιακά. Μετάφραση (Athens 1935).

*Mariani, L. *Le Olimpiache di Pindaro* (Naples 1887). Translation.

*Mayne, C. *Pindar, Olympian Odes*. Translated into English verse (London 1906).

Mommsen, C. J. T. *Annotationis criticae supplementum ad Pindari Olympias* (Berlin 1864).

[C. F. Schnitzer, *Eos(S)* 2 (1866) 269–93.]

Morice, F. D. *The Olympian and Pythian Odes of Pindar*. Translated into English verse (London 1876, 1893²).

*Pápari, T. V. *Cinque odi olimpiche*, recate in versi e brevemente annotate (Rome 1930).

Patricio de Berguizas, D. F. *Obras poéticas de Píndaro en metro castellano con el texto griego y notas críticas* (Madrid 1798).

*Pereira, J. F. *Odes olimpicas de Pindaro* (Lisbon 1890). Text and translation in prose and verse.

Perrotta, G. *Pindaro* (Rome 1958) 145–303. Translation and commentary on *O*. 1–13.

*Petri, V. F. L. *Pindars Olympische Siegshymnen*, in gereimten Versen verdeutscht und mit erklärendem Commentare versehen (Rotterdam 1853).

[R. Rauchenstein, *JPh* 77 (1858) 406–7.]

Rauchenstein, R. *Commentationum Pindaricarum particula altera. Annotationes in Pindari Olympia* (Aarau 1845).

*Ruhe, J. *Pindars Segersånger, Olympia* (Malmö 1856). Translation.

Schmidt, M. *Pindar's Siegesgesänge. Mit prolegomenis über pindarische Kolometrie und Textkritik*. Vol. 1: *Olympische Siegesgesänge*. Griechisch und deutsch. (Jena 1869).

[E. Krüger, *PA* 2 (1870) 285–8 and 494–506.]

Schwickert, J. J. *Pindar's olympische Siegesgesänge in durchgreifend geläutertem Texte auf der Grundlage kritisch-exegetischer Untersuchungen nebst begleitender Übersetzung und einem dreifachen Anhange mit zahlreichen pythischen, nemäischen, isthmischen, sophokleischen und homerischen Emendationen* (Trier 1878).

*de Sinner, L. *Pindare, Olympiques*, texte grec d'après la seconde édition de Boeckh avec un choix de scolies anciennes et des notes en français (Paris 1841).

*Sjöström, A. G. *Olympiorum ex Pindaro adumbratio* (Helsingfors 1832).

Sommer, E. *Pindare. Les Olympiques*, expliquées littéralement, traduites en français et annotées. Texte grec revu par T. Fix (Paris 1847, 1878²).

*de Sozzi, L. F. *Les Olympiques de Pindare*, traduites... avec des remarques historiques (Paris 1754).

*Sudorius, N. *Pindari Olympia, latino carmine reddita* (Paris 1623).

Tafel, T. L. F. *Dilucidationum Pindaricarum volumina duo. Volumen prius Olympia et Pythia* (all publ.), 2 pts. (Berlin 1824–27).

Triadú, J. *Píndar, Odes I: Olímpiques*. Text revisat i traducció (Barcelona 1957). Odes 1–5.

[A. Tovar, *Emerita* 27 (1959) 188; M. F. Galiano, *EClás* 4 (1958) 384–6.]

Triadú, J. *Píndar, Odes II: Olímpiques*. Text revisat i traducció (Barcelona 1959). Odes 6–14.

[M. F. Galiano, *EClás* 5 (1960) 387.]

Wheeler, G. B. *Pindari Carmina Olympica*, ex recensione et cum notis Heynii, Boeckhii, Dissenii, et Walker (Dublin 1840).

OLYMPIAN ONE

General

*Bach, E. C. C. *Pindari Olympiorum carmen 1 in Hieronem Aetnaeum* (Jena 1805).

Boeckh, A. *Observationes criticae in Pindari primum Olympicum carmen* (Heidelberg 1811).

Camarda, N. *Gerone e la prima Olimpica di Pindaro* (Palermo 1878).

*Camarda, N. *Gerone I o la prima Olimpica et le tre prime Pizie di Pindaro con un appendice* (Palermo 1880).

Furtwängler, W. *Die Siegesgesänge des Pindaros in einer Auswahl nach den wesentlichen Gesichtspunkten erklärt* (Freiburg 1859).

de Jongh, A. See under "General and Miscellaneous." Text, Latin translation, and commentary.

Jurenka, H. *Pindars erste und dritte olympische Ode. Proben einer exegetisch-kritischen Ausgabe* (Vienna 1894) 1–18.

[G. Fraccaroli, *BFC* 1 (1895) 244–5.]

Jurenka, H. "Der Mythus in Pindars erster olympischer Ode und Bakchylides III," *Philologus* 59 (1900) 313–5.

Kakridis, J. T. "Die Pelopssage bei Pindar," *Philologus* 85 (1930) 463–77.

Klausen, R. H. "Ueber den Mythus vom Pelops," *Philologus* 7 (1852) 495–510.

Lavagnini, B. "Gerone e Terone nelle due prime Olimpiche di Pindaro," *ASSO* 2nd S., 9 (1933) 5–14 (5–9).

Lübbert, E. *Meletemata de Pindari carminum quibus Olympiae origines canit fontibus* (Progr. Bonn 1882).

Lübbert, E. *Prodromus in Pindari locum de Pelopis pueritia* (Bonn 1888).

Palm, J. "Zu Pindar Ol. 1," *Opuscula Atheniensia* 4 (Lund 1962) 1–7.

*Petri, V. F. L. *Observationes aliquot in Pindari hymnum Olympicum primum* (Progr. Brunswick 1831).

*Schwickert, J. J. *Quaestiones ad carminis Pindarici Olympici primi emendationem spectantes atque explanationem* (Fribourg 1898).

[R. Harmand, *REG* 12 (1899) 432–3.]

Segal, C. P. "God and Man in Pindar's First and Third Olympian Odes," *HSCP* 68 (1964) 211–67.

*Suedelius, P. G. *Pindari Olympiorum ode 1 interpretandi conamen* (Uppsala 1803).

Welcker, F. G. *Observationes in Pindari carmen Olympicum primum* (Giessen 1806).

Translations

ARENA, A. See under "Metre" (306–12).

*BARJAU Y PONS, F. & DE LEON Y MARAGALL, F. L. *Pindaro: Las Olimpicas, Oda primera* (Madrid n.d.)
    [G. Leroux, *REG* 27 (1914) 329.]

*CAPOCASA, S. *Quattro odi di Pindaro volte in lingua italiana* (Rome 1894).

*DÜHR, A. *Pindars erste Olympische Ode*, übersetzt mit Anmerkungen (Progr. Friedland 1865).

FAGLES, R. "Two Odes of Pindar," *Arion* 3, No. 1 (1964) 24–41 (24–31).

GALLI, B. *Pindaro restituito alla natia consonanza e tradotto in versi italiani* (Florence 1882).

GARTEN, F. "Pindar's 1. Olympische Ode auf Hieron den König von Syrakus," *JPP(S)* 8 (1842) 319–20.

*GAZZANI, A. *Saggio di un volgarizzamento delle odi di Pindaro* (Bologna 1884).

*HAMM, J. *Pindari carmen olympicum 1 a Ludovico Legionensi Hispanice redditum adiunctis in verba Graeca et Hispanica adnotationibus* (Diss. Berlin 1846).

OSTERWALD, W. "Pindar's Olympische Siegesgesänge in modernen Maassen übersetzt," *JPP(S)* 9 (1843) 141–52 (141–4).

*PASQUALE, M. "Odi Pindariche," *Clizia. Rassegna bimestrale di varia letteratura e filosofia* 3 (1957) 1009–11.

ROSING, M. "Prøver paa en Oversaettelse af Pindars Oder," *Tidskrift for Philologi og Paedagogik* 3 (1862) 25–31 (25–9).

SCHENK VON STAUFFENBERG, A. "Pindars Olympische Oden I–III," *Robert Boehringer. Eine Freundesgabe* (Tübingen 1957) 625–33 (625–8).

*SÖDERHOLM, J. A. *Pindari Olympiorum Ode 1 in sermonem Suecanum conversa* (Helsingfors 1849).

*WEIDMANN, J. G. *Pindars erster Olympische Siegesgesang im Versmaasse des Originals übersetzt und mit einer Einleitung versehen* (Progr. Würzburg 1830).

Specific Verses

1–6. FRÄNKEL, H. "A Thought Pattern in Heraclitus," *AJP* 59 (1938) 309–37 (326 n. 38).

   3. VON DER MÜHLL, P. See under "*O*. 7 General" (203–4).

   7. JURENKA, H. "Analecta Pindarica," *ZOEG* 45 (1894) 1065–75 (1065–66).
      [G. Fraccaroli, *BFC* 1 (1895) 244.]

   NABER, S. A. "Pindarica," *Mnem* NS 12 (1884) 24–43 (25–8).

   8. HAND, F. *Commentatio critica in Pindari carmina* (Jena 1850) 3–5. This is the title recorded by Engelmann and Preuss, but none is given on the Programm.

   HÄNDLER, E. A. "De duobus Pindari locis, prolusio exegetica," *JPP(S)* 1 (1831) 149–55 (149–50).

   8–9. ASTIUS, F. "Observationes et coniecturae in Pindari Olympiaca. Specimen primum," *Commentarii Societatis Philologicae Lipsiensis* ed. C. D. Beckius, vol. 2, pt. 1 (Leipzig 1802) 1–39 (1–3).

   MOEBIUS, A. See under "*O*. 3.17–18" (10–11).

9–10. LAVAGNINI, B. "Nuove interpretazioni pindariche," *ASNP* 2nd S., 1 (1932) 271–82 (272).
10. AHLWARDT, C. W. See under "*P.* 1.52–3" (127–8).
12. HILLER, E. "Zu Pindar Ol. I," *Philologus* 52 (1894) 719–22 (719–20).
24. HILLER, E. See under "*O.* 1.12" (720).
27. KENNA, V. E. G. "The Return of Orestes," *JHS* 81 (1961) 99–104 (100 n. 10).
    LORIMER, H. L. "Gold and Ivory in Greek Mythology," *Greek Poetry and Life. Essays presented to Gilbert Murray on his seventieth birthday, January 2, 1936* (Oxford 1936) 14–33 (30–33).
28–9. CERRATO, L. "Questione di varianti in un luogo controverso di Pindaro (Olimp., I, 28 sq.)," *RFIC* 14 (1886) 107–23.
    FRIEDERICHS, K. *Pindarische Studien* (Berlin 1863) 3–4.
    MEZGER, F. "Zu Pindar," *Philologus* 28 (1869) 717–20 (717–18).
    SCHNITZER, C. F. *De Pindaro nuperrime emendato* (Ellwangen 1867) 13–14.
    [*PA* 1 (1869) 39–42.]
28–36. NENCI, G. "Una risposta delfica alla metodologia ecataica (Pindaro, Olimpica 1, vv. 28–36)," *CS* 3 (1964) 269–86.
28b. FLACH, H. "Zu Pindaros," *JPh* 119 (1879) 460.
    FRITZSCHE, T. "Zu Pindaros," *JPh* 119 (1879) 684.
41. GRUMME, A. See under "*O.* 10.9" (12).
41–2. JURENKA, H. "Textkritisches zur ersten olympischen Ode des Pindar," *WS* 15 (1893) 152–5.
    [G. Fraccaroli, *BFC* 1 (1895) 242–3.]
43–5. VILJOEN, G. VAN N. "A Note on Two Details in Pindar's Myth of Pelops," *PACA* 4 (1961) 22–6.
46–51. FRIEDERICHS, K. See under "*O.* 1.28–9" (4–7).
48. HARTMAN, J. J. See under "*P.* 3.38" (451).
50. BURY, J. B. "Etymologisches," *BKIS* 18 (1892) 292–5.
    HAND, F. See under "*O.* 1.8" (7–9).
    HILLER, E. See under "*O.* 1.12" (720–1).
    JURENKA, H. See under "*O.* 1.41–2."
    SCHEER, E. *Miscellanea critica* (Progr. Ploen 1887) 7–8.
50–1. ASTIUS, F. See under "*O.* 1.8–9" (3–4).
52. HUTCHINSON, W. M. L. Review of J. Sandys, *The Odes of Pindar*, *CR* 31 (1917) 99.
    WADE-GERY, H. T. "The Spartan Rhetra in Plutarch Lycurgus VI," *CQ* 37 (1943) 62–72 (70).
56–57b. LUPPINO, A. "Esegesi pindarica," *PP* 14 (1959) 359–64 (359–61).
56–8. ASTIUS, F. See under "*O.* 1.8–9" (4–6).
56–64. COMPARETTI, D. "Die Strafe des Tantalus nach Pindar (Ol. I 56 ff.)," *Philologus* 32 (1873) 227–51.
    [G. Müller, *RFIC* 1 (1873) 30–2.]
57. JURENKA, H. See under "*O.* 1.41–2."
    *SCHMIDT, M. *Miscellaneorum philologicorum particula quarta* (Jena 1880).

57–57b. Von der Mühll, P. See under "*O.* 1.111–2" (52–3).
  57b. Hartman, J. J. See under "*P.* 3.38" (450).
  58. Garrod, H. W. "On Four Passages of Pindar," *CQ* 1 (1907) 144–7 (144).
59–60. Friederichs, K. See under "*O.* 1.28–9" (7–8).
    Griset, E. *Saggio d'interpretazione estetica ed esoterica di un famoso passo pindarico* (Pinerolo n.d.).
      [J. Sitzler, *PhW* 46 (1926) 1409–10.]
    Lambert, G. Μετὰ τριῶν τέταρτον πόνον, *LEC* 2 (1933) 182–94.
59–64. Schwickert, J. J. See under "*O.* 11.4" (16–22).
  60. Camarda, N. *Osservazioni alle parole* μετὰ τριῶν τέταρτον πόνον *di Pindaro; Olimp. I., strofa 3a, v. 3* (Messina 1873).
      [L. Jeep, *RFIC* 2 (1874) 537–9; F. Mezger, *PA* 8 (1877) 33–4.]
    Cerrato, L. *De quarta Tantali poena apud Pindarum* (Casali S. Evasii apud Monferratenses 1884).
    del Grande, C. "Il quarto travaglio di Tantalo," *Filologia Minore* (Milan & Naples 1956) 121–4.
    Mesk, J. "Tantalos bei Pindar," *Charisteria Alois Rzach* (Reichenberg 1930) 142–7.
    Schroeder, O. Μετὰ τριῶν τέταρτον πόνον (Pind. Olymp. 1. 60), *ARW* 21 (1922) 47–57.
    Stoessl, F. "Zu Pindar Ol. 1. 60," *WS* 50 (1932) 171–3.
    Tarditi, G. "Il ΤΕΤΑΡΤΟΣ ΠΟΝΟΣ di Tantalo," *PP* 9 (1954) 204–11.
62–4. Nairn, J. A. "On Pindar's Olympian Odes," *CR* 15 (1901) 10–15 (10).
63–4. *Schmidt, M. "Emendationum Pindaricarum heptas," *Miscellaneorum philologicorum particula tertia* (Jena 1879) 3–14.
    Young, D. See under "*I.* 8.40" (18).
  64. Jurenka, H. See under "*O.* 1.41–2."
    Nairn, J. A. "On some passages of Pindar," *PCPS* 55–57 (1900) 15–16.
67–74. Kakridis, J. T. "Des Pelops und Iamos Gebet bei Pindar," *Hermes* 63 (1928) 415–29.
71–4. Riess, E. See under "Religion and Myth" (425–6).
  87. Lavagnini, B. See under "*O.* 1.9–10" (272).
    Young, D. See under "*I.* 8.40" (17).
  89. Hiller, E. See under "*O.* 1.12" (721).
    Voigt, T. *De Atrei et Thyestae fabula* (Diss. Halle 1885). Also in *Dissertationes philologicae halenses* 6 (Halle 1886) 307–478 (335–8).
93–5. Jurenka, H. See under "*O.* 1.7" (1068–69).
94–5. Lavagnini, B. See under "*O.* 1.9–10" (272–3).
103–5. Nairn, J. A. See under "*O.* 1.62–4" (10).
  104. Friederichs, K. See under "*O.* 1.28–9" (8–10).
    Nairn, J. A. See under "*O.* 1.64."
    *Schmidt, M. See under "*O.* 1.57."

Von der Mühll, P. See under "*O.* 7 General" (202–3).
Young, D. See under "*I.* 8.40" (20–21).
104–10. Astius, F. See under "*O.* 1.8–9" (7–12).
105. Hiller, E. See under "*O.* 1.12" (721–2).
Jurenka, H. See under "*O.* 1.7" (1066–68).
Pearson, A. C. "Pindarica," *CQ* 18 (1924) 151–7 (151).
106–7. Rauchenstein, R. "Zu Pindar," *Philologus* 36 (1877) 64–72 (64).
106–8. Lavagnini, B. See under "*O.* 1.9–10" (273–5).
Semitelos, D. Διορθωτικὰ εἰς Πίνδαρον καὶ Σοφοκλέα, *Mélanges Henri Weil* (Paris 1898) 429–44 (429–33).
Wiskemann, A. *Beiträge zur Erklärung Pindar's* (Progr. Marburg 1876) 1–2.
[E. von Leutsch, *PA* 7 (1875) 507–8.]
107. Grumme, A. See under "*O.* 10.9" (12–13).
Rauchenstein, R. "Zu Pindar," *RhM* 18 (1863) 464–5.
107–11. Jurenka, H. See under "*O.* 1.7" (1069–70).
108–10. Moorhouse, A. C. See under "*N.* 7.68" (5–6).
109–10. van Herwerden, H. See under "*O.* 2.71" (38).
111–2. Von der Mühll, P. "Kleine Bemerkungen zu Pindars Olympien," *MH* 11 (1954) 52–6 (52–3).
113. von Blumenthal, A. "Beobachtungen zu griechischen Dichtern: 4. Zum Pindartext," *Hermes* 69 (1934) 458.
Jurenka, H. See under "*O.* 1.41–2."
Nairn, J. A. See under "*O.* 1.62–4" (10–11).
Turyn, A. "Lyrica Graeca," *Eos* 27 (1924) 110–12.
115–16. Astius, F. See under "*O.* 1.8–9" (12–13).
Rousopoulos, A. Ἐπιστασία κριτικὴ καὶ ἑρμηνευτικὴ εἰς μίαν λέξιν Πινδάρου (Athens 1898).
115b. Garrod, H. W. "Notes on Pindar," *CQ* 9 (1915) 129–34 (129).

OLYMPIAN TWO

General

Bastgen, P. *Quo tempore et consilio Pindarus carmen olympicum secundum et tertium composuerit* (Diss. Monasterii 1883).
Bollack, J. "L'or des rois; le mythe de la Deuxième Olympique," *RPh* 37 (1963) 234–54.
*Camenz, C. W. T. *Pindari olympicum carmen II.* (Penicii 1806).
Carrière, J. "Lueurs nouvelles sur la Seconde Olympique de Pindare," *Pallas: Annales de la Faculté des Lettres de Toulouse* 11 (1962) 29–45.
Dieterich, A. *Nekyia. Beiträge zur Erklärung der neuentdeckten Petrusapokalypse* (Leipzig 1893, 1913²).
Ehnmark, E. "Some Remarks on the Idea of Immortality in Greek Religion," *Eranos* 46 (1948) 1–21 (12–14).

del Grande, C. "Lettura della seconda olimpica," *Filologia Minore* (Milan & Naples 1956) 77–112.
Grumme, A. *De Pindari Ol. II commentatio* (Göttingen 1862).
Hampe, R. "Zur Eschatologie in Pindars zweiter olympischer Ode," Ἑρμηνεία. *Festschrift Otto Regenbogen* (Heidelberg 1952) 46–65.
Härter, E. *Die zweite olympische Ode Pindar's, übersetzt und erklärt* (Progr. Stendal 1870).
> [E. von Leutsch, *PA* 3 (1871) 577–81.]

Impellizzeri, S. "La II Olimpica e i frammenti di Θρῆνοι di Pindaro," *SIFC* 16 (1939) 105–10.
Jaeger, W. "The Greek Ideas of Immortality," *HTR* 52 (1959) 135–47 (140–1). Also in *Humanistische Reden und Vorträge* (Berlin 1960²) 287–99 (292–3).
*Karsten, S. *Pindari carmina tria: Olympiorum II et VI, Pythiorum I.* (Diss. Traiecti ad Rhenum and Leipzig 1825).
Lavagnini, B. See under "*O.* 1 General" (9–14).
*Le Bidois, G. "Études d'analyse critique appliquée aux poètes grecs. La deuxième Olympique," *L'Enseignement chrétien* 11 (1892) 23–9.
van Leeuwen, J. *Pindarus' Tweede Olympische Ode*, 2 vols. (Assen 1964).
> [A. Garzya, *P&I* 7 (1965) 255–6; R. W. B. Burton, *CR* NS 15 (1965) 267–8; P. Von der Mühll, *MH* 22 (1965) 240; É. des Places, *RPh* 3rd S., 40 (1966) 114–15; C. Pavese, *A&R* NS 11 (1966) 175–7.]

Long, H. S. *A Study of the Doctrine of Metempsychosis in Greece from Pythagoras to Plato* (Diss. Princeton 1948) 29–44.
Malten, L. "Elysium und Rhadamanthys," *JAI* 28 (1913) 35–51.
McGibbon, D. "Metempsychosis in Pindar," *Phronesis* 9 (1964) 5–11.
Perosa, A. "La seconda ode olimpica di Pindaro," *SIFC* NS 18 (1941) 25–53.
da Rocha Pereira, M. H. *Concepções Helénicas de Felicidade no Além de Homero a Platão* (Coimbra 1955) 63–7, 125–49, 195–6.
Rohde, E. See under "Religion and Myth."
*Schwickert, J. J. *Kritisch-exegetische Untersuchungen zu Pindars zweitem olympischen Siegesgesange* (Progr. Trier 1891).
Thiemann, K. *Die platonische Eschatologie in ihrer genetischen Entwicklung* (Progr. Berlin 1892).

Translations

Arena, A. "Pindaro Olimpica II," *MC* NS 6 (1952) 79–84.
Arena, A. See under "Metre" (313–20).
Bippart, G. "Uebersetzungsproben," *JPP(S)* 17 (1851) 524–7.
Boeken, J. H. "Het tweede Olympisch zege-Lied voor Theron, den Akragantijn," *De Nieuwe Gids* 9, 2 (1894) 412–5.
*Cowley, A. *The Second Olympic and First Nemean Odes of Pindar paraphrased* (London 1656).
*Donnini, P. *La II Olimpica. A Terone d'Agrigento per la vittoria con la quadriga* (Naples 1938).

FAGLES, R. See under "*O*. 1 Translations" (32–41).
*FRITZSCHE, H. *Pindars zweite olympische Siegeshymne* (Leipzig 1861).
*VON HUMBOLDT, W. *Pindars zweite olympische Ode metrisch übersetzt* (Berlin 1792).
OSTERWALD, W. See under "*O*. 1 Translations" (145–8).
*PALMSTEIN, R. "Olympijka II," *KK* 8 (1934) 103–7.
PAPAKONSTANTINOS, P. G. Τὸ δεύτερον Πινδαρικὸν 'Ολύμπιον καὶ ὁ ἐν αὐτῷ ἐξυμνούμενον Θήρων, *Syll* 31 (1909) 89–95.
PELIAS, H. "Second Olympic Ode, Pindarus for Theron of Acragas Winner in Chariot Race 476 B.C.," *Athene* 26 (1965) 26.
PETRI, V. F. L. "Probe einer Uebersetzung der Oden von Pindar," *JPP(S)* 10 (1844) 626–9.
*POUSETTE, K. *Specimen acad. sistens Odam secundam Pindari Olympiorum in latinam conversam* (Uppsala 1790).
*REUSS, K. J. *Pindars zweite Olympie, nach dem Heyneschen Texte übersetzt* (Würzburg 1809).
ROMAGNOLI, E. "La seconda Olimpia di Pindaro," *A&R* 16 (1913) 321–9.
SCHENK VON STAUFFENBERG, A. See under "*O*. 1 Translations" (628–31).
*WEIDMANN, J. G. *Pindars zweiter olympische Siegesgesang im Versmaasse des Originals übersetzt und mit einer Einleitung versehen* (Progr. Würzburg 1836).

Metre

BOWRA, C. M. "The Metre of Pindar, Olympian II," *CQ* 30 (1936) 94–9.
MAAS, P. See under "Metre" (Responsionsfreiheiten, 13–31).

Specific verses

6. PEARSON, A. C. See under "*O*. 1.105" (153).
8–10. JURENKA, H. See under "*O*. 12.13–16" (190–1).
10. GARROD, H. W. See under "*O*. 1.115b" (129).
15–17. ASTIUS, F. See under "*O*. 1.8–9" (13–14).
FRITZSCHE, T. "Zu Pindaros Epinikien," *JPh* 125 (1882) 145–55 (145–6).
17. MCCARTNEY, E. S. "Father Time," *CP* 23 (1928) 187–8.
19. NABER, S. A. See under "*O*. 1.7" (28).
21–2. ROBINSON, D. M. "The Wheel of Fortune," *CP* 41 (1946) 207–16 (207).
26. JURENKA, H. See under "*O*. 1.7" (1070).
OELSCHLAEGER, F. *Aliquot Pindari loci tractantur* (Progr. Suevofurti 1858) 13.
30–2. SCHMIDT, M. "Zu den griechischen Lyrikern," *Philologus* 1 (1846) 639–44 (643–4).
30–6. ASTIUS, F. See under "*O*. 1.8–9" (14–15).
35–46. LAVAGNINI, B. See under "*O*. 1.9–10" (275–6).
41. JURENKA, H. See under "*O*. 1.7" (1070–1).
42–3. VON LEUTSCH, E. "Pind. Ol. II, 49," *Philologus* 30 (1870) 72.
43. VAN HERWERDEN, H. "Varia," *Mnem* NS 29 (1901) 209–18 (211).

46. von Leutsch, E. "Pind. Ol. II, 46," *Philologus* 30 (1870) 193.
51–4. Astius, F. See under "*O*. 1.8–9" (15–16).
52. Bowra, C. M. See under "*O*. 2 Metre" (97–8).
    Housman, A. E. *ΣΩΦΡΟΝΗ, CR* 2 (1888) 242–5.
53–4. von Wilamowitz-Moellendorff, U. "Lesefrüchte cxxiii," *Hermes* 44 (1909) 445–6. Also in *Kleine Schriften IV* (Berlin 1962) 224–5.
54. Erbse, H. See under "*O*. 10.9" (27–31).
    Garrod, H. W. See under "*O*. 1.58" (144–5).
    Von der Mühll, P. See under "*O*. 1.111–2" (55–6).
54–6. Wright, F. A. "Two Passages in Pindar," *AJP* 43 (1922) 164–5.
55–6. Cornford, F. M. "On Pindar, Olymp. II. 58–66," *PCPS* 61–63 (1902) 9.
55–60. Maass, E. "Aischylos und Pindar," *Orpheus* (Munich 1895) 261–78.
56. Donaldson, J. W. See under "*P*. 2.76–7" (221–22).
    Dreykorn, J. *Commentationum Pindaricarum specimen* (Progr. Landau 1863) 17.
    Fritzsche, T. See under "*O*. 2.15–17" (146–8).
    Hand, F. See under "*O*. 1.8" (5–7).
    Rauchenstein, R. See under "*O*. 1.106–7" (64–5).
    Wiskemann, A. See under "*O*. 1.106–8" (3).
56–7. Lavagnini, B. See under "*O*. 1.9–10" (276–7).
56–60. Deas, H. T. "A Note on Pindar, Olympian II. 56–60," *CQ* 24 (1930) 191–2.
    Mezger, F. See under "*O*. 1.28–9" (718–19).
    Nilsson, M. P. "Early Orphism and Kindred Religious Movements," *HTR* 28 (1935) 181–230 (214–16).
    Oelschlaeger, F. See under "*O*. 2.26" (14–15).
56–63. van Herwerden, H. See under "*O*. 2.43" (211–12).
56–100. Gray, A. "On Pindar, Ol. II 56-end," *TCPS* 2 (1881–82) 183–5.
57. Altenhoven, P. "Notes sur trois passages de Pindare," *AIPhO* 5 (1937) 13–18 (13–14).
57–60. Deubner, L. "Totengericht (Pind. Ol. II 57–60)," *Hermes* 43 (1908) 638–42.
    Garrod, H. W. See under "*O*. 1.58" (145–6).
    Garrod, H. W. See under "*O*. 1.115b" (130).
    Lübbert, E. *Commentatio de Pindaro dogmatis de migratione animarum cultore* (Bonn 1887).
57–63. Goodrich, W. J. "A Passage of Pindar Reconsidered," *CQ* 2 (1908) 31–3.
57–70. Schroeder, O. "Pindars Olympien II 57 ff.," *PhW* 24 (1904) 924–6.
61–2. Rose, H. J. "The Date of Iambulos," *CQ* 33 (1939) 9–10.
    Woodbury, L. "Equinox at Acragas: Pindar, Ol. 2.61–62," *TAPA* 97 (1966) 597–616.
62. Bowra, C. M. See under "*O*. 2 Metre" (98–9).
63. Mommsen, T. "Zu Pindar," *RhM* 18 (1863) 303–6.

63–4. LAVAGNINI, B. See under "*O*. 1.9–10" (277).
  65. HUTCHINSON, W. M. L. See under "*O*. 1.52."
      LEHRS, K. "Adversarien über Madvig's Adversarien I," *RhM* 30 (1875) 91–6 (91). Also in his *Kleine Schriften* (Königsberg 1902) 170–4.
      MADWIG, J. N. *Adversaria critica ad scriptores Graecos et Latinos*, Vol. I (Hauniae 1871) 186–8 (186).
      NAIRN, J. A. See under "*O*. 1.62–4" (11).
68–70. BLUCK, R. S. See under "Fr. 133 General."
      VON FRITZ, K. "'Εστρὶς ἑκατέρωθι in Pindar's Second Olympian and Pythagoras' Theory of Metempsychosis," *Phronesis* 2 (1957) 85–9.
68–77. BIANCHI, U. "Razza aurea, mito delle cinque razze ed Elisio. Un' analisi storico-religiosa," *SMSR* 34 (1963) 143–210 (195–202).
      CAPELLE, P. "Elysium und Inseln der Seligen: I," *ARW* 25 (1927) 245–64 and II, 26 (1928) 17–40.
69–70. STETTNER, W. *Die Seelenwanderung bei Griechen und Römern* (Stuttgart 1934) 24–8.
  70. CAPELLE, P. *De luna stellis lacteo orbe animarum sedibus* (Halle 1917) 38–9.
      HUNT, D. W. S. "Feudal Survivals in Ionia," *JHS* 67 (1947) 68–75 (73).
70–1. GRIFFITHS, J. G. "In Search of the Isles of the Blest," *G&R* 16 (1947) 122–6.
  71. VAN HERWERDEN, H. "Pindarica," *Mnem* NS 25 (1897) 37–58 (38).
      ROCHA PEREIRA, M. H. "Notas a um passo de Pindaro," *Humanitas* 4 (1952) 7–12.
76–7. KAIBEL, G. "Sententiarum liber tertius," *Hermes* 19 (1884) 246–63 (247–8).
      ROCHA PEREIRA, M. H. "Textkritisches zu Pindar Ol. 2, 76–77," *Miscellanea critica* 1 (Leipzig 1964) 240–3.
      SCHNITZER, C. F. See under "*O*. 1.28–9" (16–17).
      SEMITELOS, D. See under "*O*. 1.106–8" (433–9).
  85. OELSCHLAEGER, F. See under "*O*. 2.26" (15).
85–8,92. CORNFORD, F. M. "Hermes-Nous and Pan-Logos in Pindar, Ol. II," *CR* 26 (1912) 180–1.
86–7. DAWES, R. See under "*P*. 6 General" (84–88 and 650).
86–8. BOECKH, A. *De Pindari sententia Olymp. II. v. 94 sqq. = 86 sqq. ad litterarum quoque studia spectante* (Berlin 1820). Also in his *Gesammelte Kleine Schriften* 4 (Leipzig 1874) 157–8.
      FRIEDERICHS, K. See under "*O*. 1.28–9" (10–11).
      LAVAGNINI, B. See under "*O*. 1.9–10" (277–8).
      RÜDIGER, H. "Rivalisierende Dichter (Pindar-Dante-Greene)," *Prolegomena* 1 (1952) 122–7.
  87. NAIRN, J. A. See under "*O*. 1.62–4" (11–13).
95–7. ASTIUS, F. See under "*O*. 1.8–9" (17–19).
      RAUCHENSTEIN, R. See under "*O*. 1.106–7" (65).
      WISKEMANN, A. See under "*O*. 1.106–8" (3–5).
95–8. JURENKA, H. See under "*O*. 3.42–5" (7–9).

95–100. BERGK, T. "Conjecturen zu Pindaros," *JPh* 99 (1869) 181–92 (181–3).
    97. NABER, S. A. See under "*O.* 1.7" (30–1).
    NAIRN, J. A. See under "*O.* 1.64."
    SCHRÖDER, O. See under "*I.* 3/4 General" (8).
   97–8. KAIBEL, G. See under "*O.* 2.76–7" (248–9).
97–100. NAIRN, J. A. See under "*O.* 1.62–4" (13).
    98. McCARTNEY, E. S. "Vivid Ways of Indicating Uncountable Numbers," *CP* 55 (1960) 79–89 (81).

Scholia
   87e. GRASSI, E. "Schol. ad Pind. Ol. II 53 ss.," *A&R* NS 6 (1961) 137.

OLYMPIAN THREE

General
BASTGEN, P. See under "*O.* 2 General."
FRAENKEL, H. See under "*N.* 7.1–2" (394–7). On the Theoxenia.
FURTWÄNGLER, W. See under "*O.* 1 General."
JURENKA, H. See under "*O.* 1 General" (18–24).
LÜBBERT, E. See under "*O.* 1 General" (1882).
SEGAL, C. P. See under "*O.* 1 General."

Translations
ARENA, A. See under "'Metre'" (321–4).
BOEKEN, J. H. "Het derde Olympisch zegelied voor Theron, den Akragantijn," *De Nieuwe Gids* 9, 2 (1894) 266–8.
FAGLES, R. "Three Odes of Pindar," *Arion* 3, No. 2 (1964) 28–45 (28–33).
HÄNDLER, E. A. "Pindars olympischer Gesänge," *JPP(S)* 1 (1832) 637–40 (637–8).
OSTERWALD, W. See under "*O.* 1 Translations" (148–50).
PELIAS, H. "Third Olympic Ode of Pindaros for Theron of Acragas," *Athene* 27, No. 2 (1966) 16.
SCHENK VON STAUFFENBERG, A. See under "*O.* 1 Translations" (632–3).
*WEIDMANN, J. G. *Pindars dritter olympische Siegesgesang im Versmaasse der Urschrift nebst einer Einleitung* (Progr. Würzburg 1846).

Specific verses
    4. ASTIUS, F. See under "*O.* 1.8–9" (19–20).
    NABER, S. A. See under "*O.* 1.7" (38).
    *SCHMIDT, M. See under "*O.* 1.63–4."
  6–10. JURENKA, H. See under "*O.* 1.7" (1071–72).
   8a. HUDE, C. See under "Schol. *O.* 6.154d."

8–9. FENNELL, C. A. M. "Pindar Ol. III 8, 9," *TCPS* 1 (1881) 166.
13–18. FRIEDERICHS, K. "Erklärungen zu Pindar's Epinikien," *Philologus* 15 (1860) 30–7 (30–1).
FRIEDERICHS, K. See under "*O.* 1.28–9" (12–13).
PEARSON, L. "Herodotus on the Source of the Danube," *CP* 29 (1934) 328–37 (337).
16–18. ASTIUS, F. See under "*O.* 1.8–9" (20).
17. *SCHMIDT, M. See under "*O.* 1.63–4."
17–18. JURENKA, H. See under "*O.* 1.7" (1072).
MOEBIUS, A. *Animadversiones in Pindari carmina. Specimen I* (Susati 1802) 5.
19–20. UNGER, G. F. "Tages Anfang," *Philologus* 51 (1892) 14–45 (28).
19–22. KAKRIDIS, J. T. Ἑρμηνευτικὰ καὶ διορθωτικὰ εἰς τὸν Πίνδαρον (Athens 1925). Also in Ἀθηνᾶ 36 (1925) 245–53.
[J. Sitzler, *PhW* 47 (1927) 33–4.]
KAKRIDIS, J. T. "Abermals zu Pindars Ol. III 19 ff. und XIII, 44," *PhW* 47 (1927) 988–9.
25. BOSSLER, C. See under "Syntax" (4).
NABER, S. A. See under "*O.* 1.7" (28).
*SCHMIDT, M. See under "*O.* 1.63–4."
26. FRIEDERICHS, K. See under "*O.* 1.28–9" (13–14).
ROSE, H. J. "Pindar, Olymp. iii. 26," *CR* 57 (1943) 13.
27. DEVEREUX, G. "The Exploitation of Ambiguity in Pindaros O. 3.27," *RhM* 109 (1966) 289–98.
29. RIDGEWAY, W. "The legend of Herakles and the Hind with the golden horns (Pindar, Ol. III 31)," *PCPS* 37–39 (1894) 14–15.
35. BOWRA, C. M. See under "Metre" (177).
38–9. GARROD, H. W. See under "*O.* 1.115b" (130).
JURENKA, H. See under "*O.* 1.7" (1072).
42–5. JURENKA, H. See under "*O.* 1.7" (1073–4).
JURENKA, H. "Novae lectiones Pindaricae," *WS* 15 (1893) 1–34 (2–3).
[G. Fraccaroli, *BFC* 1 (1895) 243.]
44. NORWOOD, G. "Pindarica," *CQ* 9 (1915) 1–6 (1–2).
45. BOWRA, C. M. See under "Metre" (86–7).
NABER, S. A. See under "*O.* 1.7" (28–9).
TYRRELL, R. Y. "Pindarica," *Hermathena* 5 (1885) 351–3.

Scholia

33a. FOTHERINGHAM, J. K. "Cleostratus" and "Cleostratus (III)," *JHS* 39 (1919) 164–84 (177–8) and 45 (1925) 78–83 (83).
SCHMIDT, M. See under "*O.* 2.30–2" (644).
VON WILAMOWITZ-MOELLENDORFF, U. *Commentariolum grammaticum IV* (Göttingen 1889) 10. Also in *Kleine Schriften IV* (Berlin 1962) 670.

OLYMPIAN FOUR

General

GALIANO, M. F. "Psaumis en las Olimpicas de Pindaro," *Emerita* 10 (1942) 112-48.
GARROD, H. W. "Pindarica. I. The Date of the Fourth and Fifth Olympian Odes," *CR* 36 (1922) 101-2.
JURENKA, H. "Psaumidea. Ein Beitrag zur höheren Kritik und zur Exegese des Pindar," *WS* 17 (1895) 1-20.
    [G. Fraccaroli, *BFC* 3 (1897) 28.]
*PFAFF, H. L. *Pindari carmen IV Olympicum perpetua adnotatione* (Jena 1787).
ROBERT, C. See under "O. 5.6" (182-3).
*SCHWICKERT, J. J. *Kritisch-exegetische Erörterungen zu Pindar*, pt. 2 (Progr. Trier & Leipzig 1884) 1-5.
    [L. Cerrato, *RFIC* 13 (1885) 82-5.]
*SÜVERN, I. W. *Pindari carmen in Psaumidem, sive Olympiorum IV cum commentariis* (Lemgo 1796).
WELCKER, F. G. See under "General and Miscellaneous" (387-90 or 212-14).

Translations

ARENA, A. "Pindaro: Olimpica IV," *RSC* 11 (1963) 306-7.
BOEKEN, J. H. "Het vierde Olympisch zege-Lied voor Psaumis, der Kamarineër," *De Nieuwe Gids* 9, 2 (1894) 416-7.
VAN GRONINGEN, B. A. "Twee Oden van Pindarus," *De Gids* 110 (1947) 100-10. Also in *Over Hellas en Hellenen* (Amsterdam 1964) 247-58.
HÄNDLER, E. A. See under "O. 3 Translations" (639).
OSTERWALD, W. See under "O. 1 Translations" (150-1).

Specific verses

9. VON LEUTSCH, E. "Pind. Ol. IV, 9," *Philologus* 29 (1870) 604.
10-11. OLDFATHER, W. A. "Pindar Ol. 4. 10 and the Intransitive Use of 'ὀχεῖν'," *CR* 24 (1910) 82-3.
    RAUCHENSTEIN, R. See under "O. 1.106-7" (65).
11. WISKEMANN, A. See under "O. 1.106-8" (6).
11-12. SCHWICKERT, J. J. See under "O. 11.4" (29-31).
18. GILDERSLEEVE, B. L. "Brief Mention," *AJP* 28 (1907) 480-1.
18-27. BEAZLEY, J. D. "A Hoplitodromos Cup," *ABSA* 46 (1951) 7-15.
19. FRIEDERICHS, K. See under "O. 1.28-9" (14-15).

OLYMPIAN FIVE

General

BOWRA, C. M. *Pindar* (Oxford 1964) 414-20.
*DAHL, C. *Pindari Olympiorum ode quinta — ode undecima* (Uppsala 1797).
GALIANO, M. F. See under "O. 4 General."

GARROD, H. W. See under "*O. 4 General.*"
HERMANN, G. "Ueber Pindars fuenfte olympische Ode," *Berichte der k. sächs. Gesellschaft der Wiss. zu Leipzig* 1 (1847) 322–32. Also in *Opuscula* 8 (Leipzig 1877) 99–110.
HOEKSTRA, S. "Het vaderschap van het vijfde olympische zegelied van Pindarus," *Verslagen en mededeelingen der kon. Akademie van Wetenschappen. Afdeeling Letterkunde* 3rd S., 1 (1884) 109–27.
JURENKA, H. See under "*O.4 General.*"
VON LEUTSCH, E. "Ist die fünfte Olympische ode von Pindar?" *Philologus* 1 (1846) 116–27.
MANCUSO, U. See under "*N. 3 General*" (183–91).
SCHWICKERT, J. J. See under "*O. 11.4*" (31–3).
*SCHWICKERT, J. J. See under "*O. 4 General*" (6–12).

Translations

ARENA, A. "Pindaro: Olimpica V," *RSC* 11 (1963) 308–9.
HÄNDLER, E. A. See under "*O. 3 Translations*" (639–40).
OSTERWALD, W. See under "*O. 1 Translations*" (151–2).
Z, Y. See under "*P. 6 Translations*" (261–6).

Specific verses

    6. MIE, F. See under "Games" (Festordnung, 170–4).
       MIE, F. See under "Games" (Quaestiones, 28–32).
       ROBERT, C. "Die Ordnung der olympischen Spiele und die Sieger der 75.–83. Olympiade," *Hermes* 35 (1900) 141–95 (149–50).
       SCHONE, J. "De dialecto Bacchylidea," *LSCP* 19 (1899) 179–309 (278).
 6–7. FRIEDERICHS, K. See under "*O. 1.28–9*" (15–16).
   7. NABER, S. A. See under "*O. 1.7*" (41–2).
  11. PACE, B. "L'Oanis," *RSA* 11 (1907) 292–4.
  12. SCHMIDT, J. H. H. *Synonymik der griechischen Sprache*, vol. 4 (Leipzig 1886) 642–4. See also Gildersleeve's comments in *AJP* 7 (1886) 407.
  13. VAN HERWERDEN, H. See under "*O. 2.43*" (212).
  16. OELSCHLAEGER, F. See under "*O. 2.26*" (15–16).
17–18. HAMPE, R. "'Idaeische Grotte' in Olympia?" *Studies Presented to D. M. Robinson on his Seventieth Birthday* 1 (Saint Louis 1951) 336–50.
23–4. ASTIUS, F. See under "*O. 1.8–9*" (20–2).

Scholia

  42a. BERGK, T. "Demetrius Scepsius ap. schol. Pind. Olymp. 5, 42," *Kleine philologische Schriften* 2 (Halle 1886) 287–8.
      VOLKMANN, R. *Observationes miscellae* (Progr. Jauer 1872).

OLYMPIAN SIX

General

ANDREWES, A. "Sparta and Arcadia in the Early Fifth Century," *Phoenix* 6 (1952) 1–5.
BORNEMANN, L. "Pindar's sechste olympische Ode," *Philologus* 47 (1889) 589–98.
FRIESLAND, E. *Quaestionum Pindaricarum specimen* (Diss. Halle 1864) 1–39.
FURTWÄNGLER, W. See under "*O.* 1 General."
JURENKA, H. "Zur Kritik und Erklärung der sechsten olympischen Ode des Pindar," *ZOEG* 44 (1893) 1057–66.
  [G. Fraccaroli, *BFC* 1 (1895) 243–4.]
*KARSTEN, S. See under "*O.* 2 General."
TACCONE, A. "Per la data e per l'esegesi dell' Olimpica VI di Pindaro," *AAT* 48 (1912–13) 179–88.
VON WILAMOWITZ-MOELLENDORFF, U. ΙΑΜΟΥ ΓΟΝΑΙ, in *Isyllos von Epidauros* =*PU* 9 (1886) 162–85.
WISKEMANN, A. *De Pindari carmine Olympico VI et Pythico II* (Progr. Marburg 1871) 1–9.

Translations

ARENA, A. "Pindaro: Olimpica VI," *RSC* 11 (1963) 70–6.
BORCHARDT, R. See under "*P.* 9 Translations" (125–30).
BORCHARDT, R. "Siegeslied Pindars auf Agesias von Syrakus wegen Sieges mit dem Rennwagen," *Die Antike* 9 (1933) 49–53.
FAGLES, R. "Two Odes of Pindar," *Arion* 4 (1965) 52–63 (52–61).
ISTVÁN, H. "Pindaros V.I. olympiai ódája," *EPK* 10 (1886) 57–63.
PETRI, V. F. L. "Proben einer Uebersetzung der Oden von Pindar," *JPP(S)* 11 (1845) 164–8.
ROMAGNOLI, E. "La sesta ode olimpica di Pindaro," *Athenaeum* 4 (1916) 143–9.
TACCONE, A. "L'ode pindarica d'Iamo (Olimpica VI)," *Miscellanea della Facoltà di Lettere e Filosofia dell' Università di Torino* 1 (Turin 1936) 1–13.

Specific verses

7. JURENKA, H. See under "*O.* 1.7" (1074–5).
15. BERGK, T. *Meletematum Lyricorum specimen* (Halle 1859) 4.
  DAVIES, G. "Note on Pindar, Ol. VI. 15, 16 (23, 24)," *CR* 13 (1899) 9.
  FRAENKEL, E. See under "*I.* 6.17" (284).
  FURTWAENGLER, W. "Zur Kritik und Erklärung des Pindaros," *JPh* 73 (1856) 785–95 (785–6).
  NABER, S. A. See under "*O.* 1.7" (30).
  ROBERTSON, D. S. See under "*P.* 2 General."
  STONE, W. A. "Three Notes on Pindar," *CR* 43 (1929) 115–6.
  VERRALL, A. W. "On Pindar," *PCPS* 12 (1885) 27.

15–16. Meinel, G. See under "*P.* 2 General" (31–2).
19. Furtwaengler, W. See under "*O.* 6.15" (786–8).
22. Heller, H. See under "*P.* 4.210" (267–9).
24. von Leutsch, E. "Pind. Ol. VI, 24," *Philologus* 30 (1870) 652.
28. Bowra, C. M. See under "Metre" (178).
    Garrod, H. W. See under "*O.* 1.115b" (131)
31. Friederichs, K. "Erklärungen zu Pindar's Epinikien," *Philologus* 12 (1857) 412–24 (412).
38. van Herwerden, H. See under "*P.* 5.121."
42. Peek, W. "Pindar, Ol. VI 42," *Philologus* 102 (1958) 319–20.
43. Bergk, T. See under "*O.* 2.95–100" (183).
    Moebius, A. See under "*O.* 3.17–18" (8–10).
44. Astius, F. See under "*O.* 1.8–9" (22).
53–4. Boeckh, A. *Specimen emendationum in Pindari carmina* (Heidelberg 1810). Also in his *Commentationum acad. II. cont. specim. emend. in Pindari carmina* (Leipzig 1811) 10.
55. Platt, A. "Two Emendations," *CQ* 5 (1911) 53.
    Rauchenstein, R. "Zu Pindaros Ol. VI 55," *JPh* 91 (1865) 656.
55–6. van Herwerden, H. See under "*O.* 2.71" (38–9).
57–62. Kakridis, J. T. See under "*O.* 1.67–74."
58–61. Riess, E. See under "Religion and Myth" (425–6).
60. Von der Mühll, P. "Weitere pindarische Notizen," *MH* 20 (1963) 101–2.
62. Furtwaengler, W. See under "*O.* 6.15" (788–90).
    Garrod, H. W. See under "*O.* 1.58" (146–7).
    van Herwerden, H. See under "*O.* 2.71" (39).
    Maguire, T. "Some passages in Pindar and Homer," *Hermathena* 3 (1879) 374–86 (374–9).
70. Amandry, P. *La mantique apollinienne à Delphes* (Paris 1950) 107 n. 4.
73–4. Fennell, C. A. M. "Pindar Ol. VI 73, 74," *TCPS* 1 (1881) 166–7.
    Maguire, T. See under "*O.* 6.62" (380).
74. Headlam, W. "Emendations and Explanations," *JP* 30 (1907) 290–319 (297).
77. Bury, J. B. "Agesias of Syracuse and Stymphalos," *CR* 4 (1890) 480–1.
78. Chantraine, P. "Un tour archaïque chez Pindare," *RPh* 3rd S., 27 (1953) 16–20.
82. Headlam, W. See under "Fr. 112 General" (438).
    Pearson, A. C. "Pindar, Ol. 6. 82," *CR* 45 (1931) 209.
    Stanford, W. B. "In Lexicographos: Another Heresy," *G&R* 5 (1936) 155–9.
    Verrall, A. W. See under "*O.* 6.15."
82–3. Beattie, A. J. "Pindar, Ol. 6. 82 f.," *CR* NS 6 (1956) 1–2.
    Furtwaengler, W. See under "*O.* 6.15" (790–5).

WOODBURY, L. "The Tongue and the Whetstone: Pindar, Ol. 6. 82–83," *TAPA* 86 (1955) 31–9.

82–6. DOVER, K. J. "Pindar, Olympian Odes 6. 82–86," *CR* NS 9 (1959) 194–6.
82–8. NORWOOD, G. "Pindar Olympian vi. 82–88," *CP* 36 (1941) 394–6.
83. PAVESE, C. "Pindarica," *Maia* 16 (1964) 307–12 (307–8).
84–6. KAMBYLIS, A. See under "Style and Imagery" (113–14).
84–90. FRIEDERICHS, K. See under "*O.* 6.31" (412–13).
86. NABER, S. A. See under "*O.* 1.7" (31).
89–90. NORWOOD, G. See under "*O.* 3.44" (2–3).
92. JURENKA, H. See under "*O.* 3.42–5" (5–6).
94. VAN BROCK, N. See under "*N.* 3.18" (191–2).
SCHULTZ, H. "Das koloristische Empfinden der älteren griechischen Poesie," *NJA* 27 (1911) 11–22 (16).
95. RADKE, G. "Die ΛΕΥΚΑΙ ΚΟΡΑΙ in Delphi und ähnliche Gottheiten," *Philologus* 92 (1937) 387–402 (399 n. 44).
100. BOWRA, C. M. See under "Metre" (181).
VAN HERWERDEN, H. See under "*O.* 2.71" (39–40).
103–5. PIERACCIONI, D. "Un nuovo papiro pindarico della raccolta fiorentina," *Maia* 1 (1948) 287–8.
104. HARTMAN, J. J. "Varia ad varios" *Mnem* NS 46 (1918) 334–6.

Scholia

154d. HUDE, C. "In scholia Pindarica," *NTF* 12 (1904) 108.

OLYMPIAN SEVEN

General

FERNÁNDEZ LLORENS, M. DEL C. "Comentarios Estéticos de la Séptima Olímpica," *Helmantica* 7 (1956) 357–77.
FRITZSCHE, T. *Beiträge zur Kritik und Erklärung des Pindar. Spec. 1. Pind. Olymp. VII* (Progr. Güstrow 1880).
GRAUX, C. "Une Olympique de Pindare écrite à l'encre d'or," *RPh* 5 (1881) 117–21. Also in his *Notices bibliographiques et autres articles* (Paris 1884) 302–7.
GREEN, E. L. "A Family of Athletes," *CJ* 13 (1918) 267–71.
JURENKA, H. "Pindars Diagoras-Lied und seine Erklärer," *WS* 17 (1895) 180–96. [G. Fraccaroli, *BFC* 3 (1897) 28–9.]
LAWALL, G. "The Cup, the Rose, and the Winds in Pindar's Seventh Olympian," *RFIC* NS 39 (1961) 33–47.
MYLONAS, G. E. "Athletic Honors in the Fifth Century," *CJ* 39 (1944) 278–89.
*PFRETZSCHNER, C. T. *Observationes nonnullae in Pindari carmen Olymp. VII* (Progr. Plauen 1826).
RIVIER, A. See under "Religion and Myth" (75–81).

Von der Mühll, P. "Weitere pindarische Notizen," *MH* 20 (1963) 197–204 (197–202).
Welcker, F. G. See under "General and Miscellaneous" (381–7 or 206–12).

Translations

Balbes, S. D. Πινδάρου ὁ ἕβδομος τῶν Ὀλυμπιονικῶν, Ἁρμονία 1 (1900) 96–104.
Fagles, R. See under "*O*. 3 Translations" (34–43).
*Gazzani, A. See under "*O*. 1 Translations."
Massini Correas, C. & Granero, I. "Pindaro Olimpicas VII y XIV," *REC* 5 (1952) 109–33 (109–27).
Ruck, C. A. P. & Matheson, W. H. "For Diagoras of Rhodes: Victory in Boxing (Pindar, Olympia VII)," *Arion* 4 (1965) 404–14.

Specific verses

    1. Jurenka, H. See under "*O*. 3.42–5" (9–11).
  1–3. Fritzsche, T. See under "*O*. 2.15–17" (148–50).
       Naber, S. A. See under "*O*. 1.7" (26–7).
  1–4. Macurdy, G. H. "The Grammar of Drinking Healths," *AJP* 53 (1932) 168–71.
  1–5. Lavagnini, B. See under "*O*. 1.9–10" (278–9).
 1–10. Pieraccioni, D. See under "*O*. 6.103–5."
    7. Kambylis, A. See under "Style and Imagery" (114–15).
11–12. Bergk, T. See under "*O*. 6.15" (4–6).
  20–4. Lavagnini, B. See under "*O*. 1.9–10" (279).
    33. Schnitzer, C. F. See under "*O*. 1.28–9" (20).
    34. Astius, F. See under "*O*. 1.8–9" (22).
35–50. Lavagnini, B. See under "*O*. 1.9–10" (280).
    40. Astius, F. See under "*O*. 1.8–9" (23).
  43–4. Ribezzo, F. "Ad Pind. Ol. VII 43–44," *RIGI* 9 (1925) 92.
    44. Garrod, H. W. See under "*O*. 1.115b" (131).
       Schnitzer, C. F. See "*O*. 1.28–9" (20–1).
    48. Farnell, L. R. "On the Interpretation of Aesch. Agam. 69–71," *CR* 11 (1897) 293–8 (295).
    52. Astius, F. See under "*O*. 1.8–9" (23–4).
       Moebius, A. See under "*O*. 3.17–18" (6–8).
    53. Maguire, T. See under "*O*. 6.62" (380–1).
  54–7. Robertson, D. S. "The Delphian Succession in the Opening of the Eumenides," *CR* 55 (1941) 69–70.
    58. Bergk, T. See under "*O*. 2.95–100" (183–4).
       van Herwerden, H. See under "*O*. 2.71" (40).
       Naber, S. A. See under "*O*. 1.7" (31–2).
59–60. Dawes, R. See under "*P*. 6 General" (88–92 and 650).
    68. Grumme, A. See under "*O*. 10.9" (11).

69. LAVAGNINI, B. See under "*O.* 1.9–10" (280).
71–6. BLINKENBERG, C. *POΔOY KTIΣTAI, Hermes* 48 (1913) 236–49.
74. GARROD, H. W. See under "*O.* 1.115b" (131–2).
84–5. ASTIUS, F. See under "*O.* 1.8–9" (24).
86. BOWRA, C. M. See under "Metre" (177).
93–4. HÄNDLER, E. A. See under "*O.* 1.8" (150–1).

OLYMPIAN EIGHT

General

*BUSSE, A. I. L. *De Pindari octavo Olympico epinicio* (Diss. Heidelberg 1824).
CHRIST, W. See under "Games" (22–4). Myth.
DE JONGH, A. See under "General and Miscellaneous." Text, Latin translation, and commentary.
LÜBBERT, E. *Dissertatio de Pindari carminibus Aegineticis quattuor postremis* (Kiel 1879). Date.

Translations

BIPPART, G. "Proben aus einer Uebersetzung des Pindar," *JPP(S)* 11 (1845) 317–20.

Specific verses

1–9. FRACCAROLI, G. "Di alcuni luoghi controversi di Pindaro," *RFIC* 18 (1890) 87–105 (87–91).
1–10. JURENKA, H. "Analecta Pindarica," *WS* 17 (1895) 197–203.
[G. Fraccaroli, *BFC* 3 (1897) 27–8.]
1–18. PATON, W. R. "Pindar, Olympian viii," *CR* 4 (1890) 318–9.
8. ASTIUS, F. See under "*O.* 1.8–9" (24–5).
GARROD, H. W. See under "*O.* 1.115b" (132).
RAUCHENSTEIN, R. See under "*O.* 1.106–7" (65).
WISKEMANN, A. See under "*O.* 1.106–8" (7).
15–16. BOECKH, A. See under "*O.* 6.53–4" (10–11).
16. AHRENS, H. L. "Coniecturae Pindaricae," *Philologus* 16 (1860) 52–9 (52).
FRITZSCHE, T. See under "*O.* 2.15–17" (150–1).
20. GARROD, H. W. See under "*O.* 1.115b" (132).
25–7. LAVAGNINI, B. See under "*O.* 1.9–10" (281).
37–46. HILL, D. E. "Pindar, Olympian 8. 37–46," *CR* NS 13 (1963) 2–4.
38–9. RAUCHENSTEIN, R. See under "*O.* 1.106–7" (65–6).
WISKEMANN, A. See under "*O.* 1.106–8" (7–8).
39. AHRENS, H. L. See under "*O.* 8.16" (52).
41. FRITZSCHE, T. See under "*O.* 2.15–17" (151).
GARROD, H. W. See under "*O.* 1.115b" (132).
JURENKA, H. See under "*O.* 8.1–10."

42–6. Von der Mühll, P. "Weitere pindarische Notizen," *MH* 21 (1964) 50–7 (50–5).
45. Rauchenstein, R. See under "*O*. 1.106–7" (66).
45–6. Ahrens, H. L. See under "*O*. 8.16" (52).
   Beattie, A. J. "Pindar, Ol. 8. 45–46," *CR* NS 5 (1955) 1–3.
   Jurenka, H. See under "*O*. 8.1–10."
   Wiskemann, A. See under "*O*. 1.106–8" (8).
47. Pearson, L. See under "*O*. 3.14."
52. Düring, I. "Pindarica," *Eranos* 31 (1933) 1–20 (1). In Swedish.
52–9. Fritzsche, T. See under "*O*. 2.15–17" (151–5).
53. Jurenka, H. See under "*O*. 8.1–10."
53–9. Whitmore, C. E. "Pindar, O. VIII, 53 ff.," *Studies in Philology, Univ. of North Carolina* 15 (1918) 344–7.
   [B. L. Gildersleeve, *AJP* 40 (1919) 103–6.]
53–64. Forbes, P. B. R. "Pindar, O. 8, 53–64," *CR* 47 (1933) 167–8.
54. Ahrens, H. L. See under "*O*. 8.16" (52–3).
54–5. Nairn, J. A. See under "*O*. 1.62–4" (13).
54–9. Fraccaroli, G. See under "*O*. 8.1–9" (91–2).
   Friederichs, K. See under "*O*. 1.28–9" (17–18).
   Friederichs, K. See under "*O*. 3.13–18" (31–2).
54–66. Wade-Gery, H. T. See under "*P*. 8 General" (211–2).
56. Jurenka, H. See under "*O*. 8.1–10."
56–9. Wiskemann, A. See under "*O*. 1.106–8" (8–9).
58. Ahrens, H. L. See under "*O*. 8.16" (53).
   Rauchenstein, R. See under "*O*. 1.106–7" (66).
59. Jurenka, H. See under "*O*. 8.1–10."
59–61. Dörrie, H. *Leid und Erfahrung. Die Wort- und Sinn-Verbindung παθεῖν–μαθεῖν im griechischen Denken* (Wiesbaden 1956) 14–15.
68–9. Astius, F. See under "*O*. 1.8–9" (25–7).
75. Jurenka, H. See under "*O*. 8.1–10."
78. Bossler, C. See under "Syntax" (35).
82–5. Lavagnini, B. See under "*O*. 1.9–10" (281–2).

OLYMPIAN NINE

General

Bossler, K. "Ueber Pindar's neunte olympische Ode," *Philologus* 20 (1863) 193–210.
Christ, W. "Heptas antiquarish-philologischer Miscellen," *SAWM* (1900) 97–149 (143–9). Date.
Hermann, G. *Emendationes quinque carminum Olympiorum Pindari* (Progr. Leipzig 1847) 3–9. Also in *Opuscula* 8 (Leipzig 1877) 110–28 (110–16).
de Jongh, A. See under "General and Miscellaneous." Text, Latin translation, and commentary.

LÜBBERT, E. *De Pindaro Locrorum Opuntiorum amico et patrono* (Bonn 1882).
PETRES, N. Πινδαρικαὶ μελέται, *Eph* 3 (1880) 283–6 and 289–94. Myth.
PUECH, A. "Les mythes dans la IXᵉ Olympique de Pindare," *REG* 32 (1919) 415–28.
SCHWICKERT, J. J. *Neue kritisch-exegetische Bearbeitung eines Siegesgesanges aus Pindar als Probe einer vollständigern Läuterung und gründlichern Exegese der pindar'schen Dichtungen* (Progr. Diekirch 1875).
    [*PA* 8 (1877) 31–2.]

Specific verses

1–2. BAHNTJE, U. *Quaestiones Archilocheae* (Diss. Göttingen 1900) 41–3.
    DEUTICKE, P. *Archilocho Pario quid in Graecis litteris sit tribuendum* (Diss. Halle 1877) 30–5.
12. ASTIUS, F. See under "*O.* 1.8–9" (27–8).
14. BOSSLER, C. See under "Syntax" (12–13).
    NAIRN, J. A. See under "*O.* 1.64."
    NAIRN, J. A. See under "*O.* 1.62–4" (13–14).
16–18. BOECKH, A. See under "*O.* 6.53–4" (11–12).
17. BOSSLER, C. See under "Syntax" (80–2).
    SCHNITZER, C. F. See under "*O.* 1.28–9" (23).
17–18. AHRENS, H. L. See under "*O.* 8.16" (53).
32. PARKE, H. W. & BOARDMAN, J. "The Struggle for the Tripod and the First Sacred War," *JHS* 77 (1957) 276–82.
33. HARRISON, J. *Prolegomena to the Study of Greek Religion* (Cambridge 1903, 1908², 1922³, repr. New York 1955) 45.
33–5. DODDS, E. R. *The Greeks and the Irrational* (Berkeley 1951) 138 and 159 n. 18.
38–40. BORTHWICK, E. K. "Suetonius' Nero and a Pindaric Scholium," *CR* NS 15 (1965) 252–6.
38–56. GORAM, G. O. *Observationes in aliquot Pindari locos* (Progr. Merseburgi 1851) 1–13.
39. PETRES, N. See under "*O.* 9.47" (250–2).
42–6. PERPIÑÁ, R. "Los tres pensadores griegos sobre el fenómeno colonial," *Helmantica* 1 (1950) 214–37 (214–23).
47. PETRES, N. Ἑρμηνευτικά, *EPh* 2 (1879) 247–52 (247–50).
48–9. VON WILAMOWITZ-MOELLENDORFF, U. "Lesefrüchte XCVII," *Hermes* 40 (1905) 128–9. Also in *Kleine Schriften IV* (Berlin 1962) 181–3.
53–6. ASTIUS, F. See under "*O.* 1.8–9" (28–30).
    FRIESE, E. See under "Syntax" (40).
53–7. JURENKA, H. See under "*O.* 3.42–5" (11–12).
53–61. FRIEDERICHS, K. See under "*O.* 3.13–18" (32–3).
56. FRIEDERICHS, K. See under "*O.* 1.28–9" (18–19).
56–7. RAUCHENSTEIN, R. "Zu Pindaros," *Philologus* 27 (1868) 332–5.

76. Ahrens, H. L. See under "*O.* 8.16" (53).
    Post, L. A. "Emendation of Pindar Olympian 9. 82 (76)," *CP* 42 (1947) 124.
76–81. Garrod, H. W. See under "*O.* 1.115b" (133).
78. Naber, S. A. See under "*O.* 1.7" (32–5).
80–1. Goram, G. O. See under "*O.* 9.38–56" (13–17).
80–3. Rauchenstein, R. See under "*O.* 9.56–7."
83. Von der Mühll, P. See under "*O.* 1.111–2" (52).
89. Ahrens, H. L. See under "*O.* 8.16" (53–4).
    Jurenka, H. See under "*O.* 3.42–5" (15–16).
96. Kourouniotis, K. Κατάλογοι Λυκαιονικῶν, *EA* (1905) 161–78.
100–12. Lattimore, R. "Pindar Olympian 9. 100–112," *CP* 41 (1946) 230–2.
107–12. Jurenka, H. See under "*O.* 8.1–10" (202–3).
109. Ahrens, H. L. See under "*O.* 8.16" (54).
109–12. von Wilamowitz-Moellendorff, U. *Commentariolum grammaticum IV* (Göttingen 1889) 7–8. Also in *Kleine Schriften IV* (Berlin 1962) 664–7.
112. Girard, P. "Ajax fils de Télamon," *REG* 18 (1905) 1–75 (69–70).
    Goram, G. O. See under "*O.* 9.38–56" (17–23).
    Petres, N. Πινδαρικαὶ μελέται, *EPh* 4 (1881) 202–6.

Scholia

1–3. von Sybel, L. "Zu dem Kallinikos des Archilochos und den Pindarscholien," *Hermes* 5 (1871) 192–204.
59a–c. Borthwick, E. K. See under "*O.* 9.38–40."
74b. Schmid, W. "Das Scholium Pindar. Olymp. IX 74b," *RhM* 59 (1904) 320.

OLYMPIAN TEN

General

*Dahl, C. See under "*O.* 5 General."
Hermann, G. See under "*O.* 9 General" (9–13 or 116–21).
de Jongh, A. See under "General and Miscellaneous." Text, Latin translation, and commentary.
Lavagnini, B. See under "*O.* 1. 9–10" (282).
Lübbert, E. *Dissertatio de Pindari carmine Olympico decimo* (Progr. Kiel 1881).
Lübbert, E. See under "*O.* 1 General" (Meletemata).
Meinel, G. See under "*P.* 2 General" (24–9).
Mezger, F. See under "*P.* 10 General" (24–31).
Viljoen, G. van N. *Pindaros se tiende en elfde Olympiese odes* (Diss. Leiden 1955). In Africaans with summary in English.
    [H. J. Rose, *CR* NS 6 (1956) 299–300; H. J. Rose, *Mnem* 4th S., 9 (1956) 340–2; R. van Pottelbergh, *AC* 25 (1956) 454–5.]

Specific verses

- 1–3. PACKARD, L. R. "The Beginning of a Written Literature in Greece," *TAPA* 11 (1880) 34–51 (41–2).
  ROME, A. See under "General and Miscellaneous" (524–7).
- 7–12. FRIEDERICHS, K. See under "*O.* 3.13–18" (33–5).
  - 9. BERGK, T. See under "*O.* 2.95–100" (184).
    ERBSE, H. "Beiträge zum Pindartext," *Hermes* 88 (1960) 23–33 (25–7).
    FRIEDERICHS, K. See under "*O.* 1.28–9" (19–21).
    GRUMME, A. *De lectionibus Pindaricis nuper a Tycho Mommsenio prolatis* (Progr. Bielefeld 1866) 6–7.
    RAUCHENSTEIN, R. See under "*O.* 1.106–7" (66).
    SCHNITZER, C. F. See under "*O.* 1.28–9" (24–5).
    WIESELER, F. "Zu Pindar," *Philologus* 6 (1851) 668.
- 9–10. HARDIE, W. R. See under "*N.* 1.46."
  WISKEMANN, A. See under "*O.* 1.106–8" (9–10).
- 9–12. FRACCAROLI, G. See under "*O.* 8.1–9" (92–5).
  - 15. HEADLAM, W. See under "*I.* 3/4.85" (246).
    ROSE, H. J. "Herakles and Kyknos (Pindar, O. X. 15)," *Mnem* 4th S., 10 (1957) 110–16.
  - 20. HOEKSTRA, A. See under "Syntax."
- 22–3. MOEBIUS, A. See under "*O.* 3.17–18" (5–6).
  - 25. ERBSE, H. See under "*O.* 10.9" (23–5).
    HEADLAM, W. See under "*O.* 6.74" (297–8).
    KOCH, H. A. See under "Fr. 75.14."
- 37–8. ASTIUS, F. See under "*O.* 1.8–9" (31–2).
  - 41. VAN HERWERDEN, H. See under "*O.* 2.71" (40–1).
  - 46. YOUNG, D. See under "*I.* 8.40" (22).
- 49–55. QUINCEY, J. H. See under "*P.* 1.67–8" (146).
  - 63. RAUCHENSTEIN, R. See under "*O.* 1.106–7" (66–7).
    WISKEMANN, A. See under "*O.* 1.106–8" (10–11).
  - 66. MAAS, P. See under "*O.* 14.21."
- 72–7. HEADLAM, W. See under "*I.* 3/4.53–7" (292).
  - 76. LOCKWOOD, J. F. "Two Notes," *CR* 51 (1937) 57.
- 82–3. ASTIUS, F. See under "*O.* 1.8–9" (32–3).
- 84–97. ROME, A. See under "General and Miscellaneous" (527–9).
  - 86. GARROD, H. W. See under "*O.* 1.115b" (133).
  - 93. GARROD, H. W. See under "*O.* 1.115b" (133).
  - 94. JURENKA, H. See under "*O.* 3.42–5" (30).
  - 98. VAN HERWERDEN, H. See under "*O.* 2.71" (41).
- 104–5. BOECKH, A. See under "*O.* 6.53–4" (12–13).
  - 105. GARROD, H. W. See under "*O.* 1.115b" (134).

Scholia

46f. Lübbert, E. "Scholion quoddam pindaricum (O. XI 46) in hac quaestione quid doceat," *Originum eliacarum capita selecta* (Bonn 1882) 9–11.

OLYMPIAN ELEVEN

General

Bundy, E. L. "Studia Pindarica I: The Eleventh Olympian Ode," *Univ. of California Publ. in Class. Philology* 18, 1 (Berkeley and Los Angeles 1962) 1–34.
    [G. M. Kirkwood, *CW* 56 (1962) 8; A. Garzya, *P&I* 4 (1962) 327–8; R. W. B. Burton, *CR* NS 13 (1963) 144–5; G. M. Kirkwood, *Gnomon* 35 (1963) 130–3; J. Defradas, *REG* 76 (1963) 197–9; F. Vian, *RPh* 3rd S., 37 (1963) 294–5; J. A. Davison, *AC* 32 (1963) 226–7; F. Jouan, *RBPh* 41 (1963) 235–7; W. B. Stanford, *Hermathena* 98 (1964) 116–18; W. J. Verdenius, *Mnem* 4th S., 18 (1965) 297–8.]

de Jongh, A. See under "General and Miscellaneous." Text, Latin translation, and commentary.

*Loeber, G. F. *Exercitatio critica in Pindari Olympionicarum Oden XI* (Jena 1743).

Mezger, F. See under "*P*. 10 General" (23–4).

Schwickert, J. J. *Commentationis pindaricae emendationis studiosae atque explanationis liber singularis adiecta terentiani loci selecti emendatione* (Progr. Diekirch 1878) 1–6.

Viljoen, G. van N. See under "*O*. 10 General."

von Wilamowitz-Moellendorff, U. *Commentariolum grammaticum* IV (Göttingen 1889) 8–10. Also in *Kleine Schriften IV* (Berlin 1962) 667–70.

Translations

Arena, A. "Pindaro: Olimpica XI," *RSC* 11 (1963) 310.
*Bochenski, T. "Na zwyciestwo Hegezydama (Ol. XI)," *Meander* 1 (1946) 507.
*Czuprówna, J. "Ol. XI," *KK* 7 (1933) 300.
Fagles, R. See under "*O*. 6 Translations" (62–3).
Giannoukos, J. G. Πινδάρου ᾠδὴ ιά, Ἑλλάς 5 (1895) 355.
Rosing, M. See under "*O*. 1 Translations" (29–30).

Specific verses

4. Schwickert, J. J. *Ein Triptychon klassischer kritisch-exegetischer Philologie* (Leipzig & Würzburg 1896) 12–13.
    [G. Fraccaroli, *RFIC* 25 (1897) 297–8.]

4–6. van Groningen, B. A. "La parathèse grammaticale en Grec," *Mnem* 3rd S., 9 (1941) 258–80 (258–9).

Wiskemann, A. See under "*O*. 1.106–8" (9).

4-8. Astius, F. See under "*O.* 1.8-9" (33-5).
5. Hartman, J. J. See under "*P.* 3.38" (451).
5-6. Rauchenstein, R. See under "*O.* 1.106-7" (66).
10. Grumme, A. See under "*O.* 10.9" (8-11).
20. Gildersleeve, B. L. "Brief Mention," *AJP* 12 (1891) 386-7.
van Herwerden, H. See under "*O.* 2.43" (212).

OLYMPIAN TWELVE

General

Becker, O. "Pindars Olympische Ode vom Glück," *Die Antike* 16 (1940) 38-50.
de Coster, R. "La Fortune d'Antium et l'Ode I, 35 d'Horace," *AC* 19 (1950) 65-80 (77-80).
Kapsoménos, S. G. "Un prétendant de la monarchie à Cnossos dans la poésie de Pindare," Κρητικὰ Χρονικά 15 (1963) 252-78.
Kunze, E. "Das Ergoteles-Epigram," *Bericht über die Ausgrabungen in Olympia* 5 (Berlin 1956) 153-6.
Smith, T. C. "Religious Ἀρετή in Pindar's Ol. 12," *CB* 36 (1959) 16-7.

Translations

Arena, A. "Pindaro: Olimpica XII," *RSC* 11 (1963) 311.
Bippart, G. See under "*O.* 8 Translations."
*Czuprówna, J. "Ol. XII," *KK* 7 (1933) 288.
Fagles, R. See under "*O.* 3 Translations" (44-5).
Rosing, M. See under "*O.* 1 Translations" (30-1).
Schultz, J. & Geffcken, J. *Altgriechische Lyrik in deutschem Reim* (Berlin 1895) 56-7.

Specific verses

2. Hommel, H. "Domina Roma," *Die Antike* 18 (1942) 127-58 (152-3).
6. Verdenius, W. J. ΑΝΩ ΚΑΙ ΚΑΤΩ, *Mnem* 4th S., 17 (1964) 387.
12a. Bossler, C. See under "Syntax" (14).
13-16. Jurenka, H. "Zur Klärung der Sappho-Frage," *WS* 19 (1897) 189-210 (189-90).
19. Fränkel, H. "The Immigrant's Bath," *Univ. of California Publ. in Class. Philology* 12, No. 16 (1944) 293-4. A German translation appears in *Wege und Formen frühgriechischen Denkens* (Munich 1955, 1960²) 97-9.
Norwood, G. See under "*O.* 3.44 (3-4).

OLYMPIAN THIRTEEN

General

Picard, C. "Sur le diadème d'or de Vix: L'énigme des grands pavots et des petits Pégases," *RA* (1962) 87-91.
Friederichs, K. See under "*O.* 1.28-9" (21-4).

OLYMPIAN 13

FURTWÄNGLER, W. See under "*O. 1 General.*"
HERMANN, G. See under "*O. 9 General*" (13–19 or 121–7).

Translations

PELIAS, H. "Pindar's XIII Olympic Ode (456 B.C.) for Xenophon—the Corinthian," *Athene* 23, No. 1 (1962) 18 and 52–3.

Specific verses

6–8. BOWRA, C. M. "A Prayer to the Fates," *CQ* NS 8 (1958) 231–40 (239). Also in *Greek Lyric Poetry* (Oxford 1961 [2]) 414.
10. JURENKA, H. "Analecta Pindarica," *WS* 19 (1897) 71–7.
    OELSCHLAEGER, F. See under "*O. 2.26*" (16).
13–17. DÜRING, I. See under "*O. 8.52*" (1–2).
18–19. ADAMS, S. M. "Pindar and the Origin of Tragedy," *Phoenix* 9 (1955) 170–4.
    FERNANDES, R. M. R. "Nota a Pindaro," *Euphrosyne* 3 (1961) 199–201.
    PICKARD-CAMBRIDGE, A. W. *Dithyramb, Tragedy and Comedy* (Oxford 1927) 6–7 and 21–2.
20. VAN HERWERDEN, H. See under "*O. 2.43*" (212–3).
30–1. BOECKH, A. See under "*O. 6.53–4*" (22–4).
37–9. CHRIST, W. See under "Games" (11–16).
38–9. MAGUIRE, T. See under "*O. 6.62*" (381).
40–2. NAIRN, J. A. See under "*O. 1.62–4*" (14).
41–2. JURENKA, H. See under "*O. 13.10.*"
43–6. KAKRIDIS, J. T. See under "*O. 3.19–22.*"
44. KAKRIDIS, J. T. See under "*O. 3.19–22.*"
44–6. ASTIUS, F. See under "*O. 1.8–9*" (35–6).
48. DÜRING, I. See under "*O. 8.52*" (2–3).
49–53. JURENKA, H. See under "*O. 13.10.*"
52. BOSSLER, C. See under "Syntax" (44–5).
53–4. HARTMAN, J. J. "Ad Pindari Ol. XIII, 53," *Mnem* NS 46 (1918) 414.
55. JURENKA, H. See under "*O. 13.10.*"
69. JURENKA, H. See under "*O. 13.10.*"
76. BOECKH, A. See under "*O. 6.53–4*" (21).
83. BOSSLER, C. See under "Syntax" (58).
86. LAVAGNINI, B. See under "*O. 1.9–10*" (282).
89. VAN HERWERDEN, H. See under "*O. 2.71*" (41).
92. ASTIUS, F. See under "*O. 1.8–9*" (36–7).
98–9. STONE, W. A. "Notes on Pindar," *CR* 49 (1935) 123–5.
99. BOECKH, A. See under "*O. 6.53–4*" (24–5).
    BOSSLER, C. See under "Syntax" (15).
    GARROD, H. W. See under "*O. 1.115b*" (134).
101–6. RIBEZZO, F. "Ad Pind. Ol. XIII 102 sqq.," *RIGI* 10 (1926) 58.
105–8. ASTIUS, F. See under "*O. 1.8–9*" (38–9).

106. Jurenka, H. See under "*O.* 13.10."
106–13. Fraccaroli, G. See under "*O.* 8.1–9" (95–8).
107. Jurenka, H. See under "*O.* 3.42–5" (21).
107–8. Nairn, J. A. See under "*O.* 1.62–4" (14–15).
Schnitzer, C. F. See under "*O.* 1.28–9" (28 and 77).
113. Christ, W. "Zu Pindar," *Philologus* 45 (1886) 190–1.
113–14. Robertson, D. S. See under "*P.* 2 General."
114. Garrod, H. W. See under "*O.* 1.115b" (134).
Pearson, A. C. See under "*O.* 1.105" (151–2).
Young, D. See under "*I.* 8.40" (19–20).
114–15. Jurenka, H. See under "*O.* 13.10."

Scholia

74f. *Wuerth, B. *Der anonyme Pindarkommentar im Schol. Eurip. Medea 9* (Diss. Freiburg 1938).

OLYMPIAN FOURTEEN

General

Dawes, R. See under "*P.* 6 General" (103–8). Metre.
Eichinger, P. F. *Die Chariten von Orchomenos* (Progr. Augsburg 1892).
Furtwängler, W. See under "*O.* 1 General."
Gervais, J. "La quatorzième olympique de Pindare," *L'Enseignement secondaire au Canada*, Univ. Laval, Québec 19 (1940) 448–59. Text, translation, and commentary.
del Grande, C. "Lettura della quattordécesima olimpica," *Filologia Minore* (Milan & Naples 1956) 115–20.
van Groningen, B. A. "Een Ode van Pindarus," *De Gids* 105 (1942) 77–83. Also in *Over Hellas en Hellenen* (Amsterdam 1964) 239–46.
Hermann, G. See under "*O.* 9 General" (19–20 or 127–8).
Robert, C. See under "*O.* 5.6" (183). Date.
Schwickert, J. J. See under "*O.* 11 General" (6–16).

Translations

Arena, A. "Pindaro: Olimpica XIV," *RSC* 11 (1963) 312–13.
*Czuprówna, J. "Ol. XIV," *KK* 7 (1933) 282.
*Gazzani, A. See under "*O.* 1 Translations."
*van Groningen, B. A. "Veertiende Olympische Ode," *Muziek der Spheren*, ed. by H. Wagenvoort (Utrecht 1944) 65.
István, H. "A 14-ik olympiai óda (lyd hangnem). Pindaros," *EPK* 6 (1882) 178–9.
Massini Correas, C. & Granero, I. See under "*O.* 7 Translations" (129–33).
Papacostea, C. "Pindar Olympica 14," *RCl* 4–5 (1932–33) 272.
*Pasquale, M. See under "*O.* 1 Translations."

ZILLIACUS, E. "Pindaros' hyllning till Chariterna," *Festskrift til Francis Bull på 50 Årsdagen* (Oslo 1937) 381–5.

Specific verses
- 5–6. BERGK, T. See under "*O*. 2.95–100" (184–5).
- 7. AHRENS, H. L. See under "*O*. 8.16" (54).
- 11. AHRENS, H. L. See under "*O*. 8.16" (54).
- 13–16. PLATT, A. "On τε etc., with Vocatives," *CR* 23 (1909) 105–6.
- 14–15. VAN DER VALK, M. *Researches on the Text and Scholia of the Iliad* 2 (Leiden 1964) 630–1.
- 15. AHRENS, H. L. See under "*O*. 8.16" (54).
  SHACKLE, R. J. "Some Emendations of Pindar," *CR* 34 (1920) 85–7.
- 17. VAN GRONINGEN, B. A. "Pindari Olymp. XIV 17," *Mnem* 3rd S., 10 (1942) 221–4.
- 20–21. HEADLAM, W. "Notes on the Greek Lyric Poets," *CR* 14 (1900) 5–14 (10).
  HEADLAM, W. See under "*I*. 3/4.85" (249).
- 21. AHRENS, H. L. See under "*O*. 8.16" (54–5).
  MAAS, P. "Nachlese zu Pindar," *JPhV* 42 (1916) 102–4.
- 22–4. VON WILAMOWITZ-MOELLENDORFF, U. See under "History and Politics" (1308–9).

8. PYTHIAN ODES

General

Bennett, H. C. "On the Systematization of Scholia Dates for Pindar's Pythian Odes," *HSCP* 62 (1957) 61–78.

Burton, R. W. B. *Pindar's Pythian Odes, Essays in Interpretation* (Oxford 1962).

[J. Delande, *LEC* 30 (1962) 445; G. M. Kirkwood, *CW* 56 (1962) 8; D. E. Gerber, *Phoenix* 17 (1963) 152–3; J. A. Davison, *JHS* 83 (1963) 160–1; J. Irigoin, *Gnomon* 35 (1963) 763–5; J. Defradas, *REG* 76 (1963) 199–202; F. Vian, *RPh* 3rd S., 37 (1963) 124–6; W. B. Stanford, *Hermathena* 98 (1964) 116–18; S. L. Radt, *Mnem* 4th S., 17 (1964) 395–6; K. J. McKay, *AUMLA* No. 21 (1964) 91–2.]

Cerrato, L. *Le Odi di Pindaro. Testo, versione e commento. Parte II, Pitiche* (Sestri Ponente 1916).

[N. Terzaghi, *RIGI* 2 (1918) 183–4; C. Cessi, *BFC* 24 (1918) 63–5; D. Bassi, *RFIC* 46 (1918) 283–4; A. Beltrami, *Athenaeum* 5 (1917) 181–6.]

*Chabanon, M. *Les odes pythiques de Pindare*, traduites avec des remarques (Paris 1772).

*Costa, Giovanni & Costa, Giuseppe. *Pindaro, Le Pitiche*, con versione poetica latina e italiana (Asiago 1936).

[A. Taccone, *MC* 6 (1936) 215–16.]

*De Haes, J. *Puthische Oden* (Bruges 1945). Translation.

[J. van Ooteghem, *LEC* 14 (1946) 136.]

Gautier, G. Πυθιονῖκαι. *I vincitori pizj di Pindaro*. Tradotti in Italiane canzoni ed illustrati con postille (Rome 1765).

*Gedicke, F. *Pindars pythische Siegshymnen*, mit erklärenden und kritischen Anmerkungen (Berlin & Leipzig 1779).

Gildersleeve, B. L. See under "Olympian Odes, General."

Gurlitt, J. *Pindars pythische Siegesgesänge*, übersetzt mit Anmerkungen (Hamburg 1816).

*Mariani, L. *Le Pitiòniche di Pindaro* (Naples 1888). Translation.

Morice, F. D. See under "Olympian Odes, General."

*Paton, W. R. *Five Odes of Pindar* (Aberdeen 1904). Translation of Odes 1–4 and 9.

[J. P. Postgate, *CR* 19 (1905) 411.]

*Rosing, M. *Pindars sex første pythiske Oder* (Progr. Sorø 1890). Translation.

*Rosing, M. *Pindars sex sidste pythiske Oder* (Progr. Sorø 1891). Translation.

*Schjøtt, P. O. *Pindars Pythiske Oder oversat* (Christiania 1871). Also in *Forhandlinger i Videnskabs Selbskabet i Christiana* (1870) 281–312.

Schroeder, O. *Pindars Pythien* (Leipzig 1922).

[P. Shorey, *CP* 19 (1924) 192–3; K. Pr., *LZB* 73 (1922) 933; H. Fränkel, *DLZ* 43 (1922) 466–9; E. Bethe, *NJA* 51 (1923) 61–2; J. Sitzler, *PhW* 44 (1924) 193–8.]

Sommer, E. *Pindare. Les Pythiques*, expliquées littéralement, traduites en français et annotées. Texte grec revu par T. Fix (Paris 1847, 1887²).
Tafel, T. L. F. See under "Olympian Odes, General."
Wade-Gery, H. T. & Bowra, C. M. *Pindar, Pythian Odes* (London 1928).
  [D. S. Robertson, *CR* 42 (1928) 177–8.]

PYTHIAN ONE

General

*Bach, E. C. C. *Pindari Pythiorum carmen primum in Hieronem Aetnaeum* (Erfurt 1804).
Barford, W. *In Pindari primum Pythium dissertatio* (Cambridge 1751).
*Baumann, J. *Pindars Dichtungen als Ausdruck des dorischen Stammcharakters, nachgewissen an dem ersten Pythischen Siegesgesange* (Progr. Offenburg 1845).
*van den Bergh, H. *Uebersetzung und Erklärung der ersten pythischen Ode des Pindaros* (Stralsund 1867).
Brower, R. A. "The Theban Eagle in English Plumage," *CP* 43 (1948) 25–30.
Camarda, N. "Gerone e le tre odi Pizie di Pindaro," *ASS* NS 4 (1879) 259–84.
*Camarda, N. See under "*O*. 1 General."
Christ, W. "Der Aetna in der griechischen Poesie," *SAWM* (1888) 349–98.
Christ, W. "Bacchylides und die Pythiadenrechnung," *Hermes* 36 (1901) 107–12.
Dornseiff, F. See under "*I*. 5.1" (70–2).
*Fani, E. *La prima Ode Pitica di Pindaro. Saggio di commento* (Florence 1874).
  [*RFIC* 3 (1875) 615–6.]
Focke, F. "Aischylos' Prometheus," *Hermes* 65 (1930) 259–304 (287–94).
*Fraccaroli, G. *L'ode Pitia I di Pindaro dichiarata e tradotta* (Verona 1885).
Friedländer, P. *Die Melodie zu Pindars erstem pythischen Gedicht* (Leipzig 1934).
  [C. del Grande, *Dioniso* 6 (1937) 67–8; R. Wagner, *Gnomon* 12 (1936) 496–504; C. del Grande, *BFC* 42 (1936) 235–7; E. Kalinka & W. Fischer, *PhW* 55 (1935) 961–7; J. F. Mountford, *CR* 49 (1935) 62–3; M. Lenchantin, *RFIC* 63 (1935) 410–11; A. Puech, *REG* 48 (1935) 609; R. P. Winnington-Ingram, *JHS* 55 (1935) 264–5.]
Friedländer, P. & Birtner, H. "Pindar oder Kircher?" *Hermes* 70 (1935) 463–75.
Friedländer, P. "Adnotatiunculae I. Die Melodie zu Pindars erstem pythischen Gedicht," *Hermes* 87 (1959) 385–9.
Gombosi, O. "The Melody of Pindar's 'Golden Lyre'," *Musical Quarterly* 26 (1940) 381–92.
*Heimsoeth, F. *Pindars erste pythische Ode* (Bonn 1859).
*Hesselgren, B. *Primam Pythiorum Pindari versione et notis illustratam* (Uppsala 1796).
*Karsten, S. See under "*O*. 2 General."
*Kircher, A. *Musurgis Universalis* (Rome 1650).
Kirsten, E. "Ein politisches Programm in Pindars erstem pythischen Gedicht," *RhM* 90 (1941) 58–71.
Klingner, F. "Das erste pythische Gedicht Pindars," *Die Antike* 11 (1935) 49–66.

Kranz, W. "Der Eingang des ersten pythischen Siegesliedes," *Sok* 7 (1919) 252–4.
*Legouèz, A. *Pindare Pythiques, odes I, II, III*. Traduction littérale précédée d'une introduction et suivie d'un commentaire et d'un appendice (Paris 1876).
Lehrs, K. "Pindar und Luther über die Musik," *Wissenschaftliche Monatsblätter* 2 (1874) 128. Also in his *Kleine Schriften* (Königsberg 1902) 199.
Maas, P. & Müller-Blattau, J. "Kircher und Pindar," *Hermes* 70 (1935) 101–6.
von Mess, A. "Der Typhonmythus bei Pindar und Aeschylus," *RhM* 56 (1901) 167–74.
Mountford, J. F. "The Music of Pindar's 'Golden Lyre'," *CP* 31 (1936) 120–36.
Rome, A. "L'origine de la prétendue mélodie de Pindare," *LEC* 1 (1932) 3–11.
Rome, A. "Pindare ou Kircher?" *LEC* 4 (1935) 337–50.
Schlesinger, K. *The Greek Aulos* (London 1939) 353–60. On Kircher.
Schoder, R. V. "The Artistry of the first Pythian Ode," *CJ* 38 (1943) 401–12.
Stahl, J. M. *De Pindari carmine pythico primo* (Münster 1891).
Trumpf, J. "Stadtgründung und Drachenkampf (Exkurse zu Pindar, Pythien I)," *Hermes* 86 (1958) 129–57.
Valla, D. "Tifeo in Pindaro," *A&R* NS 9 (1928) 191–2.
Voss, J. H. "Pindar's erster pythischer Chor," *Anmerkungen und Randglossen* (Leipzig 1838) 82–94.
Wagner, R. "Zum Wiederaufleben der antiken Musikschriftsteller seit dem 16. Jahrhundert. Ein Beitrag zur Frage: Kircher oder Pindar?" *Philologus* 91 (1936) 161–73.

Translations

Bignone, E. "Dalla lirica greca," *A&R* 3rd S., 6 (1938) 245–61 (251–7).
*Bochenski, T. "Oda na zwyciestwo Hierona z Aitny," *Meander* 2 (1947) 367–72.
Borchardt, R. See under "P. 9 Translations" (131–7).
*Capocasa, S. See under "O. 1 Translations."
*Gazzani, A. See under "O. 1 Translations."
Händler, E. A. See under "O. 1.8" (151–5).
*Ivanov, V. "The First Pythian Ode of Pindar," *JMI* 324 (1899) 48–56. In Russian.
Mackowski, R. M. "Pindar on Music's Power (Prelude to Pythica 1)," *CB* 32 (1955) 7. Translation of vv. 1–33.
Minckwitz, J. See under "N. 1 Translations" (71–5).
Rosing, M. "Pindars 1ste pythiske Ode," *NTF* 3 (1877–78) 154–60.
Ruck, C. A. P. & Matheson, W. "Pindar: Pythia 1 for Hieron of Aetna: victory with chariot," *Arion* 3, No. 3 (1964) 39–43.
Teza, E. "Delle Pitie di Pindaro la prima tradotta in versi," *AIV* 66 (1906–07) 571–87.
Welkenhuysen, A. "Pindaros' Eerste Putische Zegelied," *Hermeneus* 36 (1964–65) 271–8.

Specific verses
- 1–28. VAN OOTEGHEM, J. "Invocation à la lyre (Pindare, Pyth., I, 1–28)," *LEC* 11 (1942) 361–72.
- 2. SEATON, R. C. "Pindar Pyth. I. 1," *CR* 2 (1888) 324.
- 6. VAN HERWERDEN, H. See under "*O.* 2.43" (213).
  MYLONAS, G. E. "The Eagle of Zeus," *CJ* 41 (1946) 203–7.
- 6–7. LA PENNA, A. "De Foscolo et Pindaro adnotatiuncula," *Maia* 7 (1955) 143–4.
- 6–8. POLLARD, J. R. T. "The Birds of Aristophanes—a Source Book for Old Beliefs," *AJP* 69 (1948) 353–76 (369).
- 9. ASTIUS, F. "Observationes et coniecturae in Pindari Carmina. Specimen secundum," *Commentarii societatis philologicae Lipsiensis* ed. C. D. Beckius. Vol. 3, pt. 2 (Leipzig 1803) 193–228 (193–4).
- 12. KRAUSE, H. "Zu Pind. Pyth. 1," *Philologus* 75 (1918) 237.
  WECKLEIN, N. "Zu Pindar und Aeschylus," *RhM* 26 (1871) 639.
- 16. NABER, S. A. See under "*O.* 1.7" (36).
- 20. WRIGHT, F. A. See under "*O.* 2.54–6."
- 35. AHRENS, H. L. See under "*O.* 8.16" (55).
  BOSSLER, C. See under "Syntax" (75–6).
- 44. KAKRIDIS, J. T. "Zu Pindars Pyth. I, 42 [83] u.f.," *PhW* 46 (1926) 654–5.
  TURYN, A. "Abermals zu Pindar Pyth. I 42 ff.," *PhW* 47 (1927) 138.
- 47. AHRENS, H. L. See under "*O.* 8.16" (55).
- 51. *SCHMIDT, M. See under "*O.* 1.63–4."
  SCHNITZER, C. F. See under "*O.* 1.28–9" (30).
- 52. AHRENS, H. L. See under "*O.* 8.16" (55).
  ASTIUS, F. See under "*P.* 1.9" (194–5).
  SHACKLE, R. J. See under "*O.* 14.15."
- 52–3. AHLWARDT, C. W. "Symbola ad augendum Schneideri Lexicon Graecum," *Acta societatis philologicae Lipsiensis* ed. C. D. Beckius. Vol. 1 (Leipzig 1811) 119–28 (121–2).
- 60. NABER, S. A. See under "*O.* 1.7" (36).
- 67. RAUCHENSTEIN, R. See under "*O.* 1.106–7" (67).
- 67–8. BOSSLER, C. See under "Syntax" (30).
  QUINCEY, J. H. "Etymologica," *RhM* 106 (1963) 142–8 (144–5).
  WISKEMANN, A. See under "*O.* 1.106–8" (11–12).
- 67–72. ASTIUS, F. See under "*P.* 1.9" (195–6).
- 68. JURENKA, H. See under "*O.* 3.42–5" (12–13).
- 71. MADWIG, J. N. See under "*O.* 2.65" (186–7).
- 72. LEHRS, K. See under "*O.* 2.65" (91–2).
- 72–9. FRIEDERICHS, K. See under "*O.* 6.31" (413–15).
- 75. DAWES, R. See under "*P.* 6 General" (93–4).
- 75–6. DREYKORN, J. See under "*O.* 2.56" (18).

75-80. ASTIUS, F. See under "*P.* 1.9" (196-7).
   FRIESE, E. See under "Syntax" (38-39).
   VON WILAMOWITZ-MOELLENDORFF, U. See under "History and Politics" (1306-8).
77. BOWRA, C. M. See under "Metre" (178-9).
   ROBERTSON, D. S. "Three notes on Pindar," *PCPS* 145-7 (1930) 2-3.
   STONE, W. A. See under "*O.* 13.98-9."
81-100 TACCONE, A. "Sulla chiusa della Pitia I di Pindaro," *BFC* 22 (1916) 270-2.
83. AHLWARDT, C. W. See under "*P.* 1.52-3" (126).
84. FRIESE, E. See under "Syntax" (39-40).
85-6. GINEVRI-BLASI, G. "Una nuova interpretazione di due versi della Pitia I di Pindaro," *BFC* 22 (1916) 251-3.
92. AHRENS, H. L. See under "*O.* 8.16" (55).
   PEARSON, A. C. See under "*O.* 1.105" (152-3).
92-4. ASTIUS, F. See under "*P.* 1.9" (197).
94. VON LEUTSCH, E. "Pindar und die Beredsamkeit," *Philologus* 17 (1861) 357-60.
   PFLIGERSDORFFER, G. "Λόγιος und die λόγιοι ἄνθρωποι bei Demokrit," *WS* 61-62 (1943-47) 5-49 (9-10).
95-6. SMYTH, W. R. "Interpretationes Propertianae," *CQ* 43 (1949) 118-25 (123-4).

Scholia

38b. SHOREY, P. "Emendation of Scholia on Pindar Pyth. 1. 20," *CP* 13 (1918) 90.

PYTHIAN TWO

General

BASSI, D. "Il mito dei Centauri secondo il risultato degli studi più recenti," *BFC* 3 (1897) 14-17.
BOWRA, C. M. "Pindar, Pythian II," *HSCP* 48 (1937) 1-28. Also in *Problems in Greek Poetry* (Oxford 1953) 66-92.
*CAMARDA, N. See under "*O.* 1 General."
CAMARDA, N. See under "*P.* 1 General."
CROISET, A. "Observations sur le sens du mythe d'Ixion dans la deuxième pythique de Pindare," *Annuaire de l'association pour l'encouragement des études grecques en France* 10 (1876) 83-96.
DRACHMANN, A. B. "Über Datierung und Veranlassung von Pindars zweiter pythischer Ode," *JPh* 141 (1890) 441-9.
GODDARD, E. H. "Pindar, Pythian II," *CR* 36 (1922) 103-6.
*LEGOUÈZ, A. See under "*P.* 1 General."

Legrand, P.-E. "Sur l'intention et la composition de la deuxième Pythique de Pindare," *Revue Universitaire* 15 (1902) 473–84.
Lübbert, E. *Dissertatio de Pindari carmine Pythico secundo* (Progr. Kiel 1880).
Meinel, G. *Beiträge zur Erklärung Pindars* (Progr. Kempten 1890) 4–17.
Mezger, F. "Pindars zweite pythische Ode," *Philologus* 35 (1876) 430–44.
Oates, J. F. "Pindar's Second Pythian Ode," *AJP* 84 (1963) 377–89.
Robertson, D. S. "On Pindar," *PCPS* 127–9 (1924) 35.
Schroeder, O. "Pindarica IV. Pindar und Hieron," *Philologus* 61 (1902) 356–73 and 636 (356–69).
Scognamiglio, R. "Contributo allo studio e alla datazione della Pitica II di Pindaro," *MC* 5 (1935) 349–54.
Urlichs, L. "Pindars zweite pythische Ode," *Eos(S)* 1 (1864) 221–4.
Von der Mühll, P. "Der Anlass zur zweiten Pythie Pindars," *MH* 15 (1958) 215–21.
Wiskemann, A. See under "*O*. 6 General" (10–12).
Woodbury, L. "The Epilogue of Pindar's Second Pythian," *TAPA* 76 (1945) 11–30.

Translations
Ruck, C. A. P. & Matheson, W. H. "For Hieron: The Poet's Apologia (Pindar, Pythia II)," *Arion* 4 (1965) 181–7.
*Schjøtt, P. O. "Pindars 2den pythiske Ode," *Forhandlinger i Videnskabs Selbskabet i Christiania* (1870) 44–59.

Specific verses
5. Nairn, J. A. "On Pindar's Pythian Odes," *CR* 15 (1901) 246–8.
7–8. Nairn, J. A. See under "*P*. 2.5."
    von Wilamowitz-Moellendorff, U. See under "History and Politics" (1309–10).
8. Nairn, J. A. See under "*O*. 1.64."
11. Robertson, D. S. "Bits and Chariots: A Note on Pindar Pythians II, 9 sqq.," *Studi in onore di Luigi Castiglioni*, vol. 2 (Florence 1960) 803–5.
    Young, D. See under "*I*. 8.40" (21).
17. Friederichs, K. See under "*O*. 1.28–9" (24–6).
    Jurenka, H. See under "*O*. 3.42–5" (4).
    Morpurgo, A. "Κτίλος (Pind., Pyth. II 17)," *RCCM* 2 (1960) 30–40.
22. Kuijper, D. "Phlegyas Admonitor," *Mnem* 4th S., 16 (1963) 162–70 (164–5).
26. Naber, S. A. See under "*O*. 1.7" (36).
28. Scarpat, G. "Varietà," *Paideia* 1 (1946) 353.
30–4. Simon, E. "Ixion und die Schlangen," *JOEAI* 42 (1955) 5–26.
    Smith, C. "The Myth of Ixion," *CR* 9 (1895) 277–80.
35–6. Sitzler, J. "Zu Pindar," *PhW* 44 (1924) 1117–8.
    Stone, W. A. See under "*O*. 6.15."

35-7. Alsina Clota, J. "Conjetura al texto de Pindaro Pítica II, 35 y siguientes," *Emerita* 23 (1955) 258-61.
Astius, F. See under "*P*. 1.9" (197-9).
36. Bossler, C. See under "Syntax" (57-8).
Cerrato, L. "Di alcuni luoghi controversi nelle Pitiche Pindariche," *RFIC* 18 (1890) 175-212 (176-8 and 211-12).
Düring, I. See under "*O*. 8.52" (3).
Fraccaroli, G. See under "*O*. 8.1-9" (98-9).
Friederichs, K. See under "*O*. 1.28-9" (26-7).
Headlam, W. See under "*O*. 6.74" (298).
Tarditi, G. "La ΥΠΕΡΒΑΣΙΑ di Issione," *PP* 11 (1956) 191-6.
45-6. Rose, H. J. "Metaphor, Ancient and Modern," *Studies in Honour of Gilbert Norwood*, Phoenix Supp. Vol. 1 (Toronto 1952) 239-47 (244).
49-56. Grimm, R. E. "Pindar and the Beast," *CP* 57 (1962) 1-9.
Hauvette, A. "Sur un passage de la deuxième Pythique de Pindare," *Mélanges Perrot. Recueil de mémoires concernant l'archéologie classique, la littérature et l'histoire anciennes dédié à Georges Perrot* (Paris 1903) 161-5.
50-1. Ridgeway, W. "Pindar, Pyth. II. 50-1," *PCPS* 46-48 (1897) 14-15.
52-6. Wyckoff, E. "Pindar Pythian 2. 52-56," *CP* 41 (1946) 160-2.
53. Schmalfeld, F. "Beiträge zur homerischen Worterklärung," *Philologus* 34 (1876) 577-98 (584).
56. Croiset, A. "Un vers de Pindare à corriger," *Annuaire de l'association pour l'encouragement des études grecques en France* 12 (1878) 63-7.
Gerber, D. E. "Pindar, Pythian 2. 56," *TAPA* 91 (1960) 100-8.
Jurenka, H. See under "*O*. 3.42-5" (14-15).
66. Friederichs, K. See under "*O*. 1.28-9" (27).
Friederichs, K. See under "*O*. 6.31" (415-16).
66-7. Jurenka, H. See under "*O*. 3.42-5" (19).
67-84. von Wilamowitz-Moellendorff, U. See under "History and Politics" (1311-7).
70. Harrison, J. E. "On Pindar Olympian II. 126: παρὰ Κρόνου τύρσιν," *PCPS* 70-72 (1905) 21-2.
72. del Grande, C. "Pitica seconda, vs. 72," *Filologia Minore* (Milan & Naples 1956) 113-14.
Headlam, W. See under "*O*. 6.74" (301-2).
van Herwerden, H. See under "*O*. 2.71" (41-2).
Luppino, A. See under "*O*. 1.56-57b" (361-3).
Matthiae, A. *De loco quodam Pindari, tum de Babrii fabulis* (Altenburg 1822) 4-5. Also in *Vermischte Schriften* (Altenburg 1842²) 98-100.
McDermott, W. C. "The Ape in Greek Literature," *TAPA* 66 (1935) 165-76 (169-70).
McDermott, W. C. *The Ape in Antiquity* (Baltimore 1938) 132.
Schmid, W. "Zu Pindaros Pythia 2, 72," *Philologus* 73 (1916) 446-7.
Schneidewin, F. W. "Pindaros," *Philologus* 7 (1852) 732.

SNELL, B. *Scenes from Greek Drama* (Berkeley 1964) 85–6.
VON DER MÜHLL, P. "Wieder zu Pindar Pythie II 72 γένοι' οἷός ἐσσι μαθών," *RhM* 72 (1917–18) 307–10.

72–3. ASTIUS, F. See under "*P.* 1.9" (199–200).
72–5. COMPARETTI, D. "Zur Hermeneutik des Pindaros," *Philologus* 28 (1869) 385–98.
FRACCAROLI, G. See under "*O.* 8.1–9" (99–104).
NORWOOD, G. "Pindar, Pythian, II, 72 ff.," *AJP* 62 (1941) 340–3.
72–85. LURIA, S. "Der Affe des Archilochos und die Brautwerbung des Hippokleides," *Philologus* 85 (1930) 1–22 (11–12).
72–88. MATTHIAE, A. *Miscellanea philologica*, vol. 1 (Leipzig and Altenburg 1809²) 28–41.
NAIRN, J. A. See under "*P.* 2.5."
76–7. DONALDSON, J. W. "On some special Difficulties in Pindar," *JCSP* 1 (1854) 210–24 (211–13).
78. FRIEDERICHS, K. See under "*O.* 1.28–9" (28).
78–80. ASTIUS, F. See under "*P.* 1.9" (200).
80. SCHNITZER, C. F. See under "*O.* 1.28–9" (32–3).
82. GILDERSLEEVE, B. L. "Brief Mention," *AJP* 28 (1907) 109–10.
HEADLAM, W. See under "*O.* 6.74" (298–9).
84. BEARE, J. I. "Miscellanea," *Hermathena* 13 (1905) 70–86 (76–8).
84–5. DORNSEIFF, F. See under "*I.* 5.1" (73–4).
89–92. PEARSON, A. C. See under "*O.* 1.105" (156–7).
90. FENNELL, C. A. M. "On Pindar Pyth. II. 161 sqq.," *CR* 12 (1898) 350.
HEADLAM, W. See under "Fr. 112 General" (437 n. 9).
WHITE, R. E. "Note on Pindar Pythian II. 161 sqq.," *CR* 12 (1898) 208.
90–1. BURY, R. G. "Pindar, Pyth. II. 90 ff.," *CR* 29 (1915) 77.
VAN HERWERDEN, H. See under "*O.* 2.43" (213–4).
NORWOOD, G. See under "*O.* 3.44" (4–5).
SHEPPARD, J. T. "Pindar, Pythian II. 90 ff.," *CR* 29 (1915) 230–3.
90–2. JÜTHNER, J. "Worterklärungen," *Ἐπιτύμβιον H. Swoboda dargebracht* (Reichenberg 1927) 107–13 (107–11).
NAIRN, J. A. See under "*O.* 1.64."

PYTHIAN THREE

General

*CAMARDA, N. See under "*O.* 1 General."
CAMARDA, N. See under "*P.* 1 General."
HEIMSOETH, F. See under "*P.* 9 General" (16–21).
HERMANN, G. *Emendationes Pindaricae* (Leipzig 1834). Also in *Opuscula* 7 (Leipzig 1839) 129–73 (129–38).
KLINGNER, F. "Über Pindars drittes Pythisches Gedicht," *Corolla L. Curtius zum sechzigsten Geburtstag dargebracht* (Stuttgart 1937) 15–19. Also in *Studien zur griechischen und römischen Literatur* (Zürich and Stuttgart 1964) 80–5.

*Legouèz, A. See under "*P.* 1 General."
Luppino, A. "Divagazioni e precisazioni sulla Pitica III di Pindaro," *RFIC* 87 (1959) 225–36.
Osann, F. *Pindari Pyth. III enarratio* (Progr. Giessen 1858).
Schroeder, O. See under "*P.* 2 General" (370–73).
Wartelle, A. "Remarques sur le style de Pindare à propos des Pythiques III, IV et V," *BAGB* 4th S. (1965) 85–93.

Translations

Borchardt, R. See under "*P.* 9 Translations" (138–43).

Specific verses

    6. Bowra, C. M. See under "Metre" (181).
  11. Hess, H. "Zwei Pindarstellen," *RhM* 88 (1939) 286–8.
      Oelschlaeger, F. See under "*O.* 2.26" (17).
14–16. Friederichs, K. See under "*O.* 1.28–9" (28–9).
  16. Bossler, C. See under "Syntax" (39).
16–19. Muth, R. "'Hymenaios' und 'Epithalamion'," *WS* 67 (1954) 5–45 (23–5).
  18. Edmonds, J. M. "Some Notes on the Homeric Hymns," *CQ* 31 (1937) 49–52 (49).
  27. Naber, S. A. See under "*O.* 1.7" (36).
  28. Astius, F. See under "*P.* 1.9" (200–1).
      Jurenka, H. See under "*O.* 3.42–5" (15).
28–9. Oelschlaeger, F. See under "*O.* 2.26" (17).
  29. van Herwerden, H. See under "*O.* 2.43" (214).
36–8. Cook, A. B. "Associated Reminiscences," *CR* 15 (1901) 338–45 (343).
  38. Astius, F. See under "*P.* 1.9" (201).
      Hartman, J. J. "Adnotatiunculas criticas ad Pindari locos quosdam," *Mnem* NS 46 (1918) 445–51 (445–6).
  40. Friederichs, K. See under "*O.* 1.28–9" (29).
40–2. Naber, S. A. See under "*O.* 1.7" (36–7).
  44. van Herwerden, H. See under "*O.* 2.71" (42).
      Jurenka, H. See under "*O.* 3.42–5" (28–9).
  48. Thomson, G. "Bad Bronze," *CR* 58 (1944) 35–7.
  57. Bergk, T. See under "*O.* 2.95–100" (185–6).
      Naber, S. A. See under "*O.* 1.7" (37).
  59. Shorey, P. See under "*P.* 5.101" (94).
  67. Dornseiff, F. See under "*I.* 5.1" (72–3).
      Farnell, L. R. "Pindar: a Reply," *CR* 47 (1933) 9–11.
      Robertson, D. S. "Pindar: a Rejoinder," *CR* 47 (1933) 61–2.
      von Wilamowitz-Moellendorff, U. *Isyllos von Epidauros* = *PU* 9 (1886) 64 n. 37.
  80. Naber, S. A. See under "*O.* 1.7" (37).

81. POSITANO, L. M. "Nugae. I. Sui versi omerici Ω 527–8," *PP* 1 (1946) 359–61.
82–3. HEADLAM, W. See under "Fr. 112 General" (436).
83. NABER, S. A. See under "*O.* 1.7" (37).
84. RADERMACHER, L. "Zu griechischen Texten," *WS* 56 (1938) 1–10.
103–6. ASTIUS, F. See under "*P.* 1.9" (201–3).
106. BERGK, T. See under "*O.* 2.95–100" (186).
BOECKH, A. See under "*O.* 6.53–4" (27).
JURENKA, H. See under "*O.* 3.42–5" (9).
SHACKLE, R. J. See under "*O.* 14.15."
112. SCHWICKERT, J. J. See under "*O.* 11.4" (22–3).

Scholia

Inscr. b (p.63 Dr.). VAN COMPERNOLLE, R. See under "Chronology" (324–30)
32c. GÜNGERICH, R. "Die antike Erklärung eines griechischen Hochzeitsspruchs," *Hermes* 65 (1930) 238–40.
137b. DODDS, E. R. See under "*O.* 9.33–5" (117).
HARRISON, J. See under "*O.* 9.33" (410).
177b. MAAS, P. "Zum Scholion Pindar, Pyth. 3, 177b," *Philologus* 90 (1935) 240.

PYTHIAN FOUR

General

CHAMOUX, F. *Cyrène sous la monarchie des Battiades* (Diss. Paris 1952).
DANIELSSON, O. A. "De carminis Pythici IV:i Pindarici locis selectis," *Eranos* 25 (1927) 1–22.
DEFRADAS, J. See under "*P.* 11 General" (242–53).
DELAGE, É. "Le mythe des Argonautes et la composition dans la IVe Pythique," *Mélanges offerts à A. M. Desrousseaux* (Paris 1937) 123–30.
FORSSMAN, B. See under "Dialect" (86–100).
FRIEDERICHS, K. See under "*O.* 1.28–9" (38–47).
HADAS, M. "The Tradition of a Feeble Jason," *CP* 31 (1936) 166–8.
HERMANN, G. See under "*P.* 3 General" (138–43).
JUNGHANS, W. *Zur Methodik. Das vierte pythische Epinikion des Pindaros* (Progr. Lüneburg 1868).
*KRÁL, J. A. *Abhandlung über die Argonautenfahrt (auf Grundlage der vierten Ode von Pindar, und der Epopöe Argonautica von Apollonius)* (Brünn 1852).
DE LANNOY, L. See under "Manuscripts."
LATTIMORE, R. "Pindar's Fourth Pythian Ode," *CW* 42 (1948) 19–25.
LINDSAY, J. *The Clashing Rocks. A Study of early Greek Religion and Culture and the Origins of Drama* (London 1965).
MALTEN, L. See under "*P.* 5.75."
MEZGER, F. "Pindar's vierte pythische Ode," *BBG* 4 (1868) 73–88.

*Minckwitz, J. *Pindars vierte pythische Ode* (Leipzig 1850).

Mitchell, B. M. "Cyrene and Persia," *JHS* 86 (1966) 99–113.

*Neander, M. *Theocriti Eidyllia. Pindari lyricorum principis Argonautica. Cum expositione grammatica de ore Mich. Neandri excerpta* (Basel? 1596).

*Palmblad, W. F. *Pindari Pythiorum ode quarta, vs. 1–151* (Progr. Uppsala 1836).

Paranikas, M. Ἀνάλυσις τῆς Δ' ᾠδῆς τῶν Πυθίων τοῦ Πινδάρου, *Syll* 22 (1889–90 and 1890–91) 190–5.

*Sjöström, A. G. *Circa Pindari Pythiorum quartum adversaria* (Progr. Helsingfors 1846).

Strosetzki, N. "Antike Rechtssymbole," *Hermes* 86 (1958) 1–17 (11–13).

Thornton, H. & A. See under "Style and Imagery" (27–35 and Fig. 2).

*Wagner, I. F. *Symbolae ad Pindari Argonautica interpretanda* (Luneburgi 1794).

Wartelle, A. See under "P. 3 General."

Wehrli, F. "Die Rückfahrt der Argonauten," *MH* 12 (1955) 154–7.

Translations

Bignone, E. "La Pitica IV di Pindaro," *A&R* 3rd S., 7 (1939) 221–37.

Borchardt, R. See under "P. 9 Translations" (108–24).

*Borgeaud, W. *Les Argonautes de Pindare. IVᵉ Pythique pour Arkésilas de Cyrène* (Geneva 1949).

Gravenhorst, C. T. *Pindar's Siegesgesang auf Arkesilas, König von Kyrene* (Progr. Bremen 1862).

Hartung, J. A. *Pindar's IV. pythische Ode*, griechisch und deutsch (Progr. Schleusingen 1854).

Houghton, H. P. "Pindar: Pythia IV; An Editing and a Rendering," *Studies Presented to D. M. Robinson on his Seventieth Birthday*. Vol. 2 (Saint Louis 1953) 514–30.

*Krüger, E. "Pindars vierte pythische Siegeshymne übersetzt," *Bremer Sonntagsblatt* (1864) No. 30.

Loenen, D. *De vierde Pythische ode van Pindaros* (Amsterdam 1940).
 [W. E. J. Kuiper, *MPh* 48 (1941) 202–4; B. A. van Groningen, *Hermeneus* 13 (1941) 35.]

*Loenen, D. *De vierde pythische ode van Pindaros, behelzende het oudste verhaal over de tocht der Argonauten* (Amsterdam 1953).

Romagnoli, E. "La quarta ode pitica di Pindaro. Versione metrica e osservazioni sulla esegesi di Pindaro," *AIV* 74 (1914–15) 641–59.

Specific verses

4. Dawes, R. See under "P. 6 General" (94–6).

7. Heller, H. See under "P. 4.210" (264–5).

20–49. Niese, B. "Herodot-Studien besonders zur spartanischen Geschichte," *Hermes* 42 (1907) 419–68 (455–9).

23. de Lannoy, L. "Enkele tekstkritische aantekeningen bij Pindaros' Vierde en Vijfde Puthische Ode," *AC* 34 (1965) 542–53 (542).

29. Long, A. A. "Sophocles Ajax 68-70. A Reply to Professor Eduard Fraenkel," *MH* 21 (1964) 228-31.
31. Archer-Hind, R. D. "Note on the fourth Pythian," *JP* 22 (1894) 267.
32-3. Sealey, R. "Thucydides, Herodotos, and the Causes of War," *CQ* NS 7 (1957) 1-12 (2-3).
36. Jurenka, H. See under "*O.* 3.42-5" (26).
*Schmidt, M. See under "*O.* 1.57."
37. van Herwerden, H. See under "*O.* 2.71" (42).
40. Oelschlaeger, F. See under "*O.* 2.26" (17-18).
42. van Herwerden, H. See under "*O.* 2.71" (42).
Hutchinson, W. M. L. See under "*N.* 3.3-5" (157 n. 2).
43-8. Kocevalov, A. See under "Syntax" (49-51).
43-9. Gercke, A. "Die Myrmidonen in Kyrene," *Hermes* 41 (1906) 447-59 (452-7).
47. van Herwerden, H. See under "*O.* 2.71" (43).
50. Bowra, C. M. See under "Metre" (84).
54. Archer-Hind, R. D. See under "*P.* 4.31."
55. Vallois, R. "Les strophes mutilées du péan de Philodamos," *BCH* 55 (1931) 241-364 (322-3).
57. van Herwerden, H. See under "*O.* 2.71" (43).
Matthiae, A. *Observationes Criticae in Tragicos, Homerum, Apollonium, Pindarum etc.* (Göttingen 1789) 39.
60. Amandry, P. See under "*O.* 6.70" (61 n. 5).
Parke, H. W. "A Note on αὐτοματίζω in Connexion with Prophecy," *JHS* 82 (1962) 145-6.
72. de Lannoy, L. See under "*P.* 4.23" (542-4).
75. Brunel, J. "Jason μονοκρήπις," *RA* 6th S., 4 (1934) 34-43.
Deonna, W. *Μονοκρήπιδες*, *RHR* 112 (1935) 50 72.
Goossens, R. "Les Étoliens chaussés d'un seul pied," *RBPh* 14 (1935) 849-54.
79. Fraenkel, E. See under "*I.* 6.17" (320 n. 1).
84. van Herwerden, H. See under "*O.* 2.71" (43).
89. Schneidewin, F. W. "Lanx satura," *RhM* 2 (1843) 294-300 (297).
96-100. Shorey, P. "On Pindar Pyth. IV. 96 ff.," *CP* 25 (1930) 280-1.
98. Röhl, H. "Zu Pindaros," *JPh* 115 (1877) 850.
98-9. Pavese, C. See under "*O.* 6.83" (308-10).
Reiter, G. *Die griechischen Bezeichnungen der Farben weiss, grau und braun* (Innsbruck 1962) 61-2.
99-100. Campbell, A. Y. "Pindarica," *CR* NS 5 (1955) 3-5.
Goossens, R. "Sur quelques passages de comédies grecques," *RBPh* 26 (1948) 92-7 (95-7).
100. Jurenka, H. See under "*O.* 3.42-5" (17).
105. von Wilamowitz-Moellendorff, U. "Parerga," *Hermes* 14 (1879) 161-86 (170-1). Also in *Kleine Schriften IV* (Berlin 1962) 8.

108. Archer-Hind, R. D. See under "*P.* 4.31."
109. Hartmann, F. "Λευκαῖς φρασί Pind. Pyth. 4, 109," *ZVS* 60 (1933) 223.
　　Maguire, T. See under "*O.* 6.62" (381).
　　Postgate, J. P. "Persius III. 43," *CR* 3 (1889) 275.
　　Reiter, G. See under "*P.* 4.98–9" (39–42).
　　Stanford, W. B. "Pelias and his Pallid Wits: on *ΛΕΥΚΑΙΣ ΦΡΑΣΙΝ* in Pindar Pythians 4. 109," *Studies in Honour of Gilbert Norwood*, Phoenix Supp. Vol. 1 (Toronto 1952) 42–5.
118. Bowra, C. M. See under "Metre" (179).
　　Jurenka, H. See under "*O.* 3.42–5" (33).
　　Lehrs, K. See under "*O.* 2.65" (92–3).
　　Madwig, J. N. See under "*O.* 2.65" (187).
　　Tyrrell, R. Y. See under "*O.* 3.45."
127–30. van Herwerden, H. See under "*O.* 2.71" (44).
131. *Schmidt, M. See under "*O.* 1.57."
139. Naber, S. A. See under "*O.* 1.7" (37).
144. Shorey, P. "The Pathos and Humor of αὖ," *CP* 23 (1928) 285–7.
145. de Lannoy, L. See under "*P.* 4.23" (544–5).
　　Wade-Gery, H. T. See under "*O.* 1.52" (71 n. 2).
145–6. Astius, F. See under "*P.* 1.9" (203).
　　van Herwerden, H. See under "*O.* 2.71" (44–5).
　　Maguire, T. See under "*O.* 6.62" (381–2).
150. van Herwerden, H. See under "*O.* 2.71" (45).
155. Schnitzer, C. F. See under "*O.* 1.28–9" (34).
156. Wade-Gery, H. T. See under "*O.* 1.52" (71).
158. Stanford, W. B. See under "*O.* 6.82."
159–62. Robertson, D. S. "The Flight of Phrixus," *CR* 54 (1940) 1–8 (7).
159–63. Messer, W. S. "A possible Source of the Dream in Pindar's Fourth Pythian," *CW* 15 (1922) 129–31.
161–2. Pearson, A. C. "Phrixus and Demodice. A Note on Pindar, Pyth. IV. 162 f.," *CR* 23 (1909) 255–7.
163. Amandry, P. See under "*O.* 6.70" (135 n. 1).
171–83. Friederichs, K. See under "*O.* 6.31" (416–18).
178–82. Friederichs, K. See under "*O.* 1.28–9" (29–31).
179. Fraser, J. "The *ΣΧΗΜΑ ΑΛΚΜΑΝΙΚΟΝ*," *CQ* 4 (1910) 25–7.
180. Schnitzer, C. F. See under "*O.* 1.28–9" (35).
182–3. Gallavotti, C. "Nomi di colori in Miceneo," *PP* 12 (1957) 5–22 (20–2).
184. Bowra, C. M. See under "Metre" (181–2).
186–7. Düring, I. See under "*O.* 8.52" (4).
　　Maguire, T. See under "*O.* 6.62" (382–3).
195–6. Friederichs, K. See under "*O.* 1.28–9" (31–2).
202. Hartman, J. J. See under "*P.* 3.38" (446–7).
　　Morrison, J. S. "Euripides, I. T. 1390 ff. and Pindar, Pythians iv. 202," *CR* 64 (1950) 3–5.

204. ASTIUS, F. See under "*P.* 1.9" (204).
205. JURENKA, H. See under "*O.* 3.42–5" (29–30).
210. HELLER, H. "Epistola ad Max. Dunkerum de particulis ἤδη et δή," *Philologus* 8 (1853) 254–308 (263–4).
211–12. BOECKH, A. See under "*O.* 6.53–4" (14–15).
212–13. FRIEDERICHS, K. See under "*O.* 6.31" (418–19).
NORWOOD, G. See under "*O.* 3.44" (6).
213. DE LANNOY, L. See under "*P.* 4.23" (545–6).
214. BURY, J. B. "῎Ιυγξ in Greek Magic," *JHS* 7 (1886) 157–60.
DE LA GENIÈRE, J. "Une roue à oiseaux du Cabinet des Médailles," *REA* 60 (1958) 27–35.
GOW, A. S. F. "῎Ιυγξ, ῥόμβος, rhombus, turbo," *JHS* 54 (1934) 1–13.
TAVENNER, E. "Iynx and Rhombus," *TAPA* 64 (1933) 109–27 (116–7).
214–15. ROBINSON, D. M. See under "*O.* 2.21–2" (210–11).
217. CHANTRAINE, P. See under "*O.* 6.78."
224–7. FRIEDERICHS, K. See under "*O.* 6.31" (419).
228. BOWRA, C. M. See under "Metre" (87).
DE LANNOY, L. See under "*P.* 4.23" (547–8).
234. DE LANNOY, L. See under "*P.* 4.23" (548–50).
NORWOOD, G. See under "*O.* 3.44" (6).
234–5. ASTIUS, F. See under "*P.* 1.9" (203–4).
DÜRING, I. See under "*O.* 8.52" (4–5).
237. MATTHIAE, A. See under "*P.* 4.57" (39).
250. WACKERNAGEL, J. "Varia," *Glotta* 4 (1912) 242–5.
250–2. JURENKA, H. See under "*O.* 3.42–5" (6–7).
253. BOSSLER, C. See under "Syntax" (42).
BOWRA, C. M. See under "Metre" (179–80).
NAIRN, J. A. See under "*O.* 1.62–4" (11).
OELSCHLAEGER, F. See under "*O.* 2.26" (18).
253–6. FRIEDERICHS, K. See under "*O.* 1.28–9" (32–4).
258. VAN HERWERDEN, H. See under "*O.* 2.43" (214).
259–69. FRIEDERICHS, K. See under "*O.* 1.28–9" (34–7).
260. ASTIUS, F. See under "*P.* 1.9" (204).
DAWES, R. See under "*P.* 6 General" (99–100).
263–8. FRIEDERICHS, K. See under "*O.* 6.31" (419–21).
263–9. SCHRÖDER, O. See under "*I.* 3/4 General" (3–5).
265. CALDER, W. M. "Pindar, Pyth. iv. 265," *CR* 57 (1943) 14.
VAN HERWERDEN, H. See under "*P.* 5.121."
266. SCHWENCK, K. "Pindarus," *RhM* 2 (1843) 462–3.
277–8. FITCH, E. "Pindar and Homer," *CP* 19 (1924) 57–66.
277–9. FRIEDERICHS, K. See under "*O.* 6.31" (421–3).
278–9. FRIEDERICHS, K. See under "*O.* 1.28–9" (37–8).
279–81. LEHRS, K. See under "*O.* 2.65" (93–5).
281. MADWIG, J. N. See under "*O.* 2.65" (187–8).
281–2. CERRATO, L. See under "*P.* 2.36" (178–9).

283. THOMAS, P. "Note sur un passage de la IVe Pythique de Pindare," *RIB* 31 (1888) 177–8.
286–7. GILDERSLEEVE, B. L. "Brief Mention," *AJP* 28 (1907) 108–9.
HEADLAM, W. See under "*O*. 6.74" (299–300).
286–90. PEARSON, A. C. See under "*O*. 1.105" (154–5).

Scholia

246b. WENTZEL, G. "Ein Pindar-Scholion und ein Philostratisches Gemälde," *Aus der Anomia. Archäologische Beitraege, Carl Robert zur Erinnerung an Berlin dargebracht* (Berlin 1890) 134–48.

PYTHIAN FIVE

General

CHAMOUX, F. See under "*P*. 4 General."
HERMANN, G. See under "*P*. 3 General" (143–53).
DE LANNOY, L. See under "Manuscripts."
MALTEN, L. See under "*P*. 5.75."
MITCHELL, B. M. See under "*P*. 4 General."
TAFEL, M. T. L. F. *Pindari carminum Pythiorum quintum cum octavo recens illustratum* (Diss. Tübingen 1819).
WARTELLE, A. See under "*P*. 3 General."

Specific verses

6–11. CERRATO, L. See under "*P*. 2.36" (179–80).
10. HEADLAM, W. See under "*O*. 14.20–21."
15–19. CAMPBELL, A. Y. "Pindar, Pythians V. 15 ff.," *CQ* 35 (1941) 148–9.
FRIEDERICHS, K. "Erklärungen zu Pindar's Epinikien," *Philologus* 13 (1858) 443–56 (443–4).
FRIEDERICHS, K. See under "*O*. 1.28–9" (47–8).
JURENKA, H. See under "*O*. 3.42–5" (17–18).
ROSE, H. J. "Two Difficulties in Pindar, Pyth. V," *CQ* 33 (1939) 69–70.
SCHRÖDER, O. See under "*I*. 3/4 General" (5–6).
SHOREY, P. ΣΥΓΓΕΝΗΣ ΟΦΘΑΛΜΟΣ, *CP* 4 (1909) 323.
17–18. BRIDGE, J. Συγγενὴς ὀφθαλμός, *HSCP* 11 (1900) 141–9. See also B. L. Gildersleeve, *AJP* 21 (1900) 475–6.
17–19. ASTIUS, F. See under "*P*. 1.9" (205–7).
CERRATO, L. See under "*P*. 2.36" (181–2).
21. HELLER, H. See under "*P*. 4.210" (264).
24. BERGK, T. "Philologische Thesen," *RhM* 19 (1864) 602. Also in *Kleine philologische Schriften* 2 (Halle 1886) 738–9.
DE LANNOY, L. See under "*P*. 4.23" (551–3).
SCHROEDER, O. "Zu Pindaros," *JPh* 115 (1877) 24.
25–6. CERRATO, L. See under "*P*. 2.36" (182–3).

26. FRIEDERICHS, K. See under "*O*. 1.28–9" (48).
31. SCHWENCK, K. "Zu Pindar," *RhM* 5 (1847) 627.
32–42. DONALDSON, J. W. See under "*P*. 2.76–7" (213–17).
    ROUX, G. "Pindare, le prétendu Trésor des Crétois et l'ancienne statue d'Apollon à Delphes," *REG* 75 (1962) 366–80.
33–9. CERRATO, L. See under "*P*. 2.36" (183–4).
40–2. FRIEDERICHS, K. See under "*O*. 1.28–9" (48).
55. ROSE, H. J. "Pindar and the Tragedians," *CR* 61 (1947) 43–4.
57–62. PEARSON, A. C. See under "*O*. 1.105" (153–4).
63–4. VAN BROCK, N. See under "*N*. 3.18" (90–1).
72–6. LÜBBERT, E. See under "*P*. 9 General."
    NAIRN, J. A. See under "*P*. 2.5."
72–81. HERMANN, G. "Ueber die Aegiden, von denen Pindar abstammte," *Berichte der k. sächs. Gesellschaft der Wiss. zu Leipzig* 1 (1847) 221–6. Also in *Opuscula* 8 (Leipzig 1877) 93–8.
    LÜBBERT, E. *Diatriba in Pindarum locum de Aegidis et sacris Carneis* (Progr. Bonn 1883).
    MOMMSEN, T. "De Pindaro Aegidarum gentili," *ZA* 3 (1845) 1–13.
    REHM, A. "Pindar und die Aigiden," *Commentationes philologicae. Conventui Philologorum Monachii Congregatorum obtulerunt Sodales Seminarii Philologici Monacensis* (Munich 1891) 146–59.
    ROBERT, K. *Oidipus. Geschichte eines poetischen Stoffs im griechischen Altertum*. Vol. 1 (Berlin 1915) 565–74.
    STUDNICZKA, F. "War Pindar ein Aigide?" *Kyrene, eine altgriechische Göttin. Archäologische und mythologische Untersuchungen* (Leipzig 1890) 73–85.
75. BORNEMANN, L. "Ueber die Aegiden, von denen angeblich Pindar stammte," *Philologus* 43 (1884) 79–85.
    MALTEN, L. *Kyrene. Sagengeschichtliche und historische Untersuchungen* = *PU* 20 (1911) 170–82.
77–81. CERRATO, L. See under "*P*. 2.36" (184–6).
    ROSE, H. J. See under "*P*. 5.15–19."
77–93. DEFRADAS, J. "Le culte des Anténorides à Cyrène," *REG* 65 (1952) 289–301.
    VIAN, F. "Les Anténorides de Cyrène et les Carneia," *REG* 68 (1955) 307–11.
82–8. BRUNEL, J. "Les Anténorides à Cyrène et l'interprétation littérale de Pindare, Pythique V, v. 82–88," *REA* 66 (1964) 5–21.
    CHAMOUX, F. "Les Anténorides à Cyrène," *Mélanges d'archéologie et d'histoire offerts à Ch. Picard* = *RA* 6th S., 29–30 (1949) 154–61.
85–7. CERRATO, L. See under "*P*. 2.36" (186–7).
87–8. PARKE, H. W. & WORMELL, D. E. W. "Notes on Delphic Oracles," *CQ* 43 (1949) 138–40.

91. Meineke, A. "Coniectanea in Aeneam Tacticum," *Hermes* 2 (1867) 174–90 (179).
96. van Herwerden, H. See under "*O.* 2.71" (45–6).
98–103. Friederichs, K. See under "*O.* 3.13–18" (35–6).
101. Shorey, P. "A Greek Analogue of the Romance Adverb," *CP* 5 (1910) 83–96 (95).
119. Naber, S. A. See under "*O.* 1.7" (37–8).
121. Hartman, J. J. See under "*P.* 3.38" (447–8).
van Herwerden, H. "Varia ad varios," *Mnem* NS 27 (1899) 378–98 (378–9).

PYTHIAN SIX

General

Bornemann, L. "Pindars sechste pythische Ode," *Philologus* 51 (1892) 465–73.
Cerrato, L. "Il disegno della sesta Pitica di Pindaro," *BSI* 1 (1889) 96–7.
Dawes, R. "Oxoniensium Pindari Editorum desideratae ἀκριβείας specimen," *Miscellanea Critica typis quinquies excusa prodeunt ex recensione et cum notis aliquanto auctioribus Thomae Kidd* (London, 1827²) 62–108 and 648–51 (62–84 and 648–50). I have not seen the first edition (Oxford 1781, pp. 37–70 and 353–66) recorded in Fabricius.
Fraccaroli, G. "Le due odi di Pindaro per Trasibulo d'Agrigento (Pitia VI ed Istmica II)," *RFIC* 15 (1887) 296–342.
Hermann, G. See under "*P.* 3 General" (153–4).
Mezger, F. See under "*P.* 10 General" (14–18).
Olivieri, A. "Note pindariche," *AAN* 9 (1926) 31–46 (31–7).

Translations

Arena, A. "Pindaro: Pitica VI," *RSC* 11 (1963) 314–16.
Z, Y. "Pindars sechster pythischer und fünfter olympischer Hymnus ins Lateinische und Deutsche übersetzt," *Athenaeum* 3 (Halle 1818) 256–66 (256–61).

Specific verses

4. Jurenka, H. See under "*O.* 3.42–5" (17).
   von Leutsch, E. "Pind. Pyth. VI, 4," *Philologus* 39 (1880) 304.
7–25. Friederichs, K. See under "*O.* 1.28–9" (49–52).
10. Jurenka, H. See under "*O.* 3.42–5" (30).
12–14. Astius, F. See under "*P.* 1.9" (207–8).
13. van Herwerden, H. See under "*O.* 2.71" (46).
   Van der Valk, M. *Researches on the Text and Scholia of the Iliad* 1 (Leiden 1963) 496.
14. Young, D. See under "*I.* 8.40" (17).
14–18. Paley, F. A. "Emendation of a passage in Pindar," *JP* 2 (1869) 152–3.

19. BURY, J. B. "Thrasybulus and the Sixth Pythian," *The Isthmian Odes of Pindar* (London 1892) 162–5.
    SANDGREN, F. "Pindars 6. Pythisches Gedicht, v. 19," *Eranos* 64 (1966) 80–2.
25/26. ASTIUS, F. See under "*P*. 1.9" (208–9).
28–42. FRAENKEL, E. "Vergil und die Aithiopis," *Philologus* 87 (1932) 242–8.
   37. HEADLAM, W. See under "*I*. 3/4.85" (246–7).
       HILLER, E. "Zu Pindaros," *JPh* 137 (1888) 455–6.
   46. GRUMME, A. See under "*O*. 10.9" (7).
   49. VON LEUTSCH, E. "Pind. Pyth. VI, 49," *Philologus* 39 (1880) 395.
       NAIRN, J. A. See under "*P*. 2.5."
   50. ASTIUS, F. See under "*P*. 1.9" (209).
       KOCH, H. A. See under "Fr. 75.14."
       SCHNITZER, C. F. See under "*O*. 1.28–9" (40–1).

PYTHIAN SEVEN

General

HERMANN, G. See under "*P*. 3 General" (155).
MEZGER, F. See under "*P*. 10 General" (20–3).
POMTOW, H. "Delphische Beilagen II. Die Datirung der VII. pythischen Ode Pindars," *RhM* 51 (1896) 577–88 and 52 (1897) 124–5.
VON WILAMOWITZ-MOELLENDORFF, U. "Das siebente pythische Gedicht des Pindaros," *Aristoteles und Athen* 2 (Berlin 1893) 323–8.

Translations

ARENA, A. "Pindaro Ode Pitica VII," *MC* NS 5 (1951) 72–3.
ARENA, A. "Pindaro: Pitica VII," *RSC* 11 (1963) 317–18.
BROZEK, M. "Megaklesowi z Aten," *Meander* 3 (1948) 251.

Specific verses

1–4. CERRATO, L. See under "*P*. 2.36" (187–8).
5/6. ASTIUS, F. See under "*P*. 1.9" (209–10).
     CERRATO, L. See under "*P*. 2.36" (188).
     GRUMME, A. See under "*O*. 10.9" (13).
     RAUCHENSTEIN, R. "Pindars siebente pythische Ode," *JPh* 83 (1861) 38–40.
     RÖHL, H. "Zu Pindaros," *JPh* 111 (1875) 608.
     SCHRÖDER, O. See under "*I*. 3/4 General" (8).
     WÖLFFLIN, E. See under "*I*. 7.28."
11/12. RAUCHENSTEIN, R. See under "*P*. 7.5/6."
18–19. RAUCHENSTEIN, R. See under "*P*. 7.5/6."

18–21. FRACCAROLI, G. See under "*O.* 8.1–9" (104–5).
20–1. CERRATO, L. See under "*P.* 2.36" (189 and 212).
21. ROSE, H. J. See under "*P.* 5.55."

PYTHIAN EIGHT

General

BORNEMANN, L. "Pindar's achte pythische Ode nebst einem Anhang über die Pythiadenrechnung," *Philologus* 50 (1891) 230–47.
BROWN, N. O. See under "History and Politics."
HERMANN, G. See under "*P.* 3 General" (155–61).
LAUER, S. See under "Style and Imagery" (32–40 and 57–8).
LÜBBERT, E. See under "*O.* 8 General." Date.
NĚMEC, J. "Pindar, Pythia VIII," *Eos* 45 (1951) 33–9. In English.
SCHLESINGER, E. "Notas a la Pítica VIII de Pindaro," *AFC* 7, 2 (1960) 29–54.
SCHROEDER, O. "Proben einer Pindarinterpretation," *JPhV* 44 (1918) 186–92.
TAFEL, M. T. L. F. See under "*P.* 5 General."
WADE-GERY, H. T. "Thucydides the Son of Melesias," *JHS* 52 (1932) 205–27 (214–5 and 224–5).

Specific verses

6–7. CERRATO, L. See under "*P.* 2.36" (189–90).
8–9. VAN HERWERDEN, H. See under "*O.* 2.71" (46).
12. JURENKA, H. See under "*O.* 3.42–5" (22).
MATTHIAE, A. See under "*P.* 4.57" (39–40).
12–13. CERRATO, L. See under "*P.* 2.36" (190–2).
MATTHIAE, A. See under "*P.* 2.72–88" (vol. 2, pt. 1, pp. 11–12).
15. ELMER, H. C. "A Note on the Gnomic Aorist," *TAPA* 25 (1894) LIX–LXIII.
25. CERRATO, L. See under "*P.* 2.36" (192).
29. VAN HERWERDEN, H. See under "*O.* 2.71" (47).
32–4. CERRATO, L. See under "*P.* 2.36" (193–4).
35–42. HESS, H. See under "*P.* 3.11."
40. ROBERTSON, D. S. "Pindar, Pyth. viii. 40," *CR* 58 (1944) 17.
41–3. ASTIUS, F. See under "*P.* 1.9" (211–12).
48–55. GINEVRI-BLASI, G. "Sui versi 48–55 della Pitia VIII di Pindaro," *RFIC* 44 (1916) 250–4.
55–60. DRACHMANN, A. B. "De duobus Pindari locis," *NTF* 1 (1892–93) 161–8 (161–3).
55–70. FLOYD, E. D. "The Performance of Pindar, Pythian 8. 55–70," *GRBS* 6 (1965) 187–200.
56–60. FRIEDERICHS, K. See under "*O.* 1.28–9" (53–4).
58–60. ROHDE, E. See under "Religion and Myth" (152–3 n. 105).
67–9. JURENKA, H. See under "*O.* 3.42–5" (24–5).

68-9. CERRATO, L. See under "*P.* 2.36" (194–5).
DÜRING, I. See under "*O.* 8.52" (5).
73-5. MEZGER, F. *Disputationes Pindaricae* (Progr. Hof 1866) 3–4.
74. CERRATO, L. See under "*P.* 2.36" (195–6).
VAN HERWERDEN, H. See under "*O.* 2.71" (47).
77. JURENKA, H. See under "*O.* 3.42–5" (25–6).
77-8. MADWIG, J. N. See under "*O.* 2.65" (188).
86-7. MICHELANGELI, L. A. "A Pindaro, Pyth. VIII, 123–125 (86–87 Bergk e Christ)," *RSA* 4 (1899) 271–7.
88-92. CERRATO, L. See under "*P.* 2.36" (196–7).
95. BACON, J. R. "Three Notes on Aeschylus, Prometheus Vinctus," *CR* 42 (1928) 115–20 (117).
JÜTHNER, J. "Zu Pindar Pyth. 8, 96," *WS* 54 (1936) 142–3.
TUROLLA, E. Σκιᾶς ὄναρ, *Orpheus* 2 (1955) 183–9. Also in *Poesia e poeti dell' antico mondo* (Catania 1956) 86–92.
95-6. BIELER, L. Σκιᾶς ὄναρ ἄνθρωπος, *WS* 51 (1933) 143–5.
95-7. STANFORD, W. B. "The Ending of the Eighth Pythian," *CJ* 37 (1942) 363–4.
97. JURENKA, H. See under "*O.* 3.42–5" (28).
MAAS, P. See under "*O.* 14.21."

PYTHIAN NINE

General

BIGNONE, E. "Saggio sui 'Satiri segugi' di Sofocle," *A&R* 3rd S., 7 (1939) 77–91 (86–8).
CHAMOUX, F. See under "*P.* 4 General."
CHRIST, W. See under "Games" (21 2).
DEFRADAS, J. See under "*P.* 11 General" (239–42).
HEIMSOETH, F. "Erklärungen zu Pindar," *RhM* 5 (1847) 1–32 (1–10).
HERMANN, G. See under "*P.* 3 General" (161–4).
VAN HOORN, G. "Met Pindarus en Herodotus te Kyrene," *Hermeneus* 29 (1957) 33–7.
LÜBBERT, E. *Prolegomena in Pindari carmen Pythium nonum* (Bonn 1883).
MALTEN, L. *Cyrenarum Origines. Caput primum* (Diss. Berlin 1904).
MALTEN, L. See under "*P.* 5.75."
STUDNICZKA, F. "Kyrene und Kallimachos," *Hermes* 28 (1893) 1–18.
WELCKER, F. G. See under "General and Miscellaneous" (372–81 or 198–206).

Translations

BORCHARDT, R. "Pindarische Gedichte," *Gesammelte Werke in Einzelbänden. Übertragungen* (Stuttgart 1958) 99–147 (99–107).
HOUGHTON, H. P. "The Ninth Pythian Ode of Pindar. An English Verse Translation," *Euphrosyne* 2 (1959) 487–92.

Specific verses
- 1–4. LUPPINO, A. See under "Style and Imagery."
- 7–11. CERRATO, L. See under "*P*. 2.36" (197–9).
- 19. CAMPBELL, A. Y. See under "*P*. 4.99–100."
  CERRATO, L. See under "*P*. 2.36" (199–200).
  ROBERTSON, D. S. See under "*P*. 1.77."
  SCHROEDER, O. "Zur Sprache Pindars," *PhW* 16 (1896) 221–4.
- 23–5. LUPPINO, A. See under "Style and Imagery."
  MACURDY, G. H. "The Dawn Songs in Rhesus (527–556) and in the Parodos of Phaethon," *AJP* 64 (1943) 408–16 (411).
- 24–5. CERRATO, L. See under "*P*. 2.36" (200–1).
- 25. VAN HERWERDEN, H. See under "*O*. 2.43" (215).
  SCHROEDER, O. See under "*P*. 9.19."
- 29. BERGK, T. See under "*O*. 2.95–100" (187–8).
  CERRATO, L. See under "*P*. 2.36" (202–3).
- 31. SCHNEIDEWIN, F. W. "Variae lectiones," *Philologus* 3 (1848) 523–42 (527–8).
- 31–2. CERRATO, L. See under "*P*. 2.36." (203–4).
- 32. NABER, S. A. See under "*O*. 1.7" (38).
- 36. VERRALL, A. W. "Death and the Horse," *JHS* 18 (1898) 1–14 (11 n. 1).
- 37. VAN HERWERDEN, H. See under "*O*. 2.71" (47–8).
- 38. GOW, A. S. F. "ΟΦΡΥΣ (Theocr. Id. xxx. 7 f.)," *CR* 58 (1944) 38–9.
- 40–1. CERRATO, L. See under "*P*. 2.36" (204–5).
- 41. BOWRA, C. M. See under "Metre" (84–5).
  NABER, S. A. See under "*O*. 1.7" (38–9).
  SITZLER, J. See under "*P*. 2.35–6."
- 46–8. MCCARTNEY, E. S. See under "*O*. 2.98."
- 62. BERGK, T. See under "*O*. 2.95–100" (188).
- 62–5. CERRATO, L. See under "*P*. 2.36" (205–8).
  JURENKA, H. "Zu Pindar Pyth. IX 62 ff. ed. Bergk," *WS* 15 (1893) 299–301.
- 64a–65. ASTIUS, F. See under "*P*. 1.9" (213–14).
- 68. VAN HERWERDEN, H. See under "*O*. 2.43" (215).
- 76–96. FARNELL, L. R. "Note by Dr. L. R. Farnell," *CQ* 25 (1931) 162–4.
  ROSE, H. J. "Iolaos and the Ninth Pythian Ode," *CQ* 25 (1931) 156–61.
- 76–100. DRACHMANN, A. B. See under "*P*. 8.55–60" (163–8).
- 77–8. GILDERSLEEVE, B. L. "Brief Mention," *AJP* 38 (1917) 335–6.
- 80. VAN HERWERDEN, H. See under "*O*. 2.43" (216).
- 84. ALLEN, F. D. "Etymological and Grammatical Notes, 4—Δαΐφρων," *AJP* 1 (1880) 133–5.
- 87. VAN HERWERDEN, H. See under "*O*. 2.71" (48).
- 87–96. FARNELL, L. R. "Pindar, Athens and Thebes: Pyth. IX. 151–170," *CQ* 9 (1915) 193–200.
- 90–2. CERRATO, L. See under "*P*. 2.36" (208–10).

90–3. MAAS, P. "Ährenlese," *ZG* (1920) 20–6 (25–6).
  96. DÜRING, I. See under "*O.* 8.52" (6).
97–100. FRIEDERICHS, K. See under "*O.* 1.28–9" (55).
  98. DÜRING, I. See under "*O.* 8.52" (6).
 100. LENDRUM, W. T. See under "*N.* 9.18–25."
103–5. ASTIUS, F. See under "*P.* 1.9" (215).
    CERRATO, L. See under "*P.* 2.36" (210–11).
 104. VAN BROCK, N. See under "*N.* 3.18" (86).
 110. DAWES, R. See under "*P.* 6 General" (96–7 and 650).
 113. VAN HERWERDEN, H. See under "*O.* 2.71" (48).
    OELSCHLAEGER, F. See under "*O.* 2.26" (18).
 119. NABER, S. A. See under "*O.* 1.7" (40).
 121. VAN HERWERDEN, H. See under "*O.* 2.43" (215).
    VAN HERWERDEN, H. See under "*O.* 2.71" (49).

PYTHIAN TEN

General

BIELER, L. "Die Sage von Perseus und das 10. Pythische Gedicht Pindars," *WS* 49 (1931) 119–28.
DUGAS, C. "Observations sur la légende de Persée," *REG* 69 (1956) 1–15 (5–6).
*ENGBERG, J. F. *Pindari Pythium carmen X explicatum* (Diss. Uppsala 1872).
*FRACCAROLI, G. *La Pitia X di Pindaro* (Verona 1880).
    [A. Arrò, *RFIC* 10 (1882) 371–4.]
FRIEDERICHS, K. See under "*O.* 1.28–9" (57–9).
VAN GRONINGEN, B. A. "Simonide et les Thessaliens," *Mnem* 4th S., 1 (1948) 1–7 (6).
HERMANN, G. See under "*P.* 3 General" (164–6).
LAUER, S. See under "Style and Imagery" (13–26 and 55–6).
MÉAUTIS, G. "Pindarica," *RPh* 3rd S., 30 (1956) 224–30.
MEZGER, F. *Disputationum Pindaricarum pars altera, Schmidtiana continens* (Augsburg 1873) 10–14.
MEZGER, F. See under "*P.* 8.73–5" (18–19).

Translations

TACCONE, A. "La Pitia X di Pindaro, Ad Ippocle tessalo giovinetto vincitore nella corsa del doppio stadio," *MC* 3 (1933) 505–8.

Specific verses

   4. BORTHWICK, E. K. See under "*O.* 9.38–40."
12–16. MEZGER, F. See under "*P.* 8.73–5" (4–5).
15–16. JURENKA, H. See under "*O.* 3.42–5" (32–3).
  16. DONALDSON, J. W. See under "*P.* 2.76–7" (216).

20. MOORHOUSE, A. C. "The Meaning and Use of ΜΙΚΡΟΣ and ΟΛΙΓΟΣ in the Greek Poetical Vocabulary," *CQ* 41 (1947) 31–45 (38).
21. SCHNEIDEWIN, F. W. See under "*P.* 9.31" (528–9).
    TYRRELL, R. Y. See under "*O.* 3.45."
21–2. DREYKORN, J. See under "*O.* 2.56" (14–16).
    FRIEDERICHS, K. See under "*O.* 1.28–9" (55–6).
21–6. MEZGER, F. See under "*P.* 8.73–5" (10–11).
28–30. JURENKA, H. See under "*O.* 3.42–5" (3).
30. VAN HERWERDEN, H. See under "*O.* 2.71" (49).
33–6. KRAPPE, A. H. Ἀπόλλων Ὄνος, *CP* 42 (1947) 223–34.
35. VON LEUTSCH, E. "Pind. Pyth. X, 34," *Philologus* 33 (1874) 631.
36. CERRATO, L. "Dell' utilità di luoghi paralleli nell' interpretazione dei classici (Pindaro, Saffo, Catullo, Alceo)," *RFIC* 26 (1898) 127–33 (127–30).
    LAWLER, L. B. "Pindar and Some Animal Dances," *CP* 41 (1946) 155–9.
    ZIELINSKI, T. "Apollon bei den Hyperboreern (zu Pind. Pyth. X), *RhM* 38 (1883) 625–7.
38–9. VON LEUTSCH, E. "Zu Pindaros," *Philologus* 29 (1870) 589.
48–50. DÜRING, I. See under "*O.* 8.52" (6–7).
55–9. FRIEDERICHS, K. See under "*O.* 1.28–9" (56–7).
60. BERGK, T. See under "*O.* 6.15" (6–7).
69. SCHNITZER, C. F. See under "*O.* 1.28–9" (43).

PYTHIAN ELEVEN

General

ALSINA, J. "Observaciones sobre la figura de Clitemestra," *Emerita* 27 (1959) 297–321 (308–10).
BORNEMANN, L. "Pindar's elfte pythische Ode, ein Sieger- und Todtenlied," *Philologus* 52 (1894) 38–48.
BOWRA, C. M. "Pindar, Pythian XI," *CQ* 30 (1936) 129–41.
BOWRA, C. M. "The Date of Pythian 11," *Pindar* (Oxford 1964) 402–5.
BULLE, C. See under "*I.* 3/4 General" (589–96).
DEFRADAS, J. *Les thèmes de la propagande delphique* (Paris 1954) 176–81.
DÜRING, I. "Klutaimestra—νηλὴς γυνά. A study of the Development of a Literary Motif," *Eranos* 41 (1943) 91–123.
*FRACCAROLI, G. *L'ode Pitia XI di Pindaro* (Verona 1886).
VAN GRONINGEN, B. A. "De Pindari carmine Pythio XI°," *Mnem* NS 59 (1931) 266–70.
GUILLON, P. "Le crime de Clytemnestre et la Pythique XI de Pindare," *Annales de la Faculté des Lettres et Sciences humaines d'Aix* 39 (1965) 5–51.
HEIMSOETH, F. See under "*P.* 9 General" (10–16).
HERMANN, G. See under "*P.* 3 General" (166–71).

MEZGER, F. See under "*P*. 8.73–5" (12–14). Date.
NASTA, M. "Considérations sur les caractères distinctifs du mètre grec," *Cahiers de linguistique théorique et appliquée* 1 (1962) 135–51 (146–51).
OLIVIERI, A. "Sul mito di Oreste nella letteratura classica," *RFIC* 26 (1898) 266–93 (272).
PERTHES, H. See under "*I*. 3/4 General" (Beiträge, 10–18).
PERTHES, H. See under "*I*. 3/4 General" (*JPh* 105.226–38).
RAUCHENSTEIN, R. "Ueber die Tendenz und die Zeit der elften pythischen Ode Pindars," *Philologus* 2 (1847) 193–211.
VON DER MÜHLL, P. "Wurde die elfte Pythie Pindars 474 oder 454 gedichtet?" *MH* 15 (1958) 141–6.

Specific verses

1–2. PLATT, A. See under "*O*. 14.13–16."
4–6. DEFRADAS, J. See under "*P*. 11 General" (61).
9. FRAENKEL, E. See under "*I*. 6.17" (131 n. 3).
17–18. FRAENKEL, E. See under "*I*. 6.17" (402 n. 2).
20. THOMSON, G. See under "*P*. 3.48."
21. DÜRING, I. See under "*O*. 8.52" (7).
24–30. RAUCHENSTEIN, R. See under "*P*. 11.54–7" (170).
28. USSHER, R. G. See under "*N*. 4.36" (235).
29–30. ALTENHOVEN, P. See under "*O*. 2.57" (15–16).
LUPPINO, A. See under "*O*. 1.56–57b" (363–4).
30. HANSSEN, J. S. T. See under "*P*. 11.42."
YOUNG, D. C. C. "Gentler Medicines in the Agamemnon," *CQ* NS 14 (1964) 1–23 (15).
36–7. STEIGER, H. "Warum schrieb Euripides seine Elektra?" *Philologus* 56 (1897) 561–600 (592–3).
37. BAYFIELD, M. A. "Note on φοναί," *CR* 15 (1901) 251–2.
38. PEARSON, A. C. See under "*O*. 1.105" (157).
40–2. EITREM, S. "Varia," *SO* 30 (1953) 108–11.
41–4. VON WILAMOWITZ-MOELLENDORFF, U. See under "History and Politics" (1317–8).
42. HANSSEN, J. S. T. "A note on Pindar, Pyth. XI 38 ff.," *Aevum* 24 (1950) 162–5.
JURENKA, H. See under "*O*. 3.42–5" (22).
42–4. VAN HERWERDEN, H. See under "*O*. 2.71" (49–50).
51. RAUCHENSTEIN, R. See under "*P*. 11.54–7" (170).
52–64. ALTENHOVEN, P. See under "*O*. 2.57" (17–18).
54–5. JURENKA, H. See under "*O*. 3.42–5" (20).
54–7. RAUCHENSTEIN, R. "Zu Pindaros," *Philologus* 27 (1868) 168–71 (168–9).
54–8. DÜRING, I. See under "*O*. 8.52" (7–9).
RAUCHENSTEIN, R. See under "*O*. 1.106–7" (67–8).
STONE, W. A. See under "*O*. 6.15."

WISKEMANN, A. See under "*O.* 1.106–8" (12–15).
55. VAN GRONINGEN, B. A. "Ad Pindari Pyth. XI vs. 55," *Mnem* 3rd S., 13 (1947) 230–3.
56–7. CERRATO, L. "Emendamento a Pitica XI, 55," *RFIC* 44 (1916) 555. Also in *BFC* 23 (1917) 151–2.
57. SHACKLE, R. J. See under "*O.* 14.15."

PYTHIAN TWELVE

General

CURTIS, J. "The Double Flutes," *JHS* 34 (1914) 89–105 (99).
DORNSEIFF, F. See under "*I.* 5.1" (27–8).
HERMANN, G. See under "*P.* 3 General" (171–3).
*KOPISCH, R. *Pindars zwölfte pythische Ode, übersetzt und erklärt. Ein Beitrag zum Verständniss dieses Dichters* (Breslau 1838).
MÉAUTIS, G. See under "*P.* 10 General."
MEZGER, F. See under "*P.* 10 General" (18–20).
ROME, A. See under "General and Miscellaneous" (529–32).
SCHLESINGER, K. See under "*P.* 1 General" (50–1 and 79–81).
WELLES, C. B. "Pindar's Religion and the Twelfth Pythian Ode," *YCS* 19 (1966) 77–100.

Translations

BOCHÉNSKIEGO, T. "Na zwyciestwo Midaesa, flecisty z Arauntu," *Meander* 3 (1948) 401–3.

Specific verses

4. GRUMME, A. See under "*O.* 10.9" (13).
11–12. KAIBEL, G. See under "*O.* 2.76–7" (246–7).
13. MCKINLAY, A. P. "On the Way Scholars Interpret 'ΑΜΑΥΡΟΣ," *AC* 26 (1957) 12–39 (26).
ROBERTSON, D. S. See under "*P.* 1.77."
14. BOSSLER, C. See under "Syntax" (25).
JURENKA, H. See under "*O.* 3.42–5" (30–1).
16. TUBBS, H. A. "Pindar, Pyth. xii. 16," *CR* 4 (1890) 69.
23. SCHROEDER, O. Πολυκέφαλος νόμος, *Hermes* 39 (1904) 315–20.
24. BOWRA, C. M. See under "Metre" (182).
29. VAN HERWERDEN, H. See under "*O.* 2.71" (50).
KAIBEL, G. See under "*O.* 2.76–7" (247).
30–1. SCHRÖDER, O. See under "*I.* 3/4 General" (7–8).

9. NEMEAN ODES

GENERAL

BURY, J. B. *The Nemean Odes of Pindar*, edited with introductions and commentary (London and New York 1890, repr. Amsterdam 1965).
    [J. E. Sandys, *CR* 5 (1891) 305–8; B. L. Gildersleeve, *AJP* 11 (1890) 528–9; G. Fraccaroli, *RFIC* 19 (1891) 529–50; A. Croiset, *REG* 4 (1891) 95–6; J. Sitzler, *NPR* (1892) 162–6.]
*CERRATO, L. *Le Odi di Pindaro, Testo, versione e commento. Parte III Nemee e Istmiche* (Sestri Ponente 1917).
    [D. Bassi, *RFIC* 46 (1918) 283–4; N. Terzaghi, *RIGI* 2 (1918) 330–1.]
GAUTIER, G. Νεμεονῖκαι. *I vincitori nemei di Pindaro*. Tradotti in Italiane canzoni ed illustrati con postille (Rome 1768).
*HOLMES, A. *The Nemean Odes of Pindar, with especial reference to Nem. VII, A Thesis* (Cambridge 1867).
OLRY, M. *Les Néméennes de Pindare*. Traduction nouvelle, avec des notes, des arguments, des études et le texte en regard (Paris 1840).
PERRAULT-MAYNAND, J. A. *Néméennes de Pindare*. Avec le texte en regard et des notes, suivies d'études sur la poésie lyrique des anciens (Paris 1856).
*ROSING, M. *Pindars nemeiske Oder* (Progr. Sorø 1892). Translation.
*SOMMER, E. *Pindare. Les Néméennes*, expliquées littéralement, traduites en français et annotées. Texte grec revu par T. Fix (Paris 1846).
*SUDORIUS, N. *Pindari opera omnia latino carmine reddita per Nic. Sudorium et eiusdem commentarius in Nemea* (Paris 1575).

NEMEAN ONE

General

FRIEDERICHS, K. See under "*O*. 1.28–9" (60–2). Myth.
HERTER, H. "Ein neues Türwunder. Zu Pind. Nem. 1 und Theokrit. id. XXIV," *RhM* 89 (1940) 152–7.
HOUGHTON, H. P. "Gildersleeve on the First Nemean," *CJ* 49 (1954) 215–20.
HUNGER, H. "Zur realistischen Kunst Theokrits," *WS* 60 (1942) 23–7. Myth.
LAUER, S. See under "Style and Imagery" (26–32 and 56–7).
LEITZMANN, A. "Briefe Friedrich Gottlieb Welckers an Wilhelm v. Humboldt," *NJA* 27 (1911) 132–49 (142–4).
VON LEUTSCH, E. "Pindarische Studien 2. Die Epinikien auf Chromios von Aetna," *Philologus* 14 (1859) 45–68.
VON LEUTSCH, E. *Additamentorum ad Lud. Disseni in Pindari carmina commentarium specimen I-IV* (Göttingen 1865–68) Spec. 1.
    [*PA* 1 (1869) 38–9.]

MEZGER, F. See under "*P.* 8.73–5" (19–20).
NOACK, T. *Pindari carmen Nemeaeum* (Progr. Cöslin 1867).
RADT, S. L. "Pindars erste Nemeische Ode," *Mnem* 4th S., 19 (1966) 148–74.
RAUCHENSTEIN, R. "Zu Pindar's Nemeen," *Philologus* 13 (1858) 245–63 and 421–42 (245–9).
RIVIER, A. See under "Religion and Myth" (69–75).

Translations
*CAPOCASA, S. See under "*O.* 1 Translations."
*COWLEY, A. See under "*O.* 2 Translations."
*GURLITT, J. *Pindars erster und zehnter nemeischer Siegesgesang*, übersetzt mit Anmerkungen (Hamburg & Leipzig 1818).
VAN IJZEREN, J. "Herakles als wiegekind bij Pindarus en bij Theocritus," *Hermeneus* 31 (1960) 230–6. Translation of vv. 33–72.
*LINDGREEN, L. A. *Pindari Nemeorum Ode 1 versione et notis illustrata* (Uppsala 1804).
MINCKWITZ, J. "Proben aus dem poetischen Hausschatze der Griechen," *JPP(S)* 14 (1848) 65–75 (68–71).

Specific verses
  1–18. ROUSE, W. H. D. "The First Triad of Nemean I," *ABSA* 37 (1936–37) 207–11.
     3. POSTGATE, J. P. "On the Nemeans of Pindar," *PCPS* 72–75 (1906) 4.
  8–9. DAWES, R. See under "*P.* 6 General" (97–8).
       WRATISLAW, A. H. "Pindar Nem. I 8, 9," *TCPS* 1 (1881) 162.
   13. HARDIE, W. R. See under "*N.* 1.46."
 14–15. ASTIUS, F. See under "*P.* 1.9" (216).
   18. DÜRING, I. See under "*O.* 8.52" (11–12).
       POSTGATE, J. P. "Nemeans of Pindar," *TCPS* 1 (1881) 252–7 (252).
       WRATISLAW, A. H. "Pindar Nem. I 18," *TCPS* 1 (1881) 162.
   24. AHRENS, H. L. See under "*O.* 8.16" (55–6).
       STONE, W. A. "Notes on Pindar," *CR* 48 (1934) 165–6.
  24–5. ASTIUS, F. See under "*P.* 1.9" (216–17).
       GILDERSLEEVE, B. L. "Brief Mention," *AJP* 30 (1909) 233–4.
       MATTHIAE, A. See under "*N.* 1.64–6" (5–6 or 97–8).
       MEZGER, F. See under "*P.* 8.73–5" (11).
   25. DÜRING, I. See under "*O.* 8.52." (12).
   31. HARTMAN, J. J. See under "*P.* 3.38" (449).
  37–8. AHRENS, H. L. See under "*O.* 8.16" (56).
   41. KAPSOMENOS, J. G. "Zu Theokrits Herakliskos," *Philologus* 94 (1940) 234–9.
   42. VON LEUTSCH, E. "Pind. Nem. I, 42," *Philologus* 22 (1865) 680.
   45. BERGK, T. See under "*O.* 2.95–100" (188–9).

46. Hardie, W. R. "Metaphors and Allusive Language in Greek Lyric Poetry: [with special reference to Mr. Bury's Ed. of the Nemean Odes of Pindar]," *CR* 5 (1891) 193–5.
Hartman, J. J. See under "*P.* 3.38" (448–9).
von Leutsch, E. "Pind. Nem. 1, 46," *Philologus* 29 (1870) 635.
Röhl, H. "Zu griechischen und lateinischen Schriftstellern," *WKPh* 29 (1912) 1324–5.
Schmidt, M. "Zu Pindarus," *RhM* 4 (1846) 462–3.
46–7. Gerber, D. E. "What Time Can Do (Pindar, Nemean 1. 46–47)," *TAPA* 93 (1962) 30–3.
46–8. Jurenka, H. See under "*O.* 3.42–5" (16).
50. Bergk, T. See under "*N.* 3.43–51" (601).
Matthiae, A. See under "*P.* 4.57" (40).
64–6. Headlam, W. See under "*O.* 6.74" (300–1).
Jurenka, H. See under "*O.* 3.42–5" (13–14).
Matthiae, A. *De nonnullis locis Pindari* (Progr. Altenburg 1823) 4–5. Also in *Vermischte Schriften* (Altenburg 1842²) 96–102 (96–7).
Mezger, F. See under "*P.* 8.73–5" (5).
Norwood, G. "Pindar Nemean I. 64 ff.," *CP* 37 (1942) 428–9.
65–6. Astius, F. See under "*P.* 1.9" (217).
von Wilamowitz-Moellendorff, U. See under "*P.* 4.105" (171). Also in *Kleine Schriften IV* (Berlin 1962) 9.
66. Ahrens, H. L. See under "*O.* 8.16" (56).
Hardie, W. R. See under "*N.* 1.46."

NEMEAN TWO

General

Christ, W. See under "*O.* 9 General."
Krischer, T. "Pindars Rhapsodengedicht (Zu Nem. 2)," *WS* 78 (1965) 32–9.
Rauchenstein, R. See under "*N.* 1 General" (249–50).
Robert, C. See under "*O.* 5.6" (183–4). Date.
Smith, K. K. "The Olympic Victory of Agias of Thessaly," *CP* 5 (1910) 169–74. Date.
von Wilamowitz-Moellendorff, U. "Die Thukydideslegende," *Hermes* 12 (1877) 326–67 (342 n. 26).

Specific verses

1. Allen, T. W. "The Homeridae," *CQ* 1 (1907) 135–43.
1–2. von Leutsch, E. "Zu Pind. Nem. II, 1," *Philologus* 18 (1862) 244.
1–3. Koller, H. "Das kitharodische Prooimion. Eine formgeschichtliche Untersuchung," *Philologus* 100 (1956) 159–206 (190–2).
Meyer, E. "Die Rhapsoden und die homerischen Epen," *Hermes* 53 (1918) 330–6 (330–1).

1–10. POSTGATE. J. P. "Ad Pindari Nemea," *Mnem* NS 53 (1925) 382–92 (382–3). See also some minor corrections and additions in *Mnem* NS 54 (1926) 386–7.
    2. DEL GRANDE, C. "Aedi e rapsodi," *Filologia Minore* (Milan & Naples 1956) 43–8.
    SHEPPARD, J. T. "Pind. Nem. ii. 1," *PCPS* (1923) 6–8.
4–8. POSTGATE, J. P. See under "*N*. 1.3."
10–12. MEINEL, G. See under "*P*. 2 General" (29–31).
    ROBERTSON, D. S. "Pindarica," *CR* 37 (1923) 5–7.
13–14. MÉAUTIS, G. See under "*P*. 10 General."
    14. MATTHIAE, A. See under "*P*. 4.57" (40).
    MONRO, D. B. "On Pindar, Nem. II. 14," *CR* 6 (1892) 3–4.
24. DÜRING, I. See under "*O*. 8.52" (12–13).
    RAUCHENSTEIN, R. See under "*P*. 11.54–7" (170–1).

Scholia

1c-e. NOTOPOULOS, J. A. "The Homeric Hymns as Oral Poetry; A Study of the Post-Homeric Oral Tradition," *AJP* 83 (1962) 337–68.
    RIZZO, J. "Adversaria II. De Cynaetho deque hymni in Apollinem Delium aetate [Ad Pindari Nem. II, 1 Scholiastam]," *RSA* 2 (1897) 12–25.

NEMEAN THREE

General

DENIS, J. See under "General and Miscellaneous" (67–72).
FRACCAROLI, G. "La terza e quarta ode Nemea," *RFIC* 21 (1893) 298–329 (298–313).
VON LEUTSCH, E. See under "*N*. 1 General" (Spec. II).
MANCUSO, U. "Un' Ode di Pindaro e un centone pindarico," *AAT* 47 (1911–12) 179–91 (179–83). Date.
MEZGER, F. See under "*P*. 8.73–5" (20–1).
POHLSANDER, H. A. "The Dating of Pindaric Odes by Comparison," *GRBS* 4 (1963) 131–40 (131–7).
SCHMIDT, E. *De Pindari carmine Nemeorum tertio* (Progr. Seehausen 1891).

Translations

BORCHARDT, R. See under "*P*. 9 Translations" (144–7).
TACCONE, A. "La Nemea III di Pindaro," *Studies Presented to D. M. Robinson on his Seventieth Birthday* 2 (Saint Louis 1953) 507–13.

Specific verses

3–5. HUTCHINSON, W. M. L. "Two Notes on Nemean III," *Essays and Studies presented to William Ridgeway* (Cambridge 1914) 222–7.

Hutchinson, W. M. L. "Pindar Nem. III. 3: A Reply," *CR* 28 (1914) 156–7.

Lendrum, W. T. "Note on Pindar," *CR* 28 (1914) 86–7.

10–14. Düring, I. See under "*O.* 8.52" (13–14).

11. Matthiae, A. See under "*P.* 4.57" (41).

12–13. Friederichs, K. See under "*O.*1.28–9" (62–3).

12–17. Rauchenstein, R. See under "*N.* 1 General" (250–1).

14. Hardie, W. R. "Pindar, Nem. iii. 14," *CR* 4 (1890) 318.
Hutchinson, W. M. L. See under "*N.* 3.3–5."

15. Matthiae, A. See under "*P.* 4.57" (41).

17. Stone, W. A. See under "*N.* 1.24."

18. van Brock, N. *Recherches sur le vocabulaire médical du grec ancien* (Paris 1961) 82 and 166.

19–26. Friederichs, K. See under "*O.* 1.28–9" (63–5).

20–6. Mezger, F. See under "*P.* 8.73–5" (6–7).

22. Cook, A. B. "Who Was the Wife of Zeus?" *CR* 20 (1906) 416–19.
Maas, P. *ΗΡΩΣ ΘΕΟΣ, MH* 11 (1954) 199.

23. Postgate, J. P. See under "*N.* 2.1–10" (383).

24–5. Jurenka, H. See under "*O.* 3.42–5" (18–19).

25. van Herwerden, H. See under "*O.* 2.71" (51).

28–9. Norwood, G. "Pindar Nemean 3. 28 f.," *CP* 38 (1943) 138–9.

29. Nairn, J. A. "Notes on the Nemeans of Pindar," *CR* 15 (1901) 195–7.
Wiskemann, A. See under "*O.* 1.106–8" (15).

29–31. Düring, I. See under "*O.* 8.52" (14).

32. Kakridis, J. T. "Zu Pind. Nem. III 32 [55] u.f.," *PhW* 46 (1926) 766–7.

32–3. Postgate, J. P. See under "*N.* 1.18" (252–3).

33. Matthiae, A. See under "*P.* 4.57" (41).

34. von Leutsch, E. "Zu Pindar," *Philologus* 15 (1860) 302.
Robertson, D. S. See under "*N.* 2.10–12."

36. Matthiae, A. See under "*P.* 4.57" (41).

39. Düring, I. See under "*O.* 8.52" (14).
Kontos, K. S. Φιλολογικὰ σύμμικτα, ’Aθηνᾶ 5 (1893) 35–129 (74).

43–8. Rauchenstein, R. See under "*N.* 1 General" (251–2).

43–51. Bergk, T. "Kritische Analekten," *Philologus* 16 (1860) 577–647 (593–600).
Friederichs, K. See under "*P.* 5.15–19" (444–50).

43–52. Friederichs, K. See under "*O.* 1.28–9" (65–70).

44–6. Rauchenstein, R. See under "*O.* 1.106–7" (68).

44–7. Wiskemann, A. See under "*O.* 1.106–8" (16).

46. *Schmidt, M. See under "*O.* 1.63–4."

47–8. van Herwerden, H. See under "*O.* 2.71" (51).
Nairn, J. A. See under "*N.* 3.29."

47–52. Robertson, D. S. "The Food of Achilles," *CR* 54 (1940) 177–80.

50–2. Salmon, E. T. "Pindar, Nemea 3. 50–2," *CW* 24 (1931) 143.
56. Schmidt, M. See under "*N.* 1.46."
58. Düring, I. See under "*O.* 8.52" (14).
59–63. Shackle, R. J. "Pindar, Nem. III. 59–63," *CR* 35 (1921) 28–9.
62. Jacobs, F. *Animadversiones in Euripidis tragoedias* (Gotha 1790) 320–21.
Walker, R. J. "Pindar, Nemean III 62," *AJP* 19 (1898) 315–16.
70–5. Cornford, F. M. "Psychology and Social Structure in the Republic of Plato," *CQ* 6 (1912) 246–65 (254–5).
Friederichs, K. See under "*O.* 1.28–9" (70–1).
Rouse, W. H. D. "Notes on the Nemeans of Pindar," *PCPS* 28–30 (1891) 16–18.
75. Grumme, A. See under "*O.* 10.9" (13–14).

Scholia

80. Schnitzer, C. F. See under "*O.* 1.28–9" (49–50).
108. Bury, J. B. "A Pindaric Scholion," *CR* 4 (1890) 47.

NEMEAN FOUR

General

Denis, J. See under "General and Miscellaneous" (72–4).
Fraccaroli, G. See under "*N.* 3 General" (313–29).
von Leutsch, E. See under "*N.* 1 General" (Spec. III).
Maloney, G. "Sur l'unité de la quatrième Néméenne de Pindare," *Phoenix* 18 (1964) 173–82.
Rauchenstein, R. See under "*N.* 1 General" (252–8).
Wade-Gery, H. T. See under "*P.* 8. General" (223–4).

Specific verses

3. Düring, I. See under "*O.* 8.52" (14–15).
Headlam, W. "Illustrations of Pindar. II," *CR* 19 (1905) 148–50.
von Leutsch, E. "Pind. Nem. VI (*sic*), 3," *Philologus* 18 (1862) 340.
4. Postgate, J. P. See under "*N.* 2.1–10" (383).
5. van Herwerden, H. See under "*O.* 2.71" (51–2).
8. Düring, I. See under "*O.* 8.52" (15).
Matthiae, A. See under "*N.* 1.64–6" (6 or 98).
9. Ahrens, H. L. See under "*O.* 8.16" (56).
16. Young, D. See under "*I.* 8.40" (16–18).
18. Postgate, J. P. See under "*N.* 1.18" (253).
23–4. Ahrens, H. L. See under "*O.* 8.16" (56–7).
Christ, W. See under "Games" (9–11).
27. Robert, C. "Alkyoneus," *Hermes* 19 (1884) 473–85.

NEMEAN 4

27–32. Koepp, F. "Herakles und Alkyoneus," *Archäologische Zeitung* 42 (1884) 31–46.
30–7. Whitmore, C. E. "On a Passage in Pindar's Fourth Nemean Ode," *HSCP* 21 (1910) 103–9.
33–43. Düring, I. See under "*O.* 8.52" (15–17).
  35. Bury, J. B. See under "*P.* 4.214."
      Gow, A. S. F. See under "*P.* 4.214."
      Von der Mühll, P. See under "*N.* 11.28–9" (128–30).
  36. Ahrens, H. L. See under "*O.* 8.16" (57).
      Donaldson, J. W. See under "*P.* 2.76–7" (219–21).
      Headlam, W. See under "*O.* 6.74" (301).
      Scheidweiler, F. ΚΑΙΠΕΡ, *Hermes* 83 (1955) 220–30 (223).
      Ussher, R. G. *The Characters of Theophrastus* (London 1960) 46.
  38. Postgate, J. P. See under "*N.* 1.18" (253–4).
47–8. Ahrens, H. L. See under "*O.* 8.16" (57).
  51. Maguire, T. See under "*O.* 6.62" (383).
54–60. Lesky, A. "Motivkontamination," *WS* 55 (1937) 21–31 (26–7).
  55. Ahrens, H. L. See under "*O.* 8.16" (57–8).
      Pearson, A. C. "Sophoclea II," *CQ* 23 (1929) 87–95 (88).
      Postgate, J. P. See under "*N.* 2.1–10" (383–4).
55–8. Headlam, W. See under "*O.* 6.74" (302–3).
57–68. Reitzenstein, R. See under "*I.* 8.27–48" (75).
  58. Matthiae, A. See under "*P.* 4.57" (41–2).
  62. Young, D. See under "*I.* 8.40" (17–18).
66–70. Ahrens, H. L. See under "*O.* 8.16" (58).
  68. Young, D. See under "*I.* 8.40" (18).
79–96. Düring, I. See under "*O.* 8.52" (17–18).
85–8. Lendrum, W. T. See under "*N.* 3.3–5."
  87. van Herwerden, H. See under "*O.* 2.71" (52).
      Stone, W. A. See under "*N.* 1.24."
89–90. Wiskemann, A. See under "*O.* 1.106–8" (17).
89–93. Ahrens, H. L. See under "*O.* 8.16" (59).
89–96. Astius, F. See under "*P.* 1.9" (217–20).
  90. Nairn, J. A. See under "*N.* 3.29."
      Postgate, J. P. See under "*N.* 2.1–10" (384).
      Rauchenstein, R. See under "*O.* 1.106–7" (68).
      Shackle, R. J. See under "*O.* 14.15."
      Young, D. See under "*I.* 8.40" (19).
  94. Knox, A. D. *Herodas, The Mimes and Fragments*, with notes by W. Headlam (Cambridge 1922, repr. 1966) 316 n. 4.

Scholia

  56b. Schnitzer, C. F. See under "*O.* 1.28–9" (51).

NEMEAN FIVE

General

DENIS, J. See under "General and Miscellaneous" (74–5).
HEIMSOETH, F. See under "*P.* 9 General" (21–32).
*HEPP, C. F. T. *Pindars fünften nemeischer Siegesgesang übersetzt und erklärt*. Hrsg. von J. Gurlitt (Hamburg 1820).
VON LEUTSCH, E. See under "*N.* 1 General" (Spec. IV).
MEZGER, F. See under "*P.* 10 General" (32–6).
RAUCHENSTEIN, R. "Erklärung der fünften nemeischen Ode Pindars," *NSM* 3 (1863) 243–54.
RAUCHENSTEIN, R. See under "*N.* 1 General" (258–61).
TACCONE, A. "Sulla data dell' ode de Bacchilide per Pitea eginese," *BFC* 12 (1905–06) 253–5.
VON WILAMOWITZ-MOELLENDORFF, U. See under "*I.* 8 General" (812–18).

Translations

BROZEK, M. "Oda Nemejska V," *Meander* 10 (1955) 225–9.
LEVI, A. "La Nemea V di Pindaro," *BSI* 6 (1894) 228–9.

Specific verses

1–6. FRIEDERICHS, K. See under "*O.* 1.28–9" (71–2).
6. DREYKORN, J. See under "*O.* 2.56" (16–17).
   FRIEDERICHS, K. See under "*O.* 3.13–18" (36).
   JURENKA, H. See under "*O.* 3.42–5" (16–17).
9–12. CHRIST, W. See under "Games" (16–18).
10. DAWES, R. See under "*P.* 6 General (100–2).
16. MATTHIAE, A. See under "*N.* 1.64–6" (6 or 98).
19–20. EBERT, J. See under "Games" (54 n. 2).
   GARDINER, E. N. "Phayllus and his Record Jump," *JHS* 24 (1904) 70–80.
20. JÜTHNER, J. "Zur Geschichte der griechischen Wettkämpfe," *WS* 53 (1935) 68–79.
22–37. REITZENSTEIN, R. See under "*I.* 8.27–48" (82–3).
26–32. LESKY, A. See under "*N.* 4.54–60."
37. MAAS, P. See under "*O.* 14.21."
41. BOWRA, C. M. See under "Metre" (87).
   SCHWARTZ, E. "Zu Bakchylides," *Hermes* 39 (1904) 630–42 (636).
41–2. BERGK, T. See under "*O.* 2.95–100" (189).
41–3. MAAS, P. See under "Metre" (Responsionsfreiheiten, 315–17).
   MEZGER, F. See under "*P.* 8.73–5" (7–8).
43. FRIEDERICHS, K. See under "*O.* 1.28–9" (73–5).
   POSTGATE, J. P. "Pind. Nem. 5. 43," *PCPS* 25–27 (1890) 8.
   POSTGATE, J. P. See under "*N.* 1.3."

SCHNITZER, C. F. See under "*O*. 1.28–9" (53).
STONE, W. A. See under "*N*. 1.24."
TUCKER, T. G. "Adversaria," *CR* 7 (1893) 198–9.
VON DER MÜHLL, P. "Weitere pindarische Notizen," *MH* 21 (1964) 96–8.
44. TYRRELL, R. Y. "On Pindar Nem. V. 44," *PCPS* 13–15 (1886) 7–8.
44–6. MEZGER, F. See under "*P*. 8.73–5" (11–12).
52. GRUMME, A. See under "*O*. 10.9" (14).
54. POSTGATE, J. P. See under "*N*. 2.1–10" (384).

Scholia
78d. SCHNITZER, C. F. See under "*O*. 1.28–9" (53).

NEMEAN SIX

General
(AUTHOR NOT GIVEN) *Pindari Nemeorum carmen sextum* (Leipzig 1845).
DENIS, J. See under "General and Miscellaneous" (75–8).
HERMANN, G. *Pindari Nemeorum carmen sextum* (Progr. Leipzig 1844). Also in *Opuscula* 8 (Leipzig 1877) 68–75.
JURENKA, H. "Pindars sechstes nemeisches Siegeslied," *Philologus* 58 (1899) 348–61.
VON KLOCH-KORNITZ, P. "Die religiöse Problematik in Pindars Nemea VI im Vergleich mit Goethes Gedichten 'Grenzen der Menschheit' und 'Das Göttliche'," *A&A* 10 (1961) 155–9.
RAUCHENSTEIN, R. See under "*N*. 1 General" (261–3).
WADE-GERY, H. T. See under "*P*. 8 General" (223–4).

Translations
*THUNBERG, C. *Pindari Nemeorum ode sexta Suethice reddita* (Uppsala 1834).

Specific verses
1. MATTHIAE, A. See under "*N*. 1.64–6" (6–7 or 98).
1–2. VON KLOCH-KORNITZ, P. "Zum Anfang von Pindars Nemea VI," *Hermes* 89 (1961) 370–1.
1–4. ROSE, H. J. See under "*P*. 5.55."
6–7. FRÄNKEL, H. See under "*O*. 1.1–6" (318 n. 18).
7–8. MATTHIAE, A. See under "*P*. 4.57" (42).
8–9. ASTIUS, F. See under "*P*. 1.9" (220–2).
13b. MAAS, P. See under "*O*. 14.21."
16. FRIEDERICHS, K. See under "*O*. 1.28–9" (75).
17. BOSSLER, C. See under "Syntax" (7–8).
18. BURY, J. B. "Emendations," *Hermathena* 5 (1885) 267–76.
30. VON LEUTSCH, E. See under "*P*. 1.94."
35. YOUNG, D. See under "*I*. 8.40" (22).

43. POSTGATE, J. P. See under "*N.* 2.1–10" (385).
   SCHNITZER, C. F. See under "*O.* 1.28–9" (56).
   YOUNG, D. See under "*I.* 8.40" (18).
45. VON LEUTSCH, E. See under "*P.* 1.94."
   PFLIGERSDORFFER, G. See under "*P.* 1.94" (10–12).
50. VON LEUTSCH, E. "Zu Pind. Nem. VI, 55 flg.," *Philologus* 17 (1861) 320.
50–1. DONALDSON, J. W. See under "*P.* 2.76–7" (217–19).
   POSTGATE, J. P. See under "*N.* 2.1–10" (385–6).
   RAUCHENSTEIN, R. "Rudolfus Rauchenstein Theodoro Bergkio S.D.P.," *ZA* 2 (1844) 405–7.
55. ROUSE, W. H. D. See under "*N.* 3.70–5."
55–7. DÜRING, I. See under "*O.* 8.52" (19).
   GILDERSLEEVE, B. L. "Brief Mention," *AJP* 39 (1918) 104–5.
   HEADLAM, W. See under "Fr. 112 General" (436).
63. ROUSE, W. H. D. See under "*N.* 3.70–5."
   SCHNITZER, C. F. See under "*O.* 1.28–9" (56–7).
65. POSTGATE, J. P. See under "*N.* 2.1–10" (386).

Scholia

85b. SCHROEDER, O. "Memnons Tod bei Lesches," *Hermes* 20 (1885) 494.

NEMEAN SEVEN

General

BORNEMANN, L. "Pindar's siebente nemeische Ode ein Siegertodtenlied," *Philologus* 45 (1886) 596–613.
DEFRADAS, J. See under "*P.* 11 General" (150–6).
FINLEY, J. H., JR. "The date of Paean 6 and Nemean 7," *HSCP* 60 (1951) 61–80.
FONTENROSE, J. "The Cult and Myth of Pyrrhos at Delphi," *Univ. of California Publ. in Class. Archeology* 4, 3 (Berkeley and Los Angeles 1960) 191–261.
*FRACCAROLI, G. *L'ode Nemea VII di Pindaro* (Messina 1892). Originally in *Atti della R. Accademia Peloritana* 7 (1889–91) 241–72.
GIANOTTI, G. F. "La Nemea Settima di Pindaro," *RFIC* 94 (1966) 385–406.
GILDERSLEEVE, B. L. "The Seventh Nemean Revisited," *AJP* 31 (1910) 125–53.
   [A. Puech, *REG* 24 (1911) 218.]
HERMANN, G. *De Sogenis Aeginetae victoria quinquertii dissertatio* (Leipzig 1822). Also in *Opuscula* 3 (Leipzig 1828) 22–36.
*HOLMES, A. See under "Nemean Odes General."
HOUGHTON, H. P. "The Seventh Nemean," *CJ* 50 (1955) 173–8.
*LEPORE, E. "La saga di Neottolemo e la VII Nemea di Pindaro," *Annali della Facoltà di Lettere e Filosofia, Università di Bari* 6 (1960) 69–85.
LÜBBERT, E. See under "*O.* 8 General." Date.
MEZGER, F. "Pindaros siebente nemeische Ode," *JPh* 93 (1866) 105–13.

Rauchenstein, R. "Pindar's Nem. VII, gedichtet auf den Aegineten Sogenes, den Sieger im Fünfkampf," *NSM* 6 (1866) 65–74.
Rauchenstein, R. See under "*N.* 1 General" (421–31).
Steffen, C. *Zu Pind. Nem. VII und zu Horat. Carm. I. 22* (Progr. Leipzig 1882) 1–14.
Trammell, E. P. "The Grave of Neoptolemus," *CJ* 44 (1949) 270–3.
Tugendhat, E. "Zum Rechtfertigungsproblem in Pindars 7. Nemeischen Gedicht," *Hermes* 88 (1960) 385–409.
Turolla, E. "A proposito di uno specchio ideale e manifestante per realtà di se stessa ignara. Osservazioni platonico-rosminiane sulla tragedia attica," *Rivista Rosminiana* 45 (1951) 177–86.
Turolla, E. "Uno specchio per gloriose imprese (γνώμη e poesia)," *Poesia e poeti dell' antico mondo* (Catania 1956) 49–62 (49–51).
Wiechers, A. "Aesop und Neoptolemos," *Aesop in Delphi* (Meisenheim 1961) 43–9.
von Wilamowitz-Moellendorff, U. "Pindar's siebentes nemeisches Gedicht," *SPAW* (1908) 328–52.

Specific verses

1–2. Fraenkel, H. "Schrullen in den Scholien zu Pindars Nemeen 7 und Olympien 3," *Hermes* 89 (1961) 385–97 (391–4).
   3. Rauchenstein, R. See under "*O.* 1.106–7" (68).
 3–4. Wiskemann, A. See under "*O.* 1.106–8" (17–18).
   6. Friederichs, K. See under "*O.* 1.28–9" (76).
11–12. Hardie, W. R. See under "*N.* 1.46."
  14. Rauchenstein, R. See under "*O.* 1.106–7" (69).
      Wiskemann, A. See under "*O.* 1.106–8" (18–19).
  17. Ridgeway, W. "Pindar, Nem. VII. 17," *CR* 1 (1887) 313.
17–18. Astius, F. See under "*P.* 1.9" (222).
17 27. Friederichs, K. See under "*O.* 1.28–9" (76–8).
17–32. Lloyd, W. W. "On a Crux in Pindar's Seventh Nemean," *CR* 2 (1888) 118.
19–20. von Leutsch, E. "Zu Pind. Nem. VII, 19," *Philologus* 20 (1863) 506.
      Postgate, J. P. See under "*N.* 2.1–10" (386–7).
20–1. Fitch, E. See under "*P.* 4.277–8."
20–7. Dornseiff, F. "Homerphilologie," *Hermes* 70 (1935) 241–4 (243).
  22. Rauchenstein, R. See under "*O.* 1.106–7" (69).
      Wiskemann, A. See under "*O.* 1.106–8" (19).
25–7. Postgate, J. P. See under "*N.* 2.1–10" (387).
  31. Gerber, D. E. "Pindar, Nemean, 7, 31," *AJP* 84 (1963) 182–8.
31–4. Wiskemann, A. See under "*O.* 1.106–8" (20–21).
31–5. Norwood, G. "Pindar, Nemean, VII, 31–35," *AJP* 64 (1943) 325–6.
      Postgate, J. P. See under "*N.* 2.1–10" (387–8).
      Rauchenstein, R. See under "*O.* 1.106–7" (69–70).
32–3. Friederichs, K. See under "*O.* 1.28–9" (79).
32–4. Düring, I. See under "*O.* 8.52" (19–20).

32-5. MEZGER, F. See under "*O*. 1.28-9" (719-20).
33. SHACKLE, R. J. See under "*O*. 14.15."
44. PLATNAUER, M. *XPHN:EXPHN, CR* 56 (1942) 2-6 (3).
48-50. FRIEDERICHS, K. See under "*O*. 1.28-9" (79-80).
50. STONE, W. A. See under "*N*. 1.24."
53. DONALDSON, J. W. See under "*P*. 2.76-7" (223-4).
60. NAIRN, J. A. See under "*O*. 1.64."
NAIRN, J. A. See under "*N*. 3.29."
61-3. HARDIE, W. R. See under "*N*. 1.46."
68. MOORHOUSE, A. C. "*"AN* with the Future," *CQ* 40 (1946) 1-10 (5).
RAEDER, H. *Ein Problem in griechischer Syntax—Die Verbindung der Partikel ἄν mit Futurum* (Copenhagen 1953).
70-3. FRIEDERICHS, K. See under "*O*. 1.28-9" (80-1).
NAIRN, J. A. See under "*N*. 3.29."
STONE, W. A. See under "*O*. 13.98-9."
70-4. EBERT, J. See under "Games" (8-10).
FLOYD, E. D. "Pindar's Oath to Sogenes (Nemean 7.70-74)," *TAPA* 96 (1965) 139-51.
HOLWERDA, A. E. J. "Olympische Studien III. Zum Pentathlon," *Archäologische Zeitung* 39 (1881) 205-16.
JÜTHNER, J. "Zu Pindar Nem. 7, 70 ff.," *WS* 50 (1932) 166-70.
LATTIMORE, R. "Pindar Nemean 7. 70-74," *CP* 40 (1945) 121-2.
77-9. FRIEDERICHS, K. See under "*O*. 1.28-9" (81).
83. TURYN, A. See under "*O*. 1.113."
YOUNG, D. See under "*I*. 8.40" (21).
84-5. POSTGATE, J. P. See under "*N*. 2.1-10" (388).
86. BURY, J. B. "Miscellen," *BKIS* 11 (1886) 331-3.
HEADLAM, W. See under "*O*. 6.74" (303).
JURENKA, H. See under "*O*. 3.42-5" (27-8).
86-105. POSTGATE, J. P. See under "*N*. 1.18" (254-6).
102-4. FRAENKEL, H. See under "*N*. 7.1-2" (385-91).
104-5. POSTGATE, J. P. See under "*N*. 2.1-10" (388-9).
106. HARDIE, W. R. See under "*N*. 1.46."

NEMEAN EIGHT

General

BROWN, N. O. See under "History and Politics."
BULLE, C. "Pindaros achte nemeische Ode," *JPh* 97 (1868) 15-25.
EHRENBERG, V. *Sophocles and Pericles* (Oxford 1954) 178-9. Date.
LLOYD, W. W. *Pindar and Themistocles: Aegina and Athens* (London 1862).
LÜBBERT, E. See under "*O*. 8 General." Date.
MEINEL, G. See under "*P*. 2 General" (17-24).

Mezger, F. "Pindaros achte nemeische und dritte isthmische Ode," *JPh* 95 (1867) 385–400 (385–92).
Rauchenstein, R. See under "*N*. 1 General" (431–4).
Von der Mühll, P. See under "General and Miscellaneous."

Translations

*Arrò, A. *La Nemea VIII di Pindaro tradotta in endecasillabi sciolti italiani* (Alba 1889).

Specific verses

    1–4. Postgate, J. P. See under "*N*. 2.1–10" (389).
    2–3. Astius, F. See under "*P*. 1.9" (223–5).
    15. Friederichs, K. See under "*O*. 1.28–9" (82).
    21. Stone, W. A. See under "*O*. 13.98–9."
  36–41. Headlam, W. See under "*N*. 4.3."
    38. Düring, I. See under "*O*. 8.52" (20).
    40. Bowra, C. M. See under "Metre" (85).
        Rauchenstein, R. See under "*O*. 1.106–7" (70).
  40–1. Postgate, J. P. See under "*N*. 2.1–10" (389).
        Wiskemann, A. See under "*O*. 1.106–8" (21–2).
    46. Friederichs, K. See under "*O*. 6.31" (423–4).
        Headlam, W. See under "*O*. 14.20–21."
  46–8. Friederichs, K. See under "*O*. 1.28–9" (82–3).
    48. Postgate, J. P. See under "*N*. 1.18" (256).
  48–9. Rauchenstein, R. See under "*O*. 1.106–7" (70).
        Wiskemann, A. See under "*O*. 1.106–8" (22).
    51. Naber, S. A. See under "*O*. 1.7" (40–1).

NEMEAN NINE

General

Czerner, B. See under "Structure and Unity" (10–12). Myth.
Herkenrath, E. "Zu Pindaros N. IX." *Hermes* 39 (1904) 311–15.
von Leutsch, E. See under "*N*. 1 General."
Lübbert, E. *Prolusio in Pindari locum de ludis Pythiis Sicyoniis* (Bonn 1883).
*Lübbert, E. *Diatriba in Pindari locum de Adrasti regno sicyonio* (Progr. Bonn 1884).
Mommsen, T. See under "Manuscripts" (1877) 6–18.
Rauchenstein, R. See under "*N*. 1 General" (434–7).

Specific verses

  1–7. von Leutsch, E. *De Pindari carminis Nemei noni prooemio adnotatiunculae* (Göttingen 1859).
    7. Friederichs, K. See under "*O*. 1.28–9" (84).
       Jurenka, H. See under "*O*. 3.42–5" (23).

15. POSTGATE, J. P. See under "*N.* 1.18" (257).
17–18. HARDIE, W. R. "Pindar, Nem. IX. 16–19," *CR* 4 (1890) 269.
18–25. LENDRUM, W. T. "Two Notes on Pindar," *CR* 22 (1908) 241–3.
20. HARTMAN, J. J. See under "*P.* 3.38" (449).
22–3. PEARSON, A. C. "Pindar, Nem. IX. 22, 23," *CR* 5 (1891) 337.
23. NABER, S. A. See under "*O.* 1.7" (41).
POSTGATE, J. P. See under "*N.* 2.1–10" (389–90).
ROBERTSON, D. S. See under "*N.* 2.10–12."
TYRRELL, R. Y. "See under "*O.* 3.45."
24–5. SHACKLE, R. J. See under "*O.* 14.15."
29. VON WILAMOWITZ-MOELLENDORFF, U. See under "*P.* 4.105" (171). Also in *Kleine Schriften IV* (Berlin 1962) 9.
34–6. CLAYTON, F. "Pindar, Nem. IX. 32," *CR* 50 (1936) 5–6.
37. VAN HERWERDEN, H. See under "*O.* 2.71" (52–3).
41. POSTGATE, J. P. See under "*N.* 1.18" (257).
42. VON LEUTSCH, E. "Pind. Nem. IX, 42," *Philologus* 21 (1864) 118.
42–3. POSTGATE, J. P. See under "*N.* 2.1–10" (390).
44. NABER, S. A. See under "*O.* 1.7" (41).
46–7. STONE, W. A. See under "*O.* 13.98–9."
47. POSTGATE, J. P. See under "*N.* 2.1–10" (390–1).
48. FRIEDERICHS, K. See under "*O.* 1.28–9" (84–5).

NEMEAN TEN

General

FRIEDERICHS, K. See under "*O.* 1.28–9." (88–91).
LENDRUM, W. T. "The Date of Pindar's Tenth Nemean," *CR* 16 (1902) 267–9.
MOMMSEN, T. See under "Manuscripts" (1877) 14–40.
PUECH, A. "La mort de Castor dans le Xe Néméenne," *REG* 43 (1930) 398–403.
RAUCHENSTEIN, R. See under "*N.* 1 General" (437–41).
RIVIER, A. See under "Religion and Myth" (81–7).
SCHADEWALDT, W. "Pindars zehnte Nemeische Ode," *Festschrift Martin Heidegger* (Pfullingen 1959) 252–63. Also in *Hellas und Hesperien* (Zürich & Stuttgart 1960) 85–94.
SEVERYNS, A. "Pindare et les 'Chants Cypriens'," *AC* 1 (1932) 261–71.
SEVERYNS, A. "Correspondance," *REG* 44 (1931) 119–20. Myth.
STAEHLIN, F. "Der Dioskurenmythus in Pindars 10. nemeischer Ode. (Ein Beispiel einer Mythenidealisierung)," *Philologus* 62 (1903) 182–95.
TACCONE, A. "Su la Nemea X di Pindaro," *BFC* 22 (1916) 42–51.

Translations

ARENA, A. "Pindaro: Nemea X," *RSC* 10 (1962) 251–8.
*GURLITT, J. See under "*N.* 1 Translations."

Specific verses

    5. BURY, J. B. "Pindar Nem. X. 5," *CR* 7 (1893) 346-7.
       HARDIE, W. R. "Pindar, Nem. X. 5," *CR* 4 (1890) 318.
       VON DER MÜHLL, P. See under "*N.* 5.43."
 9-11. BERGK, T. See under "*I.* 1.68."
12-17. FRIEDERICHS, K. See under "*O.* 1.28-9" (85-6).
  13. VAN HERWERDEN, H. See under "*O.* 2.71" (53-4).
  30. POSTGATE, J. P. See under "*N.* 1.18" (257).
  31. FRIEDERICHS, K. See under "*O.* 1.28-9" (87-8).
 37-8. VON DER MÜHLL, P. See under "*N.* 5.43."
37-42. KIECHLE, F. "Argos und Tiryns nach der Schlacht bei Sepeia," *Philologus* 104 (1960) 181-200 (190-1).
  38. ASTIUS, F. See under "*P.* 1.9" (225).
      VAN GRONINGEN, B. A. "Quelques exemples d'adverbes ou de locutions adverbiales employés comme adjectifs," *Mnem* 3rd S., 13 (1947) 236.
 41-2. BOECKH, A. See under "*O.* 6.53-4" (15).
 45-8. ROBINSON, D. M. "New Greek Bronze Vases. A Commentary on Pindar," *AJA* 46 (1942) 172-97. Abstract given in *AJA* 44 (1940) 109.
  48. POSTGATE, J. P. See under "*N.* 2.1-10" (391-2).
  60. VAN HERWERDEN, H. See under "*O.* 2.71" (54).
      VAN DER VALK, M. See under "*P.* 6.13" (348-9).
  62. HARDIE, W. R. "Pindar, Nem. X. 61-66," *CR* 4 (1890) 269-70 and 318.
      VAN DER VALK, M. See under "*O.* 14.14-15" (631-2).
  66. VAN HERWERDEN, H. See under "*O.* 2.71" (54).
  75. BOWRA, C. M. See under "Metre" (180-1).
      HEADLAM, W. See under "*I.* 3/4.85" (246).
  84. BOWRA, C. M. See under "Metre" (176-7).

NEMEAN ELEVEN

General

MOMMSEN, T. See under "Manuscripts" (1877) 40-49.
POHLSANDER, H. A. See under "*N.* 3 General" (137-9).
RAUCHENSTEIN, R. See under "*N.* 1 General" (441-2).
DE VRIES, G. J. "Het feest van Aristagoras. Een ode van Pindarus," *Hermeneus* 36 (1964-65) 149-57.
VON WILAMOWITZ-MOELLENDORFF, U. See under "*I.* 8 General" (832-5).

Specific verses

  9-11. SCHNITZER, C. F. See under "*O.* 1.28-9" (65).
   11. BOWRA, C. M. See under "Metre" (85).
11-14. FRIEDERICHS, K. See under "*O.* 1.28-9" (92-3).
   16. VERDENIUS, W. J. "Pindar Nemean XI 16," *Mnem* 4th S., 6 (1953) 299.

18. Jurenka, H. See under "*O*. 3.42–5" (31–2).
27. Bowra, C. M. See under "Metre" (85).
28–9. Von der Mühll, P. "Bemerkungen zu Pindars Nemeen und Isthmien," *MH* 14 (1957) 127–32 (127–8).
45–6. van Herwerden, H. See under "*O*. 2.71" (54–5).
46. Postgate, J. P. See under "*N*. 1.18" (257).

10. ISTHMIAN ODES

General

Bury, J. B. *The Isthmian Odes of Pindar*, edited with introduction and commentary (London and New York 1892, repr. Amsterdam 1965).
   [W. R. Hardie, *CR* 6 (1892) 388–9; B. L. Gildersleeve, *AJP* 13 (1892) 385; M. E., *REG* 5 (1892) 471; J. Sitzler, *NPR* (1893) 161–4.]
*Cerrato, L. See under "Nemean Odes General."
Gautier, G. Ἰσθμιονῖκαι. *I vincitori ismj di Pindaro*. Tradotti in Italiane canzoni ed illustrati con postille (Rome 1768).
*Rosing, M. *Pindars isthmiske Oder* (Progr. Sorø 1893). Translation.
*Sommer, E. *Pindare. Les Isthmiques*, expliquées d'après une méthode nouvelle par deux traductions françaises avec des sommaires et des notes. Texte grec revu par T. Fix (Paris 1847).

ISTHMIAN ONE

General

*Bornemann, L. *Pindar's erste isthmische Ode "An die Vaterstadt"* mit einem Vorworte über Hellenismus und Einheitsschule (Hamburg 1893).
   [H. Jurenka, *PhW* 14 (1894) 769–72; K. Löschhorn, *WKPh* 11 (1894) 373–4.]
Bundy, E. L. "Studia Pindarica II: The First Isthmian Ode," *Univ. of California Publ. in Class. Philology* 18, 2 (Berkeley and Los Angeles 1962) 35–92.
   [For reviews see Bundy, E. L., under "*O. 11* General."]

Translations

*Capocasa, S. See under "*O. 1* Translations."

Specific verses

10–11. von Leutsch, E. "Pind. Isthm. I, 10," *Philologus* 18 (1862) 486.
   11. Lendrum, W. T. See under "*N.* 9.18–25."
   14–15. Jurenka, H. See under "*O.* 3.42–5" (23–4).
   14–16. Friese, E. See under "Syntax" (41).
      Wiskemann, A. See under "*O.* 1.106–8" (22–3).
   15. Rauchenstein, R. See under "*O.* 1.106–7" (70).
   18. Rauchenstein, R. See under "*O.* 1.106–7" (70).
      *Schmidt, M. See under "*O.* 1.63–4."
      Wiskemann, A. See under "*O.* 1.106–8" (23–4).
   24–5. Rauchenstein, R. "Zu Pindars Isthmien," *Philologus* 35 (1876) 255–62 (255).

36. BERGK, T. See under "*N*. 3.43–51" (601–2).
    RAUCHENSTEIN, R. See under "*I*. 1.24–5" (255–6).
37. Gow, A. S. F. *ΜΕΤΡΑ ΘΑΛΑΣΣΗΣ, CR* 45 (1931) 10–12 (12).
40. DÖRRIE, H. See under "*O*. 8.59–61" (15–16).
41. BEATTIE, A. J. "Pindar, Isthmia, i. 41," *CR* NS 3 (1953) 77–9.
    JURENKA, H. See under "*O*. 3.42–5" (26–7).
    RAUCHENSTEIN, R. "Zu Pindaros Isthmien," *JPh* 93 (1866) 225.
    RAUCHENSTEIN, R. See under "*I*. 1.24–5" (256).
    RAUCHENSTEIN, R. See under "*O*. 1.106–7" (70).
    SHACKLE, R. J. See under "*O*. 14.15."
    STONE, W. A. See under "*N*. 1.24."
41–2. WISKEMANN, A. See under "*O*. 1.106–8" (24–5).
47–8. VAN OTTERLO, W. A. A. See under "Style and Imagery" (160).
50. NABER, S. A. See under "*O*. 1.7" (41–2).
54. RAUCHENSTEIN, R. See under "*I*. 1.24–5" (256).
63. NABER, S. A. See under "*O*. 1.7" (42).
66. VAN HERWERDEN, H. See under "*O*. 2.71" (55).
67–8. NORWOOD, G. "Two Notes on Pindar, Isthmian I and VII," *AJP* 63 (1942) 460–1.
68. BERGK, T. "Philologische Thesen," *Philologus* 14 (1859) 388. Also in *Kleine philologische Schriften* 2 (Halle 1886) 736.
    BERGK, T. See under "*N*. 3.43–51" (602).
    RAUCHENSTEIN, R. See under "*I*. 1.24–5" (256).

ISTHMIAN TWO

General

FRACCAROLI, G. See under "*P*. 6 General."
*KUBO, M. "Μοῦσα ἐργάτις (Pind. Isthm. II)," *JCS* 6 (1958) 24–32. In Japanese with resumé in English.
VON LEUTSCH, E. "Die Eparchen von Pind. Isthm. II," *Philologus* 32 (1873) 179–81.
OLIVIERI, A. See under "*P*. 6 General" (31–7).
PAVESE, C. "*ΧΡΗΜΑΤΑ, ΧΡΗΜΑΤ*' *ΑΝΗΡ* ed il motivo della liberalità nella secondo Istmica di Pindaro," *Quaderni Urbinati di cultura classica* 2 (1966) 103–12.
VON DER MÜHLL, P. See under "General and Miscellaneous."

Specific verses

1–14. VON LEUTSCH, E. *De Pindari carminis Isthmii secundi prooemio commentatio* (Göttingen 1862).
  8. FRAZER, J. G. "Coins Attached to the Face," *CR* 2 (1888) 261.
    NESTLE, W. "Ueber griechische Göttermasken. (Zu Hypereides pro Eux. 35 f. und Pindar Isthm. II 8)," *Philologus* 50 (1891) 499–506.

PATON, W. R. "Pindar, Isthm. II. 10," *CR* 2 (1888) 180.
*PATON, W. R. "Pindar's 'Silvered Faces'," *The Academy* 24 (1883) 435.
RAUCHENSTEIN, R. See under "*I.* 1.24–5" (256).
10. SCHNITZER, C. F. See under "*O.* 1.28–9" (66–7).
12. ASTIUS, F. See under "*P.* 1.9" (227–8).
RAUCHENSTEIN, R. See under "*I.* 1.24–5" (256–7).
19–20. RAUCHENSTEIN, R. See under "*I.* 1.24–5" (257).
22. DAWES, R. See under "*P.* 6 General" (102–3).
28. VILLOISON, J. "Notae et emendationes in Pindarum eiusque scholiastam ineditae," *Acta societatis philologicae Lipsiensis*, ed. C. D. Beckius, Vol. 1 (Leipzig 1811) 232–40 (233–4).
39–40. WRATISLAW, A. H. "Pindar Isth. II 39, 40," *TCPS* 1 (1881) 163.
41–2. DEAS, H. T. "Pindar, Isth. II. 41–2," *CR* 41 (1927) 211–13.
VON WILAMOWITZ-MOELLENDORFF, U. See under "*P.* 4.105" (171). Also in *Kleine Schriften IV* (Berlin 1962) 9.
42. RAUCHENSTEIN, R. See under "*I.* 1.24–5" (257).
RAUCHENSTEIN, R. See under "*I.* 1.41."

ISTHMIAN THREE/FOUR

General

BOEDEKER, J. *Pindari carmen Isthmicum tertium num in duo carmina dividendum sit* (Diss. Monasterii 1895).
BULLE, C. *Pindars dritter (und vierter) isthmischer Siegesgesang* (Progr. Bremen 1869).
BULLE, C. "Pindars dritte isthmische und elfte pythische Ode," *JPh* 103 (1871) 585–96 (585–9).
BURY, J. B. "The 'Third Isthmian'," *Hermathena* 7 (1890) 276–80.
FRIEDERICHS, K. See under "*O.* 1.28–9" (95–9).
FRIEDERICHS, K. See under "*P.* 5.15–19" (450–6).
HEIMSOETH, F. See under "*P.* 9 General" (21–32).
HERBIG, G. "Zur Chronologie der pindarischen Siegesgesänge Isth. III/IV und Isth. VII," *Commentationes philologicae. Conventui Philologorum Monachii Congregatorum obtulerunt Sodales Seminarii Philologici Monacensis* (Munich 1891) 129–45.
MEZGER, F. See under "*N.* 8 General" (392–400).
PERTHES, H. *Beiträge zur Erklärung Pindars* (Progr. Treptow 1871) 1–10.
   [E. von Leutsch, *PA* 7 (1875) 15–20.]
PERTHES, H. "Pindars dritte isthmische und elfte pythische Ode," *JPh* 105 (1872) 217–38 (217–26).
POHLSANDER, H. A. See under "*N.* 3 General" (139–40).
RAUCHENSTEIN, R. See under "*I.* 1.24–5" (257–8).
SCHNITZER, C. F. *Interpolation im Pindar* (Progr. Ellwangen 1868).
SCHNITZER, C. F. See under "*O.* 1.28–9" (68–9).
SCHRÖDER, O. *Studia Pindarica* (Progr. Berlin 1878) 1–3.

Specific verses

    5. HEADLAM, W. See under "*O.* 6.74" (303).
 19–21. BURY, J. B. "Two Literary Compliments," *CR* 19 (1905) 10–11.
        HARTMAN, J. J. See under "*P.* 3.38" (450).
   30. NORWOOD, G. See under "*O.* 3.44" (1–2).
   31. NABER, S. A. See under "*O.* 1.7" (42).
        RAUCHENSTEIN, R. See under "*O.* 1.106–7" (70).
        WISKEMANN, A. See under "*O.* 1.106–8" (25).
   36. RAUCHENSTEIN, R. See under "*I.* 1.24–5" (258).
 36–36b. WOODBURY, L. "Pindar, Isthmian 4. 19 f.," *TAPA* 78 (1947) 368–75.
 49–54. DÜRING, I. See under "*O.* 8.52" (9).
        FRIEDERICHS, K. See under "*O.* 1.28–9" (94–5).
   53. *MEINEKE, A. *Adnot. quaedam ad Pind. Isthm. III, 53* (Progr. Königsberg 1818).
  53–4. RAUCHENSTEIN, R. See under "*I.* 1.24–5" (258–9).
  53–7. HEADLAM, W. "Some Passages of Aeschylus and Others," *CR* 17 (1903) 286–95 (288–9).
   53b. LEHRS, K. See under "*O.* 2.65" (95–6).
        MADWIG, J. N. See under "*O.* 2.65" (188).
   54. SCHNITZER, C. F. See under "*O.* 1.28–9" (69).
        TYRRELL, R. Y. See under "*O.* 3.45."
  55–7. FITCH, E. See under "*P.* 4.277–8."
   59. NABER, S. A. See under "*O.* 1.7" (40).
  63–5. WISKEMANN, A. See under "*O.* 1.106–8" (25–6).
   64. STONE, W. A. See under "*O.* 13.98–9."
        YOUNG, D. See under "*I.* 8.40" (16).
   65. KELLER, O. "Zu Pindaros," *JPh* 131 (1885) 463–4.
        RAUCHENSTEIN, R. See under "*O.* 1.106–7" (70–1).
   66. BOWRA, C. M. See under "Metre" (180).
   80. FRIEDERICHS, K. See under "*O.* 1.28–9" (95).
        VAN HERWERDEN, H. See under "*O.* 2.71" (55–6).
   81. NABER, S. A. See under "*O.* 1.7" (42–3).
   85. HEADLAM, W. "Transposition of Words in MSS.," *CR* 16 (1902) 243–56 (243–4).
   89. JURENKA, H. See under "*O.* 3.42–5" (25).
        SCHNITZER, C. F. See under "*O.* 1.28–9" (70).

ISTHMIAN FIVE

General

BARTELS, C. F. *De quarto Pindari Epinicio Isthmio commentatiuncula* (Hildesheim 1823).
FINLEY, J. H. See under "History and Politics."
HEIMSOETH, F. See under "*P.* 9 General" (21–32).
VON WILAMOWITZ-MOELLENDORFF, U. See under "*I.* 8 General" (823–9).

Specific verses

    1. Dornseiff, F. *Die archaische Mythenerzählung* (Berlin & Leipzig 1933) 79–82.
  1–8. van Otterlo, W. A. A. See under "Style and Imagery" (154).
   11. Headlam, W. See under "*O*. 6.74" (303–6).
   12. Wackernagel, J. ἄλπνιστος, *ZVS* 43 (1910) 377–8.
12–14. Düring, I. See under "*O*. 8.52" (9–10).
   16. Bowra, C. M. See under "Metre" (85).
      Rauchenstein, R. See under "*I*. 1.24–5" (259).
   21. Düring, I. See under "*O*. 8.52" (10).
   28. Kerferd, G. B. "The First Greek Sophists," *CR* 64 (1950) 8–10.
34–8. Christ, W. See under "Games" (18–20).
   38. Stone, W. A. See under "*O*. 13.98–9."
   41. Bowra, C. M. See under "Metre" (178).
   43. Hartman, J. J. See under "*P*. 3.38" (450–1).
   51. van Herwerden, H. See under "*P*. 5.121."
56–8. Calogero, G. "Pindaro, Isthmia, V 56–58," *A&R* NS 6 (1925) 293–307.
      Friese, E. See under "Syntax" (41–2).
   58. Rauchenstein, R. See under "*I*. 1.24–5" (259–60).
59–60. van Herwerden, H. See under "*O*. 2.71" (56).

ISTHMIAN SIX

General

von Wilamowitz-Moellendorff, U. See under "*I*. 8 General" (818–23).

Specific verses

  1–9. Tolles, D. *The Banquet-Libations of the Greeks* (Diss. Bryn Mawr 1943) 54–6.
    4. Stone, W. A. See under "*O*. 13.98–9."
    5. Dover, K. J. "Pindar, Isthmians 6. 4," *CR* NS 1 (1951) 65–6.
      van Herwerden, H. See under "*O*. 2.71" (56).
      Schnitzer, C. F. See under "*O*. 1.28–9" (71–2).
   17. Fraenkel, E. *Aeschylus Agamemnon*. Vol. 2 (Oxford 1950) 172 n. 2.
22–3. von Blumenthal, A. "Hecatompedos," *RhM* 85 (1936) 377–83 (379–80).
31–5. Koepp, F. See under "*N*. 4.27–32."
   33. Robert, C. See under "*N*. 4.27."
   36. Rauchenstein, R. See under "*O*. 1.106–7" (71).
      Shackle, R. J. See under "*O*. 14.15."
      Tyrrell, R. Y. "See under "*O*. 3.45."
      Wiskemann, A. See under "*O*. 1.106–8" (26).
      Von der Mühll, P. See under "*N*. 11.28–9" (130–2).

42. RAUCHENSTEIN, R. See under "*I*. 1.24–5" (260).
44–7. WISKEMANN, A. See under "*O*. 1.106–8" (27–8).
45–7. MEZGER, F. See under "*P*. 8.73–5" (8–9).
46. RAUCHENSTEIN, R. See under "*I*. 1.24–5" (260).
SCHNITZER, C. F. See under "*O*. 1.28–9" (72).
WRATISLAW, A. H. "Pind. Isth. V. (VI.) 66," *JP* 2 (1869) 154–5.
46–7. RAUCHENSTEIN, R. "Pindar Isthm. V," *Philologus* 21 (1864) 679–80.
47. RAUCHENSTEIN, R. See under "*O*. 1.106–7" (71).
YOUNG, D. See under "*I*. 8.40" (19).
53. FRIEDERICHS, K. See under "*O*. 1.28–9" (99–100).
57. RAUCHENSTEIN, R. See under "*O*. 1.106–7" (71).
58. NABER, S. A. See under "*O*. 1.7" (43).
58–9. WISKEMANN, A. See under "*O*. 1.106–8" (28).
59. FRIEDERICHS, K. See under "*O*. 1.28–9" (100).
63. BOWRA, C. M. See under "Metre" (87).
SCHNITZER, C. F. See under "*O*. 1.28–9" (72–3).
66–9. SCHROEDER, O. See under "*P*. 5.24."
72. MAAS, P. "Verschiedenes," *Philologus* 72 (1913) 449–56 (456).
72–3. GRASSI, E. "Pindaro, Isthm. VI 72 ss.," *A&R* NS 6 (1961) 136–7.
74–5. KAMBYLIS, A. See under "Style and Imagery" (114).

ISTHMIAN SEVEN

General

CAMARDA, N. "Sull' Istmica VI o VII di Pindaro," *REur* 16 (1879) 319–22.
GOMME, A. W. *A Historical Commentary on Thucydides*. Vol. 1 (Oxford 1945; reprinted with corrections 1950) 318–9. Date.
MEZGER, F. See under "*P*. 8.73–5" (14–16). Date.

Translations

VAN GRONINGEN, B. A. See under "*O*. 4 Translations."
*PASQUALE, M. See under "*O*. 1 Translations."

Specific verses

3–5. MYLONAS, G. E. *Eleusis and the Eleusinian Mysteries* (Princeton 1961) 277–8.
6. TYRRELL, R. Y. Review of G. Fraccaroli, *Le odi di Pindaro dichiarate e tradotte*, in *CR* 8 (1894) 207–9.
7. HOEKSTRA, A. See under "Syntax."
8. SHACKLE, R. J. See under "*O*. 14.15."
10. GARROD, H. W. "Pindarica. II. Isthmian vii. 10," *CR* 36 (1922) 102–3.
15. BORNEMANN, L. See under "*P*. 5.75."
MALTEN, L. See under "*P*. 5.75."
16–19. FRIEDERICHS, K. See under "*O*. 1.28–9" (100).

18–19. Hardie, W. R. See under "*N.* 1.46."
  28. van Herwerden, H. See under "*O.* 2.71" (56–7).
      Matthiae, A. See under "*P.* 4.57" (42).
      Shackle, R. J. See under "*O.* 14.15."
      Wölfflin, E. "Zur Kritik Pindar's," *Philologus* 7 (1852) 209–11.
  30. Tyrrell, R. Y. See under "*I.* 7.6."
31–3. Norwood, G. See under "*I.* 1.67–8."
31–6. Bergk, T. See under "*O.* 2.95–100" (189–91).
  33. Fennell, C. A. M. "On Pindar, Isthm. VI, esp. v. 33," *PCPS* (1894) 15–16.
      Mezger, F. See under "*P.* 8.73–5" (9).
      Schnitzer, C. F. See under "*O.* 1.28–9" (73–4).
39–40. Rauchenstein, R. See under "*I.* 1.24–5" (260).
39–42. Friederichs, K. See under "*O.* 1.28–9" (101).
  44–7. Peppermüller, R. *Die Bellerophontessage. Ihre Herkunft und Geschichte* (Diss. Tübingen 1961) 55–6.

ISTHMIAN EIGHT

General

Bach, E. C. C. *Dubitationes de authentia Pindari Isthmiorum carminis octavi* (Erfurt 1806).
Finley, J. H. See under "History and Politics."
Friederichs, K. See under "*O.* 1.28–9" (102–6).
Herbig, G. See under "*I.* 3/4 General." Date.
Mezger, F. See under "*P.* 8.73–5" (16–18). Date.
Solmsen, F. *Hesiod and Aeschylus*, Cornell Studies in Classical Philology 30 (Ithaca 1949) 128–9. Myth.
Taccone, A. "Per la cronologia dell' Istmia 7ª di Pindaro e le relazioni dell' attualità col mito," *BFC* 19 (1913) 178–84.
von Wilamowitz-Moellendorff, U. "Erklärungen pindarischer Gedichte," *SPAW* (1909) 806–35 (806–12).

Translations

*Gurlitt, J. *Pindars achter isthmischer Siegesgesang*, übersetzt mit Anmerkungen (Hamburg & Leipzig 1818).
Taccone, A. "L'Istmia VIII di Pindaro," *MC* 4 (1934) 285–9.

Specific verses

  1. *Schmidt, M. See under "*O.* 1.57."
1–3. Rauchenstein, R. See under "*I.* 1.24–5" (260–1).
1–4. Wiskemann, A. See under "*O.* 1.106–8" (28–9).
1–5a. Düring, I. See under "*O.* 8.52" (10–11).
10–14. Rauchenstein, R. See under "*I.* 1.24–5" (261–2).

11. BOECKH, A. See under "*O.* 6.53–4" (15).
11–12. DÜRING, I. See under "*O.* 8.52" (11).
MEZGER, F. See under "*P.* 8.73–5" (10).
SCHNITZER, C. F. See under "*O.* 1.28–9" (74).
13. SHACKLE, R. J. See under "*O.* 14.15."
WISKEMANN, A. See under "*O.* 1.106–8" (29–31).
21–6. NORTH, H. "Pindar, Isthmian, 8, 24–28," *AJP* 69 (1948) 304–8.
27–48. REITZENSTEIN, R. "Die Hochzeit des Peleus und der Thetis," *Hermes* 35 (1900) 73–105 (74–5).
30–4. Vos, H. Θέμις (Assen 1956) 56–60.
31. BERGK, T. See under "*O.* 2.95–100" (191).
31–3. RAUCHENSTEIN, R. See under "*I.* 1.24–5" (262).
40. BERGK, T. See under "*O.* 2.95–100" (191–2).
YOUNG, D. "Notes on the Text of Pindar. III. Emendations and Defences of Readings in Pindar," *GRBS* 7 (1966) 16–22 (16).
43. WRATISLAW, A. H. "Pindar Isth. VII 43," *TCPS* 1 (1881) 163.
46–7. VON DER MÜHLL, P. "Weitere pindarische Notizen," *MH* 22 (1965) 49–52.
46a–47. RAUCHENSTEIN, R. See under "*I.* 1.24–5" (262).
SCHMIDT, M. See under "*N.* 1.46."
47. FRIEDERICHS, K. See under "*O.* 1.28–9" (101–2).
FRIEDERICHS, K. See under "*O.* 3.13–18" (36–7).
56a. DAWES, R. See under "*P.* 6 General" (88–92 and 650).
70. ERBSE, H. See under "*O.* 10.9" (31–3).
GALIANO, M. F. "A Pindaro I. VIII 70," *Emerita* 11 (1943) 134–41.
NORWOOD, G. "Pindar Isthmian 8. 77," *CP* 47 (1952) 161–2.
THEILER, W. *Die zwei Zeitstufen in Pindars Stil und Vers* (Halle 1941) 1–2.
[A. Lesky, *AAHG* 1 (1948) 37–8; F. Dornseiff, *Gnomon* 19 (1943) 161–2; E. Kalinka, *PhW* 64 (1944) 73–80.]
THUMMER, E. "Zu Pindar, Isthmia VIII, 70," *Natalicium Carolo Jax septuagenario a.d. VII. Kal. Dec. MCMLV oblatum, Pars I* (Innsbruck 1955) 165–6.

Scholia

*RESLER, J. *Ultimae Pindari Isthmiae scholia maximam partem nunc primum edita et adnotatione critica instruxit* (Diss. Vratislaviae 1847).
57b. CHARITONIDES, C. Σύμμεικτα κριτικά, *EBS* 7 (1931) 227–43 (238–9).

11. FRAGMENTS

General

Diehl, E. *Supplementum lyricum. Neue Bruchstücke von Archilochos Alcaeus Sappho Corinna Pindar Bacchylides* (Bonn 1908, 1910², 1917³).

Frassinetti, P. "Un frammento di Pindaro?" *GIF* 4 (1951) 1–5.

Headlam, W. See under "*O.* 6.74" (306). Plut. *Mor.* 586A derived from Pindar.

Lobel, E. *The Oxyrhynchus Papyri.* Part XXVI (London 1961).
   [E. G. Turner, *CR* NS 13 (1963) 268–70; B. A. van Groningen, *Gnomon* 35 (1963) 127–30; A. Tovar, *Emerita* 32 (1964) 335–7; E. des Places, *Orientalia* 32 (1963) 503; A. Swiderek, *The Journal of Juristic Papyrology* 15 (1965) 397–405.]

Mingazzini, P. "Ippocrate o Pindaro?" *RPAA* 25–26 (1949–51) 33–5.

Romagnoli, E. "I frammenti di Pindaro tradotti," *Athenaeum* 5 (1917) 263–84.

*Schneider, J. G. *Carminum Pindaricorum fragmenta* (Argentorati 1776). Text and commentary.

Schneidewin, F. W. "Supplementa corporis fragmentorum pindaricorum Boeckhiani," *Eustathii prooemium commentariorum Pindaricorum* (Göttingen 1837) 29–38.

Whitmore, C. E. "New Words in the Papyrus Fragments of Pindar," *CR* 24 (1910) 239–40.

Isthmia

When the subject of an article is limited to specific verses of a fragment, the verse numbers are given to the left of the entry.

2

Rohde, E. "Ein Fragment Pindars," *Philologus* 35 (1876) 199–201.

5

Bethe, E. "Ramenta mythographa I: De Pindari carmine quodam Isthmio deperdito," *Genethliacon Gottingense* (Halle 1888) 32–7.

Hymni

Lohan, E. "De Hymno," *Poesis melicae generum nominibus quae vis subiecta sit a classicis scriptoribus Graecis. Pars I* (Progr. Lauban 1898) 22–36.

29

VON LEUTSCH, E. "Der erste Hymnos des Pindaros," *Philologus* 11 (1856) 176–83.

SNELL, B. "Pindars Hymnos auf Zeus," *A&A* 2 (1946) 180–92. Also in *Die Entdeckung des Geistes* (Hamburg 1948), English translation by T. G. Rosenmeyer, *The Discovery of the Mind* (Oxford 1953) 71–89.

2. VIAN, F. *Les origines de Thèbes: Cadmos et les Spartes* (Paris 1963) 167. See also J. Fontenrose, *CP* 61 (1966) 192.

30

SOLMSEN, F. See under "*I.* 8 General" (67–8).

VOS, H. See under "*I.* 8.30–4."

4. CAPELLE, P. See under "*O.* 2.70" (38–9).

33c

1. GALLET DE SANTERRE, H. *Délos primitive et archaïque* (Diss. Paris 1958) 160.

6. HARVEY, A. E. "Homeric Epithets in Greek Lyric Poetry," *CQ* NS 7 (1957) 206–23 (217 n. 1).

PLATNAUER, M. See under "Style and Imagery" (160–1).

DE VRIES, G.-J. "A propos de Pindare, fr. 33b Sn.," *REG* 69 (1956) 445.

33d

10. HEADLAM, W. Review of G. S. Farnell, *Greek Lyric Poetry*, in *CR* 6 (1892) 438.

RADERMACHER, L. See under "*P.* 3.84."

35

DAIN, A. "La tripodie iambique catalectique, le *Rufulianum*," *Mélanges offerts à A.- M. Desrousseaux* (Paris 1937) 105–15 (109).

35b

DAIN, A. See under "Fr. 35" (109).

WILKINS, E. G. "Μηδὲν Ἄγαν in Greek and Latin Literature," *CP* 21 (1926) 132–48 (135–6).

36

CLASSEN, C. J. "The Libyan God Ammon in Greece before 331 B.C.," *Historia* 8 (1959) 349–55 (349–50).

37

Harrison, J. E. "Helios-Hades," *CR* 22 (1908) 12–16.

39

Herzog-Hauser, G. "Tyche und Fortuna," *WS* 63 (1948) 155–63 (160–3).

43

Adrados, F. R. "El poema del pulpo y los origenes de la colección teognidea," *Emerita* 26 (1958) 1–10.

44

Kiehl, E. J. "Een Fragment van Pindaros," *Mnem* 4 (1855) 383–6.

51 a–d

von Wilamowitz-Moellendorff, U. "Pausanias-Scholien," *Hermes* 29 (1894) 240–8 (246–8).

51b

Guillon, P. "Sur un fragment de Pindare et un faux sens de Strabon: La retraite aux trois cimes du Ptoion," *BCH* 77 (1953) 377–86.

Paeanes

Bowra, C. M. "Pindar," *New Chapters in the History of Greek Literature*, ed. J. U. Powell (Oxford 1933) 36–48.
Fairbanks, A. *A Study of the Greek Paean*, Cornell Studies in Classical Philology No. XII (Ithaca 1900).

52a

1. Housman, A. E. "On the Paeans of Pindar," *CR* 22 (1908) 8–12 (8).
3. Mulbegat-Holler, J. "Pind. Paean. 1 3 (D.)," *Eos* 30 (1927) 193.
7. Housman, A. E. See under "Fr. 52a.1" (8).

52b

von Arnim, H. "Pindars Pään für die Abderiten," *Wiener Eranos. Zur fünfzigsten Versammlung deutscher Philologen und Schulmänner in Graz 1909* (Vienna 1909) 8–19.
Hampe, R. "Zu Pindars Paian für Abdera," *Hermes* 76 (1941) 136–42.

JURENKA, H. "Pindaros neugefundener Paean für Abdera," *Philologus* 71 (1912) 173-210.

RADT, S. L. *Pindars zweiter und sechster Paian*. Text, Scholien und Kommentar (Diss. Amsterdam 1958).

[M. F. Galiano, *Emerita* 30 (1962) 154-5; J. Irigoin, *RPh* 3rd S., 35 (1961) 132-4; D. E. Gerber, *Phoenix* 15 (1961) 50-1; J. Duchemin, *FL* 2 (1961) 266-7; J. Duchemin, *REA* 63 (1961) 142-3; J. Duchemin, *RBPh* 39 (1961) 1300-2; A. Hoekstra, *Mnem* 4th S., 13 (1960) 68-70; F. Lasserre, *AC* 28 (1959) 344-5; E. Thummer, *Gnomon* 31 (1959) 724-8; G. Lieberg, *RFIC* 87 (1959) 168-74; H. T. Deas, *CR* NS 9 (1959) 233-4.]

SITZLER, J. "Zum zweiten Päan Pindars," *WKPh* 28 (1911) 586-90.

VERRALL, A. W. "The Paeans of Pindar and Other New Literature," *CR* 22 (1908) 110-18 (110-15).

29. VERRALL, A. W. "On the newly discovered Paeans of Pindar," *PCPS* 79-81 (1908) 1-2.

96-102. GILDERSLEEVE, B. L. "Brief Mention," *AJP* 29 (1908) 121. See also *AJP* 30 (1909) 112.

97. HOUSMAN, A. E. See under "Fr. 52a.1" (8).

100-1. CAMPBELL, L. "Note on Sophocles, Oedipus Tyrannus, 1218, 9," *CR* 22 (1908) 49.

52d

SITZLER, J. "Zum vierten Päan Pindars," *WKPh* 28 (1911) 698-702.

21-53. HOUSMAN, A. E. See under "Fr. 52a.1" (8-10).

50-3. VON WILAMOWITZ-MOELLENDORFF, U. "Lesefrüchte LXXXIX," *Hermes* 37 (1902) 327-8. Also in *Kleine Schriften IV* (Berlin 1962) 163-4.

52f

DEFRADAS, J. See under "*P*. 11 General" (150-6).

FINLEY, J. H., JR. See under "*N*. 7 General."

HOEKSTRA, A. "The Absence of the Aeginetans. On the Interpretation of Pindar's Sixth Paean," *Mnem* 4th S., 15 (1962) 1-14.

RADT, S. L. See under "Fr. 52b General."

SITZLER, J. "Zum sechsten Päan Pindars," *WKPh* 28 (1911) 1015-18.

TOSI, T. "Sul sesto peana di Pindaro," *A&R* 11 (1908) 201-20. Also in *Scritti di Filologia e di Archeologia* (Florence 1957) 99-114.

TOSI, T. "Ancora sul sesto peana di Pindaro," *SIFC* NS 7 (1929) 199-201

VERRALL, A. W. See under "Fr. 52b General" (115-17).

1-6. VERRALL, A. W. See under "Fr. 52b.29."

11. HOEKSTRA, A. See under "Syntax."

17. HOUSMAN, A. E. See under "Fr. 52a.1" (10-11).

50. POLAND, F. "Pindar, Paean VI 50," *PhW* 41 (1921) 332-3.

54–8. Jurenka, H. "Zu Pindars sechstem Päan," *WS* 35 (1913) 382–3.
59–61. Vollgraff, W. "Le péan delphique à Dionysos," *BCH* 49 (1925) 104–42 (121).
62–3. Housman, A. E. See under "Fr. 52a.1" (11).
76–7. Housman, A. E. See under "Fr. 52a.1" (11).
88–9. Housman, A. E. See under "Fr. 52a.1" (11).
95. Gildersleeve, B. L. "Brief Mention," *AJP* 29 (1908) 122.
105–8. Ribezzo, F. "Ad Pind. Paean. VI 105–109," *RIGI* 5 (1921) 240.
110. Mulbegat-Holler, J. "Pind. Paean. VI 110," *Eos* 30 (1927) 32.
112. Housman, A. E. See under "Fr. 52a.1" (11).
115. Housman, A. E. See under "Fr. 52a.1" (11).
118. Housman, A. E. See under "Fr. 52a.1" (11–12).
Verrall, A. W. See under "Fr. 52b.29."
125–83. Snell, B. "Identifikationen von Pindarbruchstücken," *Hermes* 73 (1938) 424–39 (425–8 and 431).

52g

1–6. Galiano, M. F. "Varia Graeca," *Humanitas* 3 (1950–51) 301–22 (304–12).

52h

Snell, B. See under "Fr. 52f.125–83" (428–30).
18–20. Friedländer, P. "Plato Phaedrus 245A," *CP* 36 (1941) 51–2.

52i

*Gennaro, S. *L'ottava peana di Pindaro* (Catania 1948).
Snell, B. "Pindars 8. Paian über die Tempel von Delphi," *Hermes* 90 (1962) 1–6.
Snell, B. See under "Fr. 52f.125–83" (432–6 and 439).
63–81. Körte, A. See under "Fr. 70a" (136–7).
70. Bergk, T. "Zu Pindar," *RhM* 8 (1853) 147–50.
Schneidewin, F. W. "Variae lectiones," *Philologus* 5 (1850) 366–78 (366–7).
Wieseler, F. "Pindar. Paean. Fr. II," *Philologus* 6 (1851) 736–7.
70–1. Miller, W. *Daedalus and Thespis. The Contributions of the Ancient Dramatic Poets to Our Knowledge of the Arts and Crafts of Greece* 1 (New York 1929) 51–2.
Vollgraff, W. "Le péan delphique à Dionysos," *BCH* 50 (1926) 263–304 (280).

52i(A)

Robert, C. "Zu Pindars VIII Paean," *Hermes* 49 (1914) 315–9.
Snell, B. See under "Fr. 52f.125–83" (437).

52k

HOUSMAN, A. E. See under "Fr. 52a.1" (12). Metre.

1–10. BOETTICHER, P. "Vermischte Bemerkungen. Zu Pindaros," *ZA* 11 (1853) 184.

FRAENKEL, E. "Lyrische Daktylen," *RhM* 72 (1917–18) 161–97 and 321–52 (176 and 328).

1–22. BLASS, F. "Pindaros Hyporchem auf die Sonnenfinsternis," *JPh* 99 (1869) 387–90.

*CIPOLLA, F. "Versioni da Pindaro," *Nozze Fraccaroli-Rezzonico* (Verona 1895) 5–10. Translation.

HERMANN, G. *De Pindari ad solem deficientem versibus* (Diss. Leipzig 1845). Also in *Opuscula* 8 (Leipzig 1877) 75–90.

HOFMANN, G. *Die in einem Fragmente des Dichters Pindar erwähnte Sonnenfinsternis* (Progr. Trieste 1889).

RIESS, E. See under "Religion and Myth" (423–5).

52m

KÖRTE, A. See under "Fr. 70a" (137–8).

52n

KÖRTE, A. "Literarische Texte mit Ausschluss der christlichen," *APF* 13 (1938) 93–5.

SNELL, B. "Drei Berliner Papyri mit Stücken alter Chorlyrik," *Hermes* 75 (1940) 177–91 (185–91).

52n(a)

9–11. SNELL, B. See under "Fr. 52f.125–83" (431–2).

52w(h)

LOBEL, E. "Two Fragments of Papyrus," *BQR* 3 (1920–22) 289–90.

DITHYRAMBI

CALDERINI, A. "Nuovi testi di Pindaro recentemente scoperti," *Nuova Antologia di Lettere, Scienze ed Arti* 6th S., 200 (1919) 379–82.

HARTUNG, J. A. "Ueber den dithyrambos," *Philologus* 1 (1846) 395–420.

*KUBO, M. "Pindarica. A Note on Dithyrambic Fragments," *JCS* 5 (1957) 51–65. In Japanese.

PICKARD-CAMBRIDGE, A. W. *Dithyramb, Tragedy and Comedy* (Oxford 1927) 32–9.

Platt, A. "On the Oxyrhynchus Papyri," *CR* 14 (1900) 18–20.
Privitera, G. A. "Intorno agli studi sul ditirambo," *A&R* NS 3 (1958) 1–25 (13–16).

70a

Körte, A. "Literarische Texte mit Ausschluss der christlichen," *APF* 7 (1923) 114–60 (134–6).

70b

Bowra, C. M. See under "Paeanes General" (48–51).
Schroeder, O. "Aus dem neusten Oxyrhynchosband (XIII)," *Sok* 7 (1919) 141–2.
Schroeder, O. *Pindars Pythien* (Leipzig 1922) 115–19.
Terzaghi, N. "Per la storia del ditirambo (Pap. Oxyrh. 1604 col. II)," *AAT* 55 (1919–20) 457–64.
1. Lawler, L. B. "'Limewood' Cinesias and the Dithyrambic Dance," *TAPA* 81 (1950) 78–88 (83–4).
2. Privitera, G. A. "L'asigmatismo di Laso e di Pindaro in Clearco fr. 88 Wehrli," *RCCM* 6 (1964) 164–70.
8–11. Cozza Luzi, G. "Della Geografia di Strabone. Frammenti scoperti in membrane palimpseste," *Gli Studi in Italia* 6, vol. 1 (1883) 808–23 (818–19).
8–18. Schubart, W. "Über den Dithyrambus," *APF* 14 (1941) 24–9.
19–23. Lawler, L. B. "Dancing Herds of Animals," *CJ* 47 (1952) 317–24.

70d

39–43. Pavese, C. See under "*O.* 6.83" (310–11).

72

Schneidewin, F. W. See under "*P.* 4.89" (298–300).
Schneidewin, F. W. See under "Fr. 75.1" (24).

75

*Cipolla, F. See under "Fr. 52k.1–22." Translation.
Hooker, G. T. W. "Pindar and the Athenian Festivals of Dionysus," *PCA* 54 (1957) 35–6.
de Timkowsky, R. "Commentatio de Dithyrambis eorumque usu apud Graecos et Romanos," *Acta societatis philologicae Lipsiensis*, ed. C. D. Beckius. Vol. 1 (Leipzig 1811) 204–31 (222–6).
1. Schneidewin, F. W. *Exercitationum criticarum in poetas Graecos minores capita quinque* (Progr. Brunswick 1836) 21.

8. SAUPPE, H. *Variae lectiones* (Göttingen 1890). Also in *Ausgewaehlte Schriften* (Berlin 1896) 807–28 (810).
13. VAN GRONINGEN, B. A. "Ad Pindari Dithyrambi fragmentum 75 S.," *Mnem* 4th S., 8 (1955) 192.
13–15. USENER, H. "Lectiones Graecae," *RhM* 23 (1868) 147–69 (148–9).
14. KOCH, H. A. "Zu Pindar, Simonides, Aeschylus," *Philologus* 6 (1851) 734–6.

76

CLAPP, E. B. Λιπαραὶ 'Αθᾶναι, *CP* 5 (1910) 100–1. Abstract in *TAPA* 39 (1908) liii.
COOK, A. B. "Iostephanos," *JHS* 20 (1900) 1–13.
GILDERSLEEVE, B. L. "Brief Mention," *AJP* 32 (1911) 366–7.
PLATNAUER, M. See under "Style and Imagery" (160).

76–77

DONNAY, G. "Pindare et Cimon, Thème et contenu politique du premier dithyrambe en l'honneur d'Athènes," *RBPh* 42 (1964) 205–6.

77

(AUTHOR NOT GIVEN) See under "Fr. 213" (423).

78

HAUPT, M. "Ueber ein Bruchstück eines pindarischen Dithyrambus," *Berichte der k. sächs. Gesellschaft der Wissenschaften* (1851) 313–16. Also in *Opuscula* 1 (Leipzig 1875) 310–14.

81

THEILER, W. See under "Fr. 169 General" (74–5).

PROSODIA

89a

VON WILAMOWITZ-MOELLENDORFF, U. "Lesefrüchte CLV," *Hermes* 54 (1919) 54–7.
ZIEGLER, K. "Zum Zeushymnus des Kallimachos," *RhM* 68 (1913) 336–54 (352–3).

91

GRIFFITHS, J. G. "The Flight of the Gods before Typhon: an unrecognized Myth," *Hermes* 88 (1960) 374–6.
ROSE, H. J. "Mythological Scraps," *CQ* 24 (1930) 107–8.

Parthenia

Rosenmeyer, T. G. "Alcman's Partheneion 1 Reconsidered," *GRBS* 7 (1966) 321–59 (328–31).

94a

Olivieri, A. See under "*P*. 6 General" (37–42).

94b

Blass, F. See under "Frr. 140a–b" (480–2).
Bowra, C. M. See under "Paeanes" (52–5).
Puech, A. "Le deuxième Parthénée de Pindare," *REG* 36 (1923) LIV–V.
Sbordone, F. "Partenii pindarici e dafneforie tebane," *Athenaeum* 2nd S., 18 (1940) 26–50.
13–15. Else, G. F. "'Imitation' in the Fifth Century," *CP* 53 (1958) 73–90 (77).

97

Kambylis, A. See under "Style and Imagery" (86–7 n. 55).

99

Uerschels, W. *Der Dionysoshymnos des Ailios Aristeides* (Diss. Bonn 1962) 33–6.

100

Timpanaro, S., Jr. "Note Serviane con contributi ad altri autori e a questioni di lessicografia latina," *StudUrb* 31 (1957) 155–98 (184–7).

104b

von Wilamowitz-Moellendorff, U. "Lesefrüchte XXXII," *Hermes* 34 (1899) 223–4. Also in *Kleine Schriften IV* (Berlin 1962) 64–6.
3. Naber, S. A. See under "*O*. 1.7" (40).

Hyporchemata

*Walther, C. H. *Commentationis de Graecorum hyporchematis pars prior* (Progr. Bochum 1874).

105

Lübbert, E. "Zu Pindar's Hyporchema an Hieron," *RhM* 41 (1886) 468–9.

106

1–2. USSHER, R. G. See under "*N.* 4.36" (68).

107(a)

ELSE, G. F. See under "Fr. 94b.13–15."

107ab

GALLAVOTTI, C. "Pindaro Hyporch. fr. 107ab," *RFIC* NS 40 (1962) 38–42.

108(b)

3. VAN HERWERDEN, H. See under "*P.* 5.121."

109

BOECKH, A. *De fragmento Pindarico a Polybio servato* (Berlin 1831). Also in *Gesammelte Kleine Schriften* 4 (Leipzig 1874) 346–9.
3. JACOBS, F. See under "Fr. 122.3–6" (42–3).
4. DAVISON, J. A. "Pindar Fr. 99b Bowra (109 Snell)," *CR* NS 16 (1966) 16.

110

1. GALIANO, F. M. "Pindaro y Galdós: influencia o coincidencia?" *EClás* 6 (1962) 550.

111

ZUNTZ, G. "A Pindar Fragment," *Hermes* 85 (1957) 401–13.

112

HEADLAM, W. "Metaphor, with a Note on Transference of Epithets," *CR* 16 (1902) 434–42 (434).

ENCOMIA

*FRAUSTADT, G. *Encomiorum in litteris Graecis historia* (Diss. Leipzig 1909).
VAN GRONINGEN, B. A. *Pindare au Banquet. Les fragments des Scolies édités avec un commentaire critique et explicatif* (Leiden 1960).
  [E. T. Vermeule, *CP* 57 (1962) 184–7; P. G. Mason, *RBPh* 40 (1962) 236–7; J. Carrière, *REA* 64 (1962) 164–5; J. Bousquet, *RPh* 3rd S., 36 (1962) 105–6; Q. Cataudella, *SicGymn* 15 (1962) 267–8; D. E. Gerber, *AJP* 82 (1961) 213–5; J. Irigoin, *Gnomon* 33 (1961)

263-6; D. S. Robertson, *CR* NS 11 (1961) 111-5: W. J. W. Koster, *Mnem* 4th S., 14 (1961) 336-9; J. T. M. F. Pieters, *Hermeneus* 32 (1960) 68-9; E. Thummer, *AAHG* 13 (1960) 148-9; F. Lasserre, *AC* 29 (1960) 183.]

IMMISCH, O. "Zur Geschichte der griechischen Lyrik, 2. ΣΚΟΛΙΑ," *RhM* 44 (1889) 558-67.

119

3. VAN HERWERDEN, H. See under "*O.* 2.71" (57).

122

BERGK, T. "De scolio Pindari in Xenophontem Corinthium dissertatio et coniecturae in poetas Graecos," *Acta Societatis Graecae*, Vol. 1 (Leipzig 1836) 187-208 (187-97).

VAN GRONINGEN, B. A. "Théopompe ou Chamaeléon? À propos de Simonide 137B, 104D," *Mnem* 4th S., 9 (1956) 11-22.

VON WILAMOWITZ-MOELLENDORFF, U. *Commentariolum grammaticum IV* (Göttingen 1889) 3-6. Also in *Kleine Schriften IV* (Berlin 1962) 660-4.

2-4. SCHNEIDEWIN, F. W. See under "Fr. 75.1" (21-2).

3-6. JACOBS, F. "Emendationes in quaedam Pindari et in Epigramma Meleagri," *BLK* 2 (1787) 40-6 (40-2).

16. CAMPBELL, A. Y. "Pindar Fr. 122 Bergk," *PCPS* 160-162 (1935) 5.

123

BERGK, T. See under "Fr. 122 General" (197-200).

COSTANZA, S. *Risonanze dell' ode di Saffo Fainetai moi kenos da Pindaro a Catullo e Orazio* (Messina 1950) 14-16.

[P. Chantraine, *RPh* 3rd S., 26 (1952) 238; M. F. Galiano, *Emerita* 20 (1952) 214-5; L. Herrmann, *Latomus* 11 (1952) 244; R. Cantarella, *Aevum* 25 (1951) 563.]

VON DER MÜHLL, P. See under "General and Miscellaneous."

VON WILAMOWITZ-MOELLENDORFF, U. See under "*I.* 8 General" (829-32).

9. VAN HERWERDEN, H. See under "*O.* 2.71" (57).
10. JACOBS, F. See under "Fr. 122.3-6" (43-4).
14. VAN HERWERDEN, H. See under "*O.* 2.71" (57).

124a-b

BLASS, F. "Zu Pindar," *RhM* 19 (1864) 306-8.

KÖRTE, A. "Bacchylidea," *Hermes* 53 (1918) 113-47 (128-30).

124c–d

NEUBECKER, A. J. "Zu Pindar Fr. 127d Snell," *Philologus* 98 (1954) 155–8.

125

3. VAN HERWERDEN, H. See under "*P.* 5.121."

126

1. MCKINLAY, A. P. See under "*P.* 12.13."

128

VON WILAMOWITZ-MOELLENDORFF, U. See under "*O.* 9.48–9."
VON WILAMOWITZ-MOELLENDORFF, U. See under "*P.* 4.105" (170).

THRENI

D'AGOSTINO, V. "Cenni di letteratura trenetica," *RSC* 1 (1953) 116–24.
REINER, E. *Die rituelle Totenklage der Griechen* (Stuttgart & Berlin 1938) 83–99.

128c

VON WILAMOWITZ-MOELLENDORFF, U. See under "*P.* 4.105" (172). Also in *Kleine Schriften IV* (Berlin 1962) 9–10.
SCHNEIDEWIN, F. W. "Ueber ein neuentdecktes Bruchstück eines pindarischen Threnos," *RhM* 2 (1834) 110–23. Included is an addendum by F. G. Welcker (121–3), reprinted in his *Kleine Schriften* 5 (Bonn 1861) 252–4.
7. MUTH, R. See under "*P.* 3.16–19" (9).

128f

KAKRIDIS, J. T. "Caeneus," *CR* 61 (1947) 77–80.

129

DIETERICH, A. See under "*O.* 2 General" (119–22).
IMPELLIZZERI, S. See under "*O.* 2 General."
PASCAL, C. "Un passo di Plutarco," *RFIC* 37 (1909) 382–4.
DA ROCHA PEREIRA, M. H. See under "*O.* 2 General" (149–56, 196–7).
TURYN, A. "The Sapphic Ostracon," *TAPA* 73 (1942) 308–18 (313–14).
1–2. KERÉNYI, K. "Zu Verg. Aen. VI, Pindar, Platon und Dante," *PhW* 45 (1925) 279–88.

4–5. PATON, W. R. "'The Golden Bough'," *CR* 25 (1911) 205.
9–10. FRÄNKEL, H. "Heraclitus on God and the Phenomenal World," *TAPA* 69 (1938) 230–44 (233 n. 8).

129–133

ROHDE, E. See under "Religion and Myth" (442–7).

130

DIETERICH, A. See under "*O*. 2 General" (119–22).
*MAJKOV, V. V. "On Pindar," Στέφανος. *Sbornik stateĭ v chest' F. F. Sokolova, k 30-lětneĭ godovchchine ego uchenoĭ děiatel' nosti* (St. Petersburg 1895) 181–2. In Russian.
PASCAL, C. See under "Fr. 129 General."
2. SEATON, R. C. "On βληχρός and ἀβληχρός," *AJP* 10 (1889) 468–9.

131a–b

OLIVIERI, A. See under "*P*. 6 General" (37–42).

131b

ADAM, J. "The Doctrine of the Celestial Origin of the Soul from Pindar to Plato," *Praelections delivered before the Senate of the University of Cambridge, 25, 26, 27 January 1906* (Cambridge 1906) 27–67 (29–33).
DODDS, E. R. See under "*O*. 9.33–5" (135 and 156 n. 1).
JAEGER, W. See under "*O*. 2 General."
KAMBYLIS, A. See under "Style and Imagery" (105–6 n. 108).
NILSSON, M. P. See under "*O*. 2.56–60."
1. VAN HERWERDEN, H. See under "*O*. 2.71" (57).

132

HEADLAM, W. See under "*I*. 3/4.53–7" (294).
4. KAYSER, C. L. *Lectiones Pindaricae* (Heidelberg 1840) 5–6.

133

BLUCK, R. S. "Plato, Pindar, and Metempsychosis," *AJP* 79 (1958) 405–14.
BLUCK, R. S. "The Phaedrus and Reincarnation," *AJP* 79 (1958) 156–64.
VON FRITZ, K. See under "*O*. 2.68–70."
LÜBBERT, E. See under "*O*. 2.57–60."
MCGIBBON, D. See under "*O*. 2 General."
NILSSON, M. P. See under "*O*. 2.56–60."

Rose, H. J. "The Ancient Grief. A Study of Pindar, Fragment 133 (Bergk), 127 (Bowra)," *Greek Poetry and Life. Essays presented to Gilbert Murray on his seventieth birthday, January 2, 1936* (Oxford 1936) 79–96.
Rose, H. J. "Note. The Grief of Persephone," *HTR* 36 (1943) 247–50.
Stettner, W. See under "*O*. 2.69–70."
1. Tannery, P. "Orphica fr. 208 Abel," *RPh* NS 23 (1899) 126–9.
2. Marcovich, M. "Zu Pind. Frg. 133 Schr. (=137 Turyn)," *RhM* 107 (1964) 364–6.
Skutsch, O. "Notes on Metempsychosis," *CP* 54 (1959) 114–16.

137

Mylonas, G. E. See under "*I*. 7.3–5" (299).

Incertorum Librorum

140a–b

Blass, F. "Literarische Texte mit Ausschluss der christlichen," *APF* 3 (1906) 266–7.
Bowra, C. M. See under "Paeanes" (51).

140b

Garrod, H. W. See under "Metre" (121–3).
Olivieri, A. See under "*P*. 6 General" (43–6).
13. Willis, W. H. "The Etymology and Meaning of ΓΛΩΣΣΑΡΓΟΣ and ΣΤΟΜΑΡΓΟΣ," *AJP* 63 (1942) 87–90.
13–15. Clapp, E. B. See under "Fr. 172" (229).
15. Else, G. F. ΥΠΟΚΡΙΤΗΣ, *WS* 72 (1959) 75–107 (79–80).
Koller, H. "Hypokrisis und Hypokrites," *MH* 14 (1957) 100–7.
Page, D. L. ὑποκριτής, *CR* NS 6 (1956) 191–2.
Zucchelli, B. ΥΠΟΚΡΙΤΗΣ. *Origine e storia del termine* (Brescia 1962) 37 and 57–8.
16. Garrod, H. W. See under "Metre" (76).

152

Ludwich, A. "Zu Herakleitos Homerischen Allegorieen. Mit einem Anhang zu griechischen Dichtern," *RhM* 37 (1882) 434–47 (446). Also in *Aristarchs Homerische Textkritik* 2 (Leipzig 1885) 642–57 (655).

156

von Wilamowitz-Moellendorff, U. "Lesefrüchte v," *Hermes* 33 (1898) 515–6. Also in *Kleine Schriften IV* (Berlin 1962) 26–7.

162

Schneidewin, F. W. See under "Fr. 75.1" (23).

166

Killy, W. "Hölderlins Interpretation des Pindarfragments 166 (Schr.)," A&A 4 (1954) 216-33.

168

Desrousseaux, A. M. "Sur deux fragments lyriques," REG 65 (1952) 40-5 (42-5).

168(b)

Headlam, W. See under "O. 14.20-21."

169

Alderisio, F. "Il Nómos di Pindaro nel Gorghias e nei Nómoi di Platone," Rassegna di Scienze Filosofiche 13 (1960) 22-46 and 123-48.

Busse, A. "Zum Pindarzitat in Platons Gorgias," Hermes 66 (1931) 126-8.

Busse, A. "Nochmals das Pindarzitat in Platons Gorgias," Hermes 66 (1931) 367-8.

Chroust, A. H. Socrates, Man and Myth. The Two Socratic Apologies of Xenophon (London 1957) 88-90.

Clapp, E. B. See under "Fr. 172" (226-9).

Gennaro, S. "Il Croiset et il frammento di Pindaro nel 'Gorgia'," SicGymn 4 (1951) 103-8.

Gigante, M. ΝΟΜΟΣ ΒΑΣΙΛΕΥΣ (Naples 1956).

*Gigante, M. "Nuovi resti dell'ode Pindarica νόμος πάντων βασιλεύς," Atti dell' XI congresso internazionale di papirologia, Milano 2-8 settembre 1965 (Milan 1966) 286-311.

Gildersleeve, B. L. "Brief Mention," AJP 40 (1919) 218-21.

Ostwald, M. "Pindar, Nomos, and Heracles," HSCP 69 (1965) 109-38.

Page, D. L. "Pindar: P. Oxy. 2450, fr. 1," PCPS NS 8 (1962) 49-51.

Schroeder, O. ΝΟΜΟΣ Ο ΠΑΝΤΩΝ ΒΑΣΙΛΕΥΣ, Philologus 74 (1917) 195-204.

Stier, H. E. ΝΟΜΟΣ ΒΑΣΙΛΕΥΣ, Philologus 83 (1928) 225-58.

Theiler, W. Νόμος ὁ πάντων βασιλεύς, MH 22 (1965) 69-80.

Treu, M. "ΝΟΜΟΣ ΒΑΣΙΛΕΥΣ: alte und neue Probleme," RhM 106 (1963) 193-214.

1-4. Croiset, A. "Le fragment de Pindare cité dans le Gorgias de Platon," REG 34 (1921) 125-8.

1–8. MENZEL, A. "Dunkle Pindarverse," *Hellenika. Gesammelte kleine Schriften* (Baden 1938) 108–24.
   3. VAN DER VALK, M. See under "*O*. 14.14–15" (286–8).
   8. METTE, H. J. "Noch einmal ἀνατεί," *Glotta* 40 (1962) 42–3.
30–2. PAVESE, C. See under "*O*. 6.83" (311–12).

172

CLAPP, E. B. "On Certain Fragments of Pindar," *CQ* 8 (1914) 225–9 (225–6). See also his review of O. Schroeder, *Pindari Carmina cum fragmentis selectis*, in *CP* 4 (1909) 465.
HERMANN, G. "Coniectanea critica," *Philologus* 2 (1847) 131–5 (135). Also in *Opuscula* 8 (Leipzig 1877) 309–14 (314).

177(a)

VAN HERWERDEN, H. See under "*O*. 2.71" (57–8).

177(d)

CLAPP, E. B. See under "Fr. 172" (226).

189

VON WILAMOWITZ-MOELLENDORFF, U. See under "*P*. 3.67" (141–2).

201

VAN HERWERDEN, H. See under "*O*. 2.71" (58).
UERSCHELS, W. See under "Fr. 99" (35–6).

203

HEADLAM, W. See under "*O*. 14.20–21."
VON WILAMOWITZ-MOELLENDORFF, U. See under "*P*. 3.67" (142).

207

EDMONDS, J. M. "Marginalia Selecta," *CQ* NS 7 (1957) 59–67 (60).
VON WILAMOWITZ-MOELLENDORFF, U. "Lesefrüchte CLXIX," *Hermes* 54 (1919) 71–2.

213

(AUTHOR NOT GIVEN) "Observationes criticae et exegeticae e libellis minoribus academicis scholasticisve excerptae," *Acta societatis philologicae Lipsiensis*, ed. C. D. Beckius. Vol. 2 (Leipzig 1812) 375–445 (413–14).

BOECKH, A. *De Platonis loco de Re publ. II. p. 365 A.B. et de Pindari fragmento ibi servato* (Berlin 1812). Also in *Gesammelte Kleine Schriften* 4 (Leipzig 1874) 61–4.
2. MOORHOUSE, A. C. "IE. *PENT- and its Derivatives," *CQ* 35 (1941) 90–6 (95).

214

CATAUDELLA, Q. Ἐλπὶς γηροτρόφος ed ἐλπὶς κουροτρόφος, *Acta Philologica III piae memoriae N. I. Herescu* (Rome 1964) 85–9.
ORTH, E. "Corollarium," *PhW* 56 (1936) 221–4 (222).

215(a)

2–3. SCHNEIDEWIN, F. W. See under "*P.* 4.89" (297–8).
4. KAMBYLIS, A. "Bemerkungen zu Pind. Fr. 215(a), 4 (Snell)," *Hermes* 94 (1966) 238–43.

221

ARNOLDT, R. "Zu griechischen Schriftstellern," *Festschrift der 48. Versammlung deutscher Philologen und Schulmänner in Hamburg dargebracht von dem Lehrerkollegium des Königlichen Christianeums zu Altona* (Altona 1905) 1–30 (3).
LIEBERG, G. "Pensiero e forma di un frammento pindarico," *RFIC* 87 (1959) 365–79.
MUTSCHMANN, H. "Pindar fragm. 221 Schroed.," *BPW* 33 (1913) 925–6.
VAN OTTERLO, W. A. A. See under "Style and Imagery" (155–7).
5. STAHL, J. M. "Zu Pindar," *RhM* 68 (1913) 631–2.

222

LENDRUM, W. T. "'Moth and Rust'—A Classical Image," *CR* 20 (1906) 307.

223+277+278

VON WILAMOWITZ-MOELLENDORFF, U. "Lesefrüchte XCVIII," *Hermes* 40 (1905) 129–30. Also in *Kleine Schriften IV* (Berlin 1962) 183–4.

225

1. VAN HERWERDEN, H. See under "*O.* 2.71" (58).

227

BOECKH, A. *Admonitio ad commilitones adhibito fragmento Pindarico [n. 250]* (Berlin 1820). Also in *Gesammelte Kleine Schriften* 4 (Leipzig 1874) 159–60.
CLAPP, E. B. See under "Fr. 172" (225–6).

234

van Otterlo, W. A. A. See under "Style and Imagery" (154).

243

Brink, K. O. "A Forgotten Figure of Style in Tacitus," *CR* 58 (1944) 43–5.

245

Ludwich, A. See under "Fr. 152."

246(b)

Headlam, W. See under "*O.* 14.20–21."

249a

Galiart, L. H. *Beiträge zur Mythologie bei Bakchylides* (Diss. Freiburg 1910) 64–6.

250a

Robertson, D. S. "An Unnoticed Pindaric Fragment," *CR* NS 9 (1959) 11–12.

260

Körte, A. See under "Fr. 52n."

279

Foerster, R. "Zu Pindar," *PhW* 25 (1905) 687.

286

Lübbert, E. See under "*N.* 9 General" (9–10).

291

Schneidewin, F. W. See under "*P.* 9.31" (529).

292

Headlam, W. See under "*O.* 14.20–21."

310

Van der Valk, M. See under "*P.* 6.13" (177).

313

Körte, A. See under "Fr. 70a" (138–9).

326

Bergk, T. "Die Geburt der Athene," *Kleine philologische Schriften* 2 (Halle 1886) 635–722 (685 n. 88).

327

Van der Valk, M. See under "*P.* 6.13" (80).

329

Keil, B. "Pindarfragment," *Hermes* 48 (1913) 319–20.

Dubia vel Spuria

333

Blass, F. "Zu den griechischen Lyrikern," *RhM* 32 (1877) 450–8.

334

Körte, A. See under "Fr. 70a" (138).

335

Körte, A. See under "Fr. 70a" (138).

337

Körte, A. See under "Fr. 52n."

339+339a

Körte, A. See under "Fr. 52n."
Zuntz, G. "Pindar and Simonides. Fragments of an Ancient Commentary," *CR* 49 (1935) 4–7.

342

Gallavotti, C. "Frammenti di un ditirambo di Pindaro in una poesia bizantina," *RFIC* 59 (1931) 377–81.

341 Bowra

Snell, B. See under "Fr. 52n" (177–83).

342 Bowra

SNELL, B. See under "Fr. 52n" (183–4).

6 Puech (vol. 4, p. 237)

EVELYN-WHITE, H. G. "Miscellanea Hesiodea," *CQ* 14 (1920) 126–8.
McKAY, K. J. "Hesiod's Rejuvenation," *CQ* NS 9 (1959) 1–5.

12. MANUSCRIPTS

Studies of a general nature on Pindaric papyri are included here.

ABEL, E. "Zur Handschriftenkunde des Pindar," *WS* 4 (1882) 224–62.
BOECKH, A. See under "*O*. 6.53–4" (15–21).
CERRATO, L. "Il codice Pindarico della collezione Ashburnham," *RFIC* 18 (1890) 213–31.
CHRIST, M. "Die älteste Textesüberlieferung des Pindar," *Philologus* 25 (1867) 607–36.
DRACHMANN, A. B. "Zur Ueberlieferung des Pindartextes," *Mélanges Bidez* = *AIPhO* 2 (Brussels 1934) 331–42.
EDMONDS, J. M. "A Note on the Fifth Century Papyrus-Codex of Pindar (Oxyrhynchus Papyri, vol. xiii, no. 1614)," *PCPS* 121–123 (1922) 1–2.
FREESE, L. *De Manuscriptis Neapolitanis Pindari* (Progr. Stargardiae 1835).
    [A. Boeckh, *Jahrbücher für wissenschaftliche Kritik* No. 87 (1835) 702–4. Also in *Gesammelte Kleine Schriften* 7 (Leipzig 1872) 514–17.]
GALIANO, M. F. "Los papiros pindáricos," *Emerita* 16 (1948) 165–200. Includes a bibliography on each papyrus.
HERZOG, R. *Die Umschrift der älteren griechischen Literatur in das ionische Alphabet* (Prog. Leipzig 1912).
HÜMMERICH, F. "Die Pindar-Handschriften B und D in Nem. und Isthm.," *Commentationes philologicae. Conventui Philologorum Monachii Congregatorum obtulerunt Sodales Seminarii Philologici Monacensis* (Munich 1891) 115–28.
IRIGOIN, J. *Histoire du texte de Pindare* (Paris 1952).
    [Q. Cataudella, *Paideia* 11 (1956) 64–5; A. Wenger, *REByz* 12 (1954) 261–3; A. G. McKay, *AJP* 76 (1955) 106–8; M. Wittek, *Scriptorium* 9 (1955) 331–4; *BCLF* 8 (1953) 105–6; P. Chantraine, *RPh* 3rd S., 28 (1954) 101–2; U. Hölscher, *ByzZ* 47 (1954) 123–7; W. J. W. Koster, *MPh* 59 (1954) 6–7; M. H. A. L. H. van der Valk, *BO* 11 (1954) 178–80; J. A. Davison, *JHS* 74 (1954) 194; É. des Places, *AC* 22 (1953) 141–2; W. Theiler, *MH* 10 (1953) 282; A. Colonna, *RFIC* 81 (1953) 151–5; M. Delcourt, *RBPh* 31 (1953) 1053–5; R. Ruelle, *LEC* 21 (1953) 257–8; J. de Romilly, *IL* 5 (1953) 154; D. S. Robertson, *CR* NS 4 (1954) 223–5; E. Wolf, *AAHG* 9 (1956) 43.]
(AUTHOR NOT GIVEN) Κατάλογος τῶν κωδίκων τῶν ἐν ᾿Αθήναις βιβλιοθηκῶν πλὴν τῆς ἐθικῆς, *Νέος Ἑλληνομνήμων* 18 (1924) 112–19 (113).
DE LANNOY, L. "Aantekeningen bij het stemma der Pindarosoverlevering voornamelijk met betrekking tot de vierde en vijfde Puthische Ode," *AC* 32 (1963) 577–86.
MOMMSEN, T. "Handschriften des Pindarus," *RhM* 6 (1848) 435–8.
MOMMSEN, T. *Einige Bemerkungen über Kritik, Exegese und Versabtheilung bei Pindar* (Oldenburg 1863) 1–26.

MOMMSEN, T. *Parerga Pindarica, quibus inter cetera continentur fragmenta quaedam Cypriorum, Euripidis, Callimachi, Menaechi Sicyonii e codd. Mss. restituta* (Progr. Frankfurt 1877) 1–6.

NASTA, M. "Pindari Carmina. Însemnări pe marginea unor ediţii," *StudClas* 2 (1960) 377–86.

NAUCK, A. "Über eine dem Herrn A. v. Hilferding gehörende griechische Hdschrift," *Bulletin de l'académie impériale des sciences de St. Pétersbourg* 6 (1863) 296–317 (296–304). Also in *Mélanges Gréco-Romains II* (St. Pétersbourg 1866) 487–518 (487–93).

NĚMEC, J. "Víceslabičné mezery v rukopisném textu pindarových epiniků," *LF* 8 (1960) 34–40. Summary in German.

RESLER, J. "Pindari codicum manuscriptorum qui Florentiae, Romae, Mediolani, Venetiis, Parisiis, Vindobonae adservantur descriptio," *Philologus* 4 (1849) 510–32.

SCHROEDER, O. "Pindarica II. Von alten und neuen Pindarhandschriften," *Philologus* 54 (1895) 274–89.

SCHROEDER, O. "Pindarica III. Zur Genealogie der Handschriften," *Philologus* 56 (1897) 78–96.

SCHROEDER, O. "Pindar. Die Wolfenbütteler Pindarhandschrift," *JPhV* 23 (1897) 284–9.

SHANGIN, M. "A manuscript of the Academy containing texts of Pindar and Aeschylus," *Bulletin de l'Académie des Sciences de l'URSS* 6th S. (1927) 499–510. In Russian.

THOMPSON, E. M. "Catalogue of Classical Manuscripts," *CR* 2 (1888) 171–4 (172).

TURYN, A. *De codicibus Pindaricis* (Cracow 1932).

> [A. Puech, *RPh* 3rd S., 8 (1934) 103; G. Coppola, *BFC* 40 (1934) 210–11; C. Gallavotti, *RFIC* 62 (1934) 552–6; M. Hombert, *RBPh* 13 (1934) 772–3; S. Stéphanou, *EO* (1934) 113; P. Maas, *Gnomon* 9 (1933) 166–8; A. B. Drachmann, *DLZ* 54 (1933) 1454–8; I. Düring, *PhW* 53 (1933) 1226–9; A. Puech, *REG* 46 (1933) 361; D. S. Robertson, *CR* 47 (1933) 239–40; *BAGB(SC)* 5 (1933) 77.]

TURYN, A. "Symbolae ad recensionem Pindaricam pertinentes," *Charisteria Gustav Przychocki a discipulis oblata* (Warsaw 1934) 210–19.

> [A. Puech, *RPh* 3rd S., 10 (1936) 362.]

TURYN, A. "Zur Pindar-Überlieferung," *Philologus* 90 (1935) 115–19.

TURYN, A. "Miscellanea 2. The Manuscript Athos Lavra M 125," *Studi in onore di Luigi Castiglioni*, Vol. 2 (Florence 1960) 1019–21.

VOLGER, E. "Eine Handschrift des Pindar zu Barcelona," *Philologus* 18 (1862) 714–5.

YOUNG, D. "Some Types of Scribal Error in Manuscripts of Pindar," *GRBS* 6 (1965) 247–73.

YOUNG, D. "Notes on the Text of Pindar. I. On the Alleged Three Mediaeval Metagrammatisms," *GRBS* 7 (1966) 5–8.

13. SCHOLIA

ABEL, E. *Scholia in Pindari Epinicia ad librorum manuscriptorum fidem.* 2 vols. (Budapest & Berlin 1884–91).
  [J. Sitzler, *NPR* (1894) 385–6.]
BENNETT, H. C. See under "Pythian Odes General."
BECK, C. D. See under "Texts."
*BERGK, T. "In Pindari scholia," *Commentationum criticarum specimen* II (Progr. Marburg 1844).
BERGK, T. "Lesefrüchte VI. Zu den pindarischen Scholien," *JPh* 117 (1878) 37–46.
BOECKH, A. See under "Text, Translation, and Commentary."
CALLIERGES, Z. See under "Texts."
DEAS, H. T. "The Scholia Vetera to Pindar," *HSCP* 42 (1931) 1–78.
DRACHMANN, A. B. *Scholia vetera in Pindari carmina.* 3 vols. (Leipzig 1903, 1910, 1927, repr. Amsterdam 1964).
  [O. Schroeder, *PhW* 24 (1904) 65–9; G. Fraccaroli, *RFIC* 33 (1905) 140–2; O. Schroeder, *PhW* 31 (1911) 1428–9; E. B. Clapp, *CP* 6 (1911) 225–7; A. Taccone, *RFIC* 39 (1911) 603–4; P. Shorey, *CP* 23 (1928) 314; M. C. van der Kolf, *MPh* 36 (1929) 260–1; A. Puech, *RPh* 3rd S., 3 (1929) 216–7; H. T. Deas, *CR* 43 (1929) 151; *BAGB* (*SC*) 1 (1929) 48–9; C. Wendel, *Gnomon* 6 (1930) 157–61.]
FEINE, P. *De Aristarcho Pindari interprete* (Diss. Leipzig 1883). Also in *Commentationes philologae Ienenses* 2 (Leipzig 1883) 253–327.
*GARPOLLAS, K. Σχόλια εἰς Πίνδαρον ἐκ τῆς ἐκδόσεως Aug. Boeckh, 2 vols. (Athens 1841).
HEADLAM, W. See under "*O.* 6.74" (306). On vol. 1, p. 3, line 13 Dr.
HEYNE, C. G. See under "Text, Translation, and Commentary."
HOPFNER, T. *Thomas Magister, Demetrius Triklinios, Manuel Moschopulos. Eine Studie über ihren Sprachgebrauch in den Scholien zu Aischylos, Sophokles, Euripides, Aristophanes, Hesiod, Pindar und Theokrit* (=*SAWW* 172, Abh. 3, 1912).
  [P. Ms., *ByzZ* 22 (1913) 541.]
HORN, E. *De Aristarchi studiis pindaricis* (Diss. Gryphiswaldiae 1883).
IRIGOIN, J. *Les scholies métriques de Pindare* (Paris 1958).
  [J. Martin, *RPh* 3rd S., 35 (1961) 295–7; J. Defradas, *REG* 74 (1961) 520–1; J. Darrouzès, *REByz* 17 (1959) 274–5; S. L. Radt, *Gnomon* 32 (1960) 221–9; D. S. Robertson, *CR* NS 10 (1960) 12–14; L. P. E. Parker, *JHS* 80 (1960) 204–5; F. Lasserre, *AC* 28 (1959) 346–8; W. J. W. Koster, *Mnem* 4th S., 13 (1960) 249–54; C. Froidefond, *REA* 62 (1960) 148–9; A. Colonna, *RFIC* 87 (1959) 278–80; R. Loriaux, *LEC* 27 (1959) 218; D. Holwerda, *MPh* 64 (1959) 214–7.]
KÖRTE, A. "Der Pindarcommentator Chrysippos," *RhM* 55 (1900) 131–8.

KOSTER, W. J. W. "De codice fragmentum scholiorum metricorum ad Pindarum continente," *Mnem* 3rd S., 1 (1934) 181–8.
LEHRS, K. *Die Pindarscholien. Eine kritische Untersuchung zur philologischen Quellenkunde. Nebst einem Anhange über den falschen Hesychius Milesius und den falschen Philemon* (Leipzig 1873).
    [E. von Leutsch, *PA* 7 (1875) 196–201.]
LEHRS, K. "Zurechtweisung für Theodor Bergk in Sachen der Pindarscholien," *Wissenschaftliche Monatsblätter* 6 (1878) 27–32. Also in *Kleine Schriften* (Königsberg 1902) 191–8.
VON LEUTSCH, E. "Pindarische Studien I. Die Quellen für die Biographie des Pindaros," *Philologus* 11 (1856) 1–35.
VON LEUTSCH, E. "Zur Vita Pindari," *Philologus* 14 (1859) 498.
LUDWICH, A. "Die metrische Lebensskizze Pindars," *RhM* 34 (1879) 357–69.
MOMMSEN, T. *Scholia Germani in Pindari Olympia e codice Caesareo Vindobonensi* (Kiel 1861).
MOMMSEN, T. *Scholia recentiora Thomano-Tricliniana in Pindari Nemea et Isthmia e codicibus antiquis* (Frankfurt 1865).
*MOMMSEN, T. *Exercitationes Sophocleae, de scholiis Pindaricis epimetrum* (Progr. Frankfurt 1865).
MOMMSEN, T. *Scholia Thomano-Tricliniana in Pindari Pythia V-XII, ex cod. Florentino edita* (Progr. Frankfurt 1867).
PATAKIS, I. G. "Coniectanea critica," *Philologus* 8 (1853) 521–8 (527–8). On vol. 3, sec. 29, pp. 300–1 Dr.
*RESLER, J. See under "*I*. 8 Scholia."
*SAKKELION, I. Πινδάρου Σχόλια Πατμιακά (Athens 1875).
SCHERER, C. "De vita Pindari metrica," *De Aelio Dionysio musico qui vocatur* (Diss. Bonn 1886) 45–9.
SCHMIDT, M. "Zu den Scholien des Pindar," *Philologus* 17 (1861) 360–1.
SCHMIDT, M. "Kritische Bemerkungen," *Philologus* 18 (1862) 226–34 (227). On vol. 1, p. 3, line 7 Dr.
SCHNEIDER, C. E. C. *Vetera in Pindarum scholia denuo ex codice Rehdigerano edita* (Progr. Vratislaviae 1843). A text of the scholia for *O*. 1 and 2.
SCHNEIDER, C. E. C. *Apparatus Pindarici supplementum ex codicibus Vratislaviensibus* (Vratislaviae 1844).

Table of Contents

    I. Thomae Mag. et Demetrii Triclinii Scholia in Pythia quattuor prima ex codice Vrat. E.
   II. Varia Olympiorum scriptura ex codicibus Vrat. A et B.
  III. Vita Pindari et Vetera in Olymp. I et II scholia ex codice Vrat. A.

SCHNEIDEWIN, F. W. *Eustathii prooemium commentariorum Pindaricorum* (Göttingen 1837).
SCHWARTZ, J. *Pseudo-Hesiodeia. Recherches sur la composition, la diffusion et la disparition ancienne d'oeuvres attribuées à Hésiode* (Leiden 1960) 138–47.

SEMITELOS, D. C. Πινδάρου σχόλια Πατμιακά, νῦν πρῶτον ἀναλώμασι τοῖς τοῦ 'Αθηναίου ἐπίκλην περιοδικοῦ συγγράμματος ἐκδιδόμενα (Athens 1875).
SNELL, B. "Zur Überlieferungsgeschichte der Pindar-Scholien," *SIFC* NS 27–28 (1956) 541–3.
*STEPHANUS, P. See under "Translations."
VON SYBEL, L. *De scholiis veteribus in Pindari carmina* (Diss. Marburg 1872).
VILLOISON, J. See under "*I*. 2.28" (235–40).
WEST, R. & WELSTED, R. See under "Translations."

14. SYNTAX

BENVENISTE, E. "La phrase nominale," *BSL* 46 (1950) 19–36 (29–31).
BOSSLER, C. *De praepositionum usu apud Pindarum* (Diss. Darmstadt 1862).
BRANDT, P. *De particularum subiunctivarum apud Pindarum usu* (Diss. Leipzig 1898).
BREYER, B. "De modorum subiectivorum usu pindarico," *Analecta Pindarica* (Diss. Vratislaviae 1880) 1–4.
BREYER, B. "De coniunctivo," *Analecta Pindarica* (Diss. Vratislaviae 1880) 5–27.
BREYER, B. "De optativo," *Analecta Pindarica* (Diss. Vratislaviae 1880) 27–43.
BURY, J. B. "The Preposition ἀνά," *The Isthmian Odes of Pindar* (London 1892) 178–85.
CLAPP, E. B. "Pindar's Accusative Constructions," *TAPA* 32 (1901) 16–42. See also *PhW* (1905) 1393.
DONOVAN, J. "The Remote Deliberative," *CR* 6 (1892) 435–7.
ERDMANN, O. *De Pindari usu syntactico* (Diss. Halle 1867).
 [K. Lehrs, *Kleine Schriften* (Königsberg 1902) 192–200.]
FRASER, J. "The ΣΧΗΜΑ ΑΛΚΜΑΝΙΚΟΝ," *CQ* 4 (1910) 25–7.
FRIESE, E. *De casuum singulari apud Pindarum usu* (Diss. Berlin 1866).
FRIESE, E. *Pindarica* (Progr. Berlin 1872) 2–38. On prepositions.
 [F. Mezger, *PA* 5 (1873) 593–602.]
GILDERSLEEVE, B. L. "Studies in Pindaric Syntax. I.–The Conditional Sentence in Pindar," *AJP* 3 (1882) 434–45.
GILDERSLEEVE, B. L. "Studies in Pindaric Syntax. II.–On AN and KEN in Pindar," *AJP* 3 (1882) 446–55.
GILDERSLEEVE, B. L. "Studies in Pindaric Syntax. III.–Aorist and Imperfect," *AJP* 4 (1883) 158–65.
GILDERSLEEVE, B. L. "Contributions to the History of the Articular Infinitive," *TAPA* 9 (1878) 5–19 (11).
GILDERSLEEVE, B. L. "On the Final Sentence in Greek," *AJP* 4 (1883) 416–44 (431–32).
GILDERSLEEVE, B. L. A note appended to E. H. Spieker, "On the so-called Genitive Absolute and its Use especially in the Attic Orators," *AJP* 6 (1885) 310–43 (318).
*GROSSE, E. *Quaestionum grammaticarum de particulis Graecis specimen I: De particulis copulativis τέ et καί apud Pindarum* (Aschersleben 1858).
GUIRAUD, C. *La phrase nominale en Grec d'Homère à Euripide* (Paris 1962).
HALLSTRÖM, R. S. A. "De usu infinitivi apud Pindarum," *Quaestiones Pindaricae* (Uppsala 1880) 1–16.
HAYDON, R. S. ΣΧΗΜΑ ΠΙΝΔΑΡΙΚΟΝ, *AJP* 11 (1890) 182–92.
HOEKSTRA, A. "A Note on the Dative of Purpose (Dativus finalis) in Greek," *Mnem* 4th S., 15 (1962) 15–23.
KEITH, A. B. "Some Uses of the Future in Greek," *CQ* 6 (1912) 121–6.
KNUENZ, I. *De enuntiatis Graecorum finalibus* (Innsbruck 1913).

KOCEVALOV, A. "Einige Beiträge zur griechischen Syntax," *RhM* 79 (1930) 44–54 (46–7). On the use of adjectives for adverbs.

MOMMSEN, T. *Beiträge zu der Lehre von den griechischen Präpositionen* (Berlin 1895) 569–78 and 780–91.

NABER, S. A. See under "*O.* 1.7" (32–5). On pronominal adjectives.

DES PLACES, É. *Le pronom chez Pindare* (Paris 1947).

[J. Humbert, *REG* 64 (1951) 362–3; D. S. Robertson, *CR* 62 (1948) 117–8; R. Lattimore, *AJP* 70 (1949) 107–8; J. W. Poultney, *CP* 44 (1949) 211–12; H. Fournier, *REA* 51 (1949) 153–6; M. Leroy, *RBPh* 27 (1949) 776–8; F. Charlier, *LEC* 16 (1948) 186; L. Deroy, *AC* 16 (1947) 396–7; P. Chantraine, *RPh* 3rd S., 23 (1949) 171.]

DES PLACES, É. "Constructions grecques de mots à fonction double (ἀπὸ κοινοῦ)," *REG* 75 (1962) 1–12.

PLATT, A. "Notes on the Homeric Genitive. III," *CR* 2 (1888) 99–102.

*PRIEWASSER, P. P. *Die präpositionen bei Kallimachus und Herondas, verglichen mit denen bei Bacchylides und dem bereits für Pindar bekannten Resultate.* 2 Teile (Progr. Halle 1903–04).

SCOTT, J. A. "Additional Notes on the Vocative," *AJP* 26 (1905) 32–43 (32–3).

SIDGWICK, A. "Remote Deliberative," *CR* 7 (1893) 97–9.

STEIN, R. *De articuli apud Pindarum usu* (Diss. Vratislaviae 1868).

*SVENSSON, E. H. *De usu pronominum reflexivorum tertiae personae apud Homerum, Hesiodum, Pindarum, Herodotum, Thucydidem* (Lund 1888).

THIERSCH, F. "Additamenta ad Hermanni editionem secundam Vigeri, necnon ad Boeckhii notas criticas in Pindarum," *Acta philologorum Monacensium* 2 (Monachii 1815–16) 99–112. On the use of ἄν.

ULLMANN, R. "L'usage de l'article dans Pindare," *SO* 1 (1922) 59–69.

VON DER MÜHLL, P. See under "*O.* 1.111–2" (52–3). On the double dative.

WEBER, P. *Entwickelungsgeschichte der Absichtssätze* (Würzburg 1884–85) 72–4.

WEILBACH, M. *Die Formen der Aufforderung in der griechischen Lyrik* (Diss. Lengerich 1938).

WILPERT, O. *De schemate pindarico et alcmanico* (Diss. Vratislaviae 1878).

WILPERT, O. *Das Schema Pindaricum und ähnliche grammatische Konstruktionen* (Progr. Oppeln 1900).

WIRTH, G. "De motione adiectivorum quae in ιος, ειος, ιμος terminantur," *LSCP* 3 (1880) 1–56 (19–20).

*ZYCHA, J. *Zum Gebrauche von περὶ bei Homer, Hesiod, Pindar, Herodot und den Tragikern* (Progr. Vienna 1886).

15. DIALECT

Arena, R. "Gli aoristi 'Eolici' in -ξα (=ion.-att. -(σ)σα)," *Helikon* 6 (1966) 125–73 (129–32).

Christ, W. "Beiträge zum Dialekte Pindars," *SAWM* (1891) 25–86. Also in *Philologische Kleinigkeiten der 41. Versammlung deutscher Philologen und Schulmänner*, ed. W. Christ and G. Oehmichen (Munich 1891) 1–62.

Forssman, B. *Untersuchungen zur Sprache Pindars* (Wiesbaden 1966).

Führer, A. "Der böotische Dialekt Pindars," *Philologus* 44 (1885) 49–60.

*Grunbaum, N. C. "La langue de Pindare et des inscriptions de Thessalie," *Philologie Classique* (Leningrad 1959) 93–102. In Russian.

Heimer, A. "De digammo Pindarico," *Studia Pindarica* (Lund 1885) 1–89.
  [F. Hanssen, *PA* 16 (1886) 202–4.]

Hermann, G. *De dialecto Pindari observationes* (Leipzig 1809). Also in *Opuscula* I (Leipzig 1827) 245–68.

van Herwerden, H. See under "*O.* 2.43" (216).

Koster, E. B. *Studia tragico-homerica* (Daventriae 1891).

Lind, J. *De dialecto Pindarica. I. Prolegomena et de vocalismo Pindarico ex proximis sonis non apto* (Lund 1893).
  [J. Sitzler, *NPR* (1895) 1–2.]

Marinone, N. "Dialetto dorico della lirica corale," *Grammatica Greca. Fonetica e morfologia* (Milan 1959) 545–65.

Mommsen, T. "Ad Pindari dialectum," *JPh* 83 (1861) 40–7.

Mucke, E. *De dialectis Stesichori, Ibyci, Simonidis, Bacchylidis aliorumque poetarum choricorum cum pindarica comparatis* (Diss. Leipzig 1879).

Peter, W. A. *De dialecto Pindari* (Diss. Halle 1866).

Schnitzer, C. F. See under "*O.* 1.28–9" (6–12).

Schone, J. See under "*O.* 5.6."

Schultz, H. *De elocutionis Pindaricae colore epico* (Diss. Göttingen 1905).
  [O. Schroeder, *PhW* 27 (1907) 1217–19; J. Sitzler, *WKPh* 23 (1906) 1025–27.]

Strunk, K. "Der böotische Imperativ δίδοι," *Glotta* 39 (1961) 114–23.

Strunk, K. "Dorisches und Hyperdorisches," *Glotta* 42 (1964) 165–9.

16. SPECIFIC WORDS

	FORSSMAN, B. *Untersuchungen zur Sprache Pindars* (Wiesbaden 1966).
ἀγαθός	GERLACH, J. *ANHP AΓAΘOΣ* (Munich 1932) 23–4.
ἀγών, ἀγώνιος	DYER, L. See under "Games" (268–70).
ἀείρω, αἴρω, ἄρνυμαι	DEWITT, N. W. "The Verbs ἀείρω, αἴρω, and ἄρνυμαι," *CP* 3 (1908) 31–8.
αἰανής	DEGANI, E. Αἰανής, *Helikon* 2 (1962) 37–56.
αἰδώς	VON ERFFA, C. E. F. *AIΔΩΣ und verwandte Begriffe in ihrer Entwicklung von Homer bis Demokrit*. Philologus Supplementband 30, Heft 2 (Leipzig 1937) 74–85.
αἰθύσσω	STANFORD, W. B. See under "Style and Imagery" (132–6).
αἰών	DEGANI, E. *AIΩN da Omero ad Aristotele* (Padova 1961) 45–51. See also *RFIC* 91 (1963) 104–10.
ἀκμή	FRIESLAND, E. See under "O. 6 General" (41–3).
ἀνάγκη	SCHRECKENBERG, H. *Ananke. Untersuchungen zur Geschichte des Wortgebrauchs* (Munich 1964).
ἄνθος	STANFORD, W. B. See under "O. 6.82."
βληχρός	SCHNEIDEWIN, F. W. See under "Fr. 75.1" (22–3).
βρέχω	FRÄNKEL, H. "Griechische Wörter," *Glotta* 14 (1925) 1–13 (1–2).
γέρας	KATLUHN, C. *ΓΕΡΑΣ* (Diss. Regimonti 1914) 22–4.
δαιμόνιος	BOWRA, C. M. "Xenophanes and the Olympic Games," *AJP* 59 (1938) 257–79 (269 n. 68). Also in *Problems in Greek Poetry* (Oxford 1953) 27 n. 1.
	BRUNIUS-NILSSON, E. *ΔΑΙΜΟΝΙΕ. An Inquiry into a Mode of Apostrophe in Old Greek Literature* (Uppsala 1955) 139–40.
δαίμων, δαιμόνιος	HEADLAM, W. See under "O. 6.74" (303–6).
δεῖ	GOODELL, T. D. See under χρή.
δόξα	GREINDL, M. See under κλέος.
ἐλπίς	MYRES, J. L. 'Ἐλπίς, ἔλπω, ἔλπομαι, ἐλπίζειν, *CR* 63 (1949) 46.
ἔμπαν	RADT, S. L. "Die Bedeutung von ἔμπαν," *Pindars zweiter und sechster Paian* (Diss. Amsterdam 1958) 200–8.
ἔρως	ROSENMEYER, T. G. "Eros-Erotes," *Phoenix* 5 (1951) 11–22 (17–22).
εὐδείελος	MÜLDER, D. "Ithaka nach der Odyssee," *RhM* 80 (1931) 1–35 (32–3).
εὐεργέτης	HEWITT, J. W. "The Terminology of 'Gratitude' in Greek," *CP* 22 (1927) 142–61 (151–3).
εὐσεβής	BOLKESTEIN, J. C. See under ὅσιος.
εὔχομαι	RITOÓK, Z. *EYXOMAI*, *AAntHung* 3 (1955) 287–99.
εὖχος	GREINDL, M. See under κλέος.

ἐφήμερος, ἐφημέριος	FRÄNKEL, H. "Man's 'Ephemeros' Nature According to Pindar and Others," *TAPA* 77 (1946) 131–45.
ἦθος	THIMME, O. See under φύσις.
θαμά, θαμάκις	INGRAM, J. K. "On θαμά and θαμάκις in Pindar," *Hermathena* 2 (1876) 217–27.
θέμις	BUCK, C. D. "Studies in Greek Noun-Formation," *CP* 13 (1918) 75–88 (77).
ἰατήρ, ἰατρός	VAN BROCK, N. See under "*N*. 3.18" (13).
ἱκέτης	VAN HERTEN, J. Θρησκεία Εὐλάβεια Ἱκέτης. *Bijdrage tot de kennis der religieuze terminologie in het grieksch* (Diss. Amsterdam 1934) 59–60.
ἰόπλοκος, ἰοπλόκαμος, ἰοβόστρυχος	PEARSON, A. C. See under "*O*. 1.105" (155).
Ἰωλκός	WEST, M. "Iolkos in der griechischen Dichtung," *Glotta* 41 (1963) 278–82.
καιρός	BRANCATO, G. "Il fren dell' arte in Pindaro," *Quattro note di filologia classica* (Messina and Florence 1960) 47–63.
	PALMER, L. R. "The Indo-European Origins of Greek Justice," *TPS* (1950) 149–68.
	UNTERSTEINER, M. See under "Concept of Poetry" (35–45 and 65–102).
κλέος	GREINDL, M. Κλέος Κῦδος Εὖχος Τιμή Φάτις Δόξα. *Eine bedeutungsgeschichtliche Untersuchung des epischen und lyrischen Sprachgebrauches* (Lengerich 1938).
κυάνεος and its compounds	LINDSAY, J. See under "*P*. 4 General" (47–60).
κῦδος	GREINDL, M. See under κλέος.
λόγος	SHOREY, P. Ἀδμήτου λόγον, *CP* 23 (1928) 188–9.
Ὀγχηστός	NIEDERMANN, M. "Zur lateinischen und griechischen Wortgeschichte," *Glotta* 19 (1931) 1–15 (13–14).
ὀξύς	FRIESLAND, E. See under "*O*. 6 General" (39–43).
ὅσιος	BOLKESTEIN, J. C. Ὅσιος en Εὐσεβής. *Bijdrage tot de godsdienstige en zedelijke Terminologie van de Grieken* (Amsterdam 1936) 11–12.
πρόφατος and related words	VON DER MÜHLL, P. See under "*O*. 1.111–2" (53–5).
σοφία	GLADIGOW, B. *Sophia und Kosmos: Untersuchungen zur Frühgeschichte von σοφός und σοφίη* (Hildesheim 1965) 39–55.
	SNELL, B. *Die Ausdrücke für den Begriff des Wissens in der vorplatonischen Philosophie* (σοφία, γνώμη, σύνεσις, ἱστορία, μάθημα, ἐπιστήμη) = *PU* 29 (1924).
σώτειρα	JANNI, P. "ΣΩΤΕΙΡΑ e ΣΩΤΗΡ in Pindaro," *StudUrb* 39 (1965) 104–9.

τελετή	Zijderveld, C. *Τελετή. Bijdrage tot de kennis der religieuze terminologie in het Grieksch* (Purmerend 1934) 7–9.
τέλος	Bayfield, M. A. "On Some Derivatives of τέλος," *CR* 15 (1901) 445–7.
	Holwerda, D. *ΤΕΛΟΣ*, *Mnem* 4th S., 16 (1963) 337–63.
τέμνω	Forssman, B. "τέμνω und τάμνω," *Glotta* 44 (1966) 5–14.
τιμή	Greindl, M. See under κλέος.
τρόπος	Thimme, O. See under φύσις.
φάτις	Greindl, M. See under κλέος.
φέγγος	Lyde, L. W. *Contexts in Pindar, with reference to the meaning of φέγγος* (Manchester 1935).
	[A. Puech, *REG* 49 (1936) 321; A. Severyns, *AC* 5 (1936) 212–3; D. M. Robinson, *CP* 31 (1936) 267–8; D. L. Page, *CR* 49 (1935) 202.]
φύσις, φυή	Beardslee, J. W. *The Use of Φύσις in Fifth-Century Greek Literature* (Diss. Chicago 1918) 6–8.
φύσις	Thimme, O. *φύσις τρόπος ἦθος. Semasiologische Untersuchung über die Auffassung des menschlichen Wesens (Charakters) in der älteren griechischen Literatur* (Diss. Quakenbrück 1935).
χάρις	Fernandes, R. M. R. See under "Religion and Myth."
	Hewitt, J. W. See under εὐεργέτης.
χεριάρης, χαλκοάρης	Dornseiff, F. See under "*I*. 5.1" (62–4).
χρή	Goodell, T. D. "*XPH* and *ΔEI*," *CQ* 8 (1914) 91–102 (94).
	Redard, G. *Recherches sur Χρή, Χρῆσθαι. Etude sémantique* (Paris 1953).
χρόνος	Accame, S. "La concezione del tempo nell' età omerica ed arcaica," *RFIC* NS 39 (1961) 359–94 (386–8).
	Fränkel, H. "Zeitauffassung in der frühgriechischen Literatur," *Wege und Formen frühgriechischen Denkens* (Munich 1955, 1960²) 1–22 (10–12 and 20–21).
	Thornton, H. & A. See under "Style and Imagery" (94–5).

17. STYLE AND IMAGERY

AVERY, H. C. "Pindar and Four Epithets," *Arion* 2 (1963) 128–9.

BECKER, O. *Das Bild des Weges und verwandte Vorstellungen im frühgriechischen Denken.* Hermes Einzelschriften 4 (Berlin 1937) 50–100.

BERNARD, M. *Pindars Denken in Bildern. Vom Wesen der Metapher* (Pfullingen 1963).
    [E. Janssens, *AC* 33 (1964) 154–5; P. Bernardini, *Maia* 17 (1965) 400–4.]

BOWRA, C. M. "The Proem of Parmenides," *CP* 32 (1937) 97–112. Also in *Problems in Greek Poetry* (Oxford 1953) 38–53.

BRÄUNING, T. F. G. *De adiectivis compositis apud Pindarum.* 2 pts. (Berlin 1880–81).

BUCCELLATO, M. "Modi etimomitologici nella 'Techne Poietike' di Pindaro" in "Linguaggio e società alle origine nel pensiero filosofico greco," *RSF* 15 (1960) 339–53 and 16 (1961) 3–32 (24–29).

BULTMANN, R. "Zur Geschichte der Lichtsymbolik im Altertum," *Philologus* 97 (1948) 1–36.

BURY, J. B. "Paronomasia in Pindar," *Hermathena* 6 (1888) 185–208.

CANTER, H. V. "The Figure ΑΔΥΝΑΤΟΝ in Greek and Latin Poetry," *AJP* 51 (1930) 32–41.

COOK, A. B. "Unconscious Iterations. II," *CR* 16 (1902) 256–67 (265–6).

DEVENTER, C. *Zu den griechischen Lyrikern. Natur und Naturgefühl bei denselben* (Progr. Gleiwitz 1887).

DIETEL, K. *Das Gleichnis in der frühen griechischen Lyrik* (Diss. Würzburg 1939) 119–52.

DORNSEIFF, F. *Pindars Stil* (Berlin 1921).
    [A. D. Nock, *CR* 39 (1925) 209; L. H. Baker, *AJP* 43 (1922) 376–7; M. Barone, *BFC* 28 (1922) 161–4; L. Derochette, *BMB* 26 (1922) 141–3; H. Fränkel, *GGA* 184 (1922) 188–99; E. von Prittwitz-Gaffron, *LZB* 72 (1921) 643–4; E. Bethe, *NJA* 49 (1922) 81–2; O. Schroeder, *PhW* 41 (1921) 745–9; G. Calògero, *RFIC* 51 (1923) 354–60; N. Terzaghi, *RIGI* 5 (1921) 280–1.]

DORNSEIFF, F. See under "I. 5.1." On the priamel.

DUCHEMIN, J. "Essai sur le symbolisme pindarique: or, lumière et couleurs," *REG* 65 (1952) 46–58.

DUCHEMIN, J. "Obscurités et difficultés de Pindare," *IL* 5 (1953) 19–26.

DUCHEMIN, J. "L'iconographie funéraire et l'exégèse pindarique," *REL* 32 (1954) 284–97.

DURANTE, M. *Saggio sulla lingua poetica greca* (Palermo 1960).

DUTOIT, E. *Le thème de l'adynaton dans la poésie antique* (Paris 1936) 10–13.

FERRANTE, D. "Immagini etimologiche nei poeti greci dell' età ionico-attica," *RIL* 99 (1965) 453–89 (461–4).

FRIESLAND, E. See under "*O.* 6 General" (43–7). Use of epithets.

GLASER, M. *Die zusammengesetzten Nomina bei Pindar* (Progr. Amberg 1898).

*Godofredus, M. *De elocutione Pindari sive de iis, quae in usu Graeci sermonis, praesertim in delectu vocabulorum et in oratione figurata apud Pindarum notabilia sunt* (Susati 1865).

del Grande, C. *Poesia ermetica nella Grecia antica* (Naples 1937) 45–9.

Goram, O. "Pindari translationes et imagines," *Philologus* 14 (1859) 241–80 and 478–98.

van Groningen, B. A. *La composition littéraire archaïque grecque* (Amsterdam 1958; 1960²) 324–86. A study primarily of *O*. 3, 7, 11, *P*. 6, 10, 11, *N*. 10, *I*. 1.

Harre, F. F. P. *De verborum apud Pindarum conlocatione* (Diss. Berlin 1867).

Hense, C. C. *Ueber personificirende Adjectiva und Epitheta bei griechischen Dichtern, insbesondere bei Pindar, Aeschylus, Sophocles* (Progr. Halberstadt 1855).

Hoey, T. "Fusion in Pindar," *HSCP* 70 (1965) 235–62.

Houghton, H. P. "Compounds in Pindar," *TAPA* 65 (1934) xxxviii–ix.

Kambylis, A. "Anredeformen bei Pindar," Χάρις Κωνστ. Ι. Βουρβέρη (Athens 1964) 95–199.

Kambylis, A. *Die Dichterweihe und ihre Symbolik. Untersuchungen zu Hesiodos, Kallimachos, Properz und Ennius* (Heidelberg 1965).

Keith, A. L. *Simile and Metaphor in Greek Poetry from Homer to Aeschylus* (Diss. Chicago 1914) 79–101.

Kienzle, E. *Der Lobpreis von Städten und Ländern in der älteren griechischen Dichtung* (Kallmünz 1936).

Kröhling, W. *Die Priamel (Beispielreihung) als Stilmittel in der griechisch-römischen Dichtung* (Greifswald 1935).

Kuhlmann, G. *De poetae et poematis Graecorum appellationibus* (Diss. Marburg 1906).

Lauer, S. *Zur Wortstellung bei Pindar* (Diss. Winterthur 1959).

Lesky, A. *Thalatta. Der Weg der Griechen zum Meer* (Vienna 1947) 206–11.

von Leutsch, E. "Homonymen in Pindar's Epinikien," *RhM* 17 (1862) 368–77.

*Lübbert, E. *De elocutione Pindari* (Diss. Halle 1853).
    [R. Rauchenstein, *JPh* 77 (1858) 243–8.]

Luppino, A. "Sullo stile di Pindaro," *PP* 12 (1957) 122–7.

Lyde, L. W. See under φέγγος.

Magnien, V. "Origines de la langue poétique grecque," *Société Toulousaine d'Études Classiques. Mélanges* 1 (1946) 23–33.

Malten, L. *Die Sprache des menschlichen Antlitzes im frühen Griechentum* (Berlin 1961) 19–21.

McCracken, G. "Pindar's Figurative Use of Plants," *AJP* 55 (1934) 340–5.

Merriam, A. C. "Alien Intrusion between Article and Noun in Greek," *TAPA* 13 (1882) 34–49 (39).

Meyer, H. *Hymnische Stilelemente in der frühgriechischen Dichtung* (Diss. Würzburg 1933) 54–69.

Moravcsik, E. "A koszorú mint költészetszimbólum Pindárosnál," (="The Wreath as a Poetic Symbol in Pindar") *Antik Tanulmanyok* 10 (1963) 167–79.
    [*BCO* 10 (1965) 130–1.]

Mugler, C. "La lumière et la vision dans la poésie grecque," *REG* 73 (1960) 40–72.

Mihály, R. "Adalékok Pindar tropikájához," *Országos Középtanodai Tanáregylet Közlönye* 4 (1871) 289–300.

*Nebel, G. "Pindar und die Heiligkeit des Ortes," *Neue Deutsche Hefte* 74 (1960) 494–504.

Norwood, G. See under "General and Miscellaneous." Symbolism.

*Olin, J. H. *Dissertatio de digressionibus Pindari* (Uppsala 1790).

van Otterlo, W. A. A. "Beitrag zur Kenntnis der griechischen Priamel," *Mnem* 3rd S., 8 (1940) 145–75.

Pannicke, E. *De sublimitate Pindari* (Progr. Küstrin 1873).

Pecz, W. Οἱ τρόποι τοῦ Πινδάρου, ΞΕΝΙΑ. *Hommage international à l'université nationale de Grèce*. Pt. 1 (Athens 1912) 42–8.

*Pecz, W. "Pindars Tropen," *UR* 2 (1913) 706–8.

Pecz, W. Συγκριτικὴ τροπικὴ τῆς ποιήσεως τῶν ἐγκρίτων χρόνων τῆς Ἑλληνικῆς λογοτεχνίας (Budapest 1913) 109–55.

    [B. L. Gildersleeve, *AJP* 35 (1914) 227–30.]

Petersen, L. *Zur Geschichte der Personifikation in griechischer Dichtung und bildender Kunst* (Würzburg 1939) 23–30.

Pierson, W. "Ueber die Tmesis der Präposition vom Verbum bei den griechischen Dichtern, insbesondere bei Dramatikern und Lyrikern," *RhM* 11 (1857) 379–400.

Platnauer, M. "Greek Colour-Perception," *CQ* 15 (1921) 153–62.

Puech, A. "La relation entre la phrase grammaticale et la période rythmique dans les poèmes de Pindare," *Mélanges offerts à A. M. Desrousseaux* (Paris 1937) 371–5.

Rickmann, E. *In cumulandis epithetis quas leges sibi scripserint poetae Graeci maxime lyrici* (Diss. Cervimontii 1884).

Ring, M. *Zur Tropik Pindar's* (Budapest 1873).

Ritter, C. *De Pindari studio nomina variandi* (Diss. Argentorati 1885). Also in *Dissertationes philologicae argentoratenses selectae* 9 (1885) 239–92.

Roever, F. *Die Übertragung des Adjektivs bei Pindar* (Progr. Stolp 1886).

Schmeier, B. *De translationibus ab homine petitis apud Aeschylum et Pindarum commentatio* (Diss. Königsberg 1882).

Schöll, A. "Das Altfränkische in Pindars Stil," *Gesammelte Aufsätze zur klassischen Literatur alter und neuer Zeit* (Berlin 1884) 1–21.

Soutar, G. *Nature in Greek Poetry* (London 1939).

Stanford, W. B. *Ambiguity in Greek Literature. Studies in Theory and Practice* (Oxford 1939) 129–36.

Stickney, T. *Les sentences dans la poésie grecque d'Homère à Euripide* (Paris 1903) 117–51.

Sulzer, A. I. *Zur Wortstellung und Satzbildung bei Pindar* (Diss. Zürich 1961).

    [V. D'Agostino, *RSC* 9 (1961) 253–4; A. J. Beattie, *CR* NS 12 (1962) 125–6; D. D. Feaver, *CW* 55 (1962) 120; A. Garzya, *P&I* 4 (1962) 199;

F. Duysinx, *RBPh* 40 (1962) 1020; J. Humbert, *REG* 75 (1962) 279; W. Theiler, *MH* 18 (1961) 238; J. A. Davison, *AC* 30 (1961) 546–8; S. Radt, *Gnomon* 35 (1963) 245–7; J. Irigoin, *RPh* 3rd S., 37 (1963) 126–8; I. Rodríguez, *Helmantica* 13 (1962) 383; R. Loriaux, *LEC* 30 (1962) 124; W. J. Verdenius, *Mnem* 4th S., 17 (1964) 308–9; R. M. Rosado Fernandes, *BF* 21 (1962–63) 138–40.]

Tarrant, D. "Greek Metaphors of Light," *CQ* NS 10 (1960) 181–7 (182–3).

*Tessing, S. *De compositis nominibus Aeschyleis et Pindaricis* (Lund 1884).

Theiler, W. See under "*I.* 8.70" (1–19).

Thesleff, H. *Studies on the Greek Superlative* (Helsingfors 1955) 27–30.

Thornton, H. & A. *Time and Style. A Psycho-Linguistic Essay in Classical Literature* (London 1962) 25–35.

Treu, M. "Licht und Leuchtendes in der archaischen griechischen Poesie," *Studium Generale* 18 (1965) 83–97.

Turolla, E. "Simbolismo e poesia nell' epinicio pindarico," *GIF* 9 (1956) 193–209. Also in *Poesia e poeti dell' antico mondo* (Catania 1956) 63–85.

Waern, I. Γῆς 'Οστέα. *The Kenning in Pre-Christian Greek Poetry* (Diss. Uppsala 1951).

Williger, E. *Sprachliche Untersuchungen zu den Komposita der griechischen Dichter des 5. Jahrhundert* (Göttingen 1928).

18. STRUCTURE AND UNITY

Arnaldi, F. *Struttura e poesia nelle odi di Pindaro* (Naples 1943).
Ausfeld, K. *De Graecorum Precationibus Quaestiones* (Leipzig 1903).
Barigazzi, A. "L'unità dell' epinicio pindarico (Storia del problema e compiti della critica)," *A&R* NS 2 (1952) 121–36.
Cerrato, L. *La tecnica composizione delle odi pindariche. Studio* (Genoa 1888).
    [G. Fraccaroli, *RFIC* 17 (1889) 409–12.]
Cerrato, L. "Ancora una parola sulla composizione tecnica delle Odi Pindariche," *RFIC* 18 (1890) 232–4.
Cessi, C. "L'esegesi artistica ed i motivi genetici degli epinici di Pindaro," *AIV* 82 (1922–23) 241–80.
Cessi, C. "L'esegesi artistica ed i motivi genetici degli epinici di Pindaro. Nota seconda," *AIV* 83 (1923–24) 611–45.
Croiset, A. "Les nomes de Terpandre et les odes de Pindare," *Annuaire de l'association pour l'encouragement des études grecques en France* 14 (1880) 99–116.
Czerner, B. *De difficultatibus quibusdam in Pindari carminibus explicandis* (Progr. Gleiwitz 1889) 1–8.
Drachmann, A. B. See under "General and Miscellaneous" (1891).
Illig, L. *Zur Form der pindarischen Erzählung. Interpretationen und Untersuchungen* (Diss. Berlin 1932).
    [D. S. Robertson, *CR* 46 (1932) 231; A. Puech, *REG* 45 (1932) 452–3; W. Schadewaldt, *DLZ* 55 (1934) 1407–12. Also in *Hellas und Hesperien* (Zürich & Stuttgart 1960) 94–8; E. Kalinka, *PhW* 53 (1933) 65–7; F. Dornseiff, *Gnomon* 9 (1933) 269–73; B. A. van Groningen, *MPh* 40 (1933) 225–6.]
Lübbert, E. *Commentatio de priscae cuiusdam epiniciorum formae apud Pindarum vestigiis* (Bonn 1885).
Lübbert, E. *Commentatio de poesis Pindaricae in archa et sphragide componendis arte* (Bonn 1885).
    [O. Crusius, *WKPh* 4 (1887) 1380–5.]
Lübbert, E. *Meletemata de Pindaro nomorum Terpandri imitatore* (Bonn 1885).
Lübbert, E. *Meletemata de Pindari studiis Terpandreis* (Bonn 1886).
    [O. Crusius, *WKPh* 4 (1887) 1385–95.]
Lübbert, E. *Commentatio de Pindaricorum carminum compositione ex Nomorum historia illustranda* (Progr. Bonn 1887).
*Macan, R. W. "Upon the Terpandrian νόμος in the Epinikia of Pindar," *TOPS* (1882–83) 16–20.
Nierhaus, R. *Strophe und Inhalt im pindarischen Epinikion* (Diss. Berlin 1936).
    [H. Bischoff, *Gnomon* 14 (1938) 43–52; F. Dornseiff, *DLZ* 58 (1937) 180–4; F. Charlier, *LEC* 6 (1937) 302–3; A. Puech, *REG* 50 (1937) 264–5; C. del Grande, *BFC* 44 (1937) 4–5; G. Tyler, *CW* 30 (1937) 147.]

*Repetto, G. *Il nomo di Terpandro e la partizione delle Odi di Pindaro* (Catania 1916).
   [C. Cessi, *RLC* 1 (1918) 159–61.]
Schadewaldt, W. *Der Aufbau des pindarischen Epinikion* (Halle 1928, repr. Tübingen 1966).
   [A. Puech, *RPh* 3rd S., 3 (1929) 424; *LZB* 80 (1929) 478; A. B. Drachmann, *DLZ* 50 (1929) 1092–1102; P. Shorey, *CP* 24 (1929) 215–6; D. S. Robertson, *CR* 44 (1930) 40–1; E. Kalinka, *PhW* 50 (1930) 529–35; H. Fränkel, *Gnomon* 6 (1930) 1–20: a revised version appears in *Wege und Formen frühgriechischen Denkens* (Munich 1955, 1960²) 350–69.]
Todde, P. "Il problema dell' unità estetica negli Epinici di Pindaro," *MC* NS 5 (1951) 129–42.
Tracy, H. L. "Thought-Sequence in the Ode," *Phoenix* 5 (1951) 108–18. Also in *Studies in Honour of Gilbert Norwood*, Phoenix Supp. Vol. 1 (Toronto 1952) 203–13.
Ziegler, K. *De precationibus apud Graecos formis quaestiones selectae* (Diss. Vratislaviae 1905).

19. METRE

Included here are studies on rhythm, colometry, prosody, music, and musical instruments. Works of a general nature on metre are omitted. See also the entries pertaining to Kircher and the musical score of *P.* 1 under "*P.* 1 General."

ARENA, A. "Pindaro Olimpiche I-II-III. Versione metrica," *RSC* 12 (1964) 293-324 (293-305). On the rhythm of Pindar's poetry.

VAN DEN BERGH, H. "Untersuchung über die wahren Werthe deutscher Silben in antiken Versmaszen nebst einer Übersetzung des ersten und Proben anderer olympischer Siegeslieder," *JPP* 96 (1867) 325-56.

BERGK, T. "Zum Anecdoton Pindaricum," *ZA* 5 (1847) 480.

BOECKH, A. *Über die Versmasse des Pindaros* (Berlin 1809).

BOECKH, A. "Selbstanzeige der Schrift über die Versmaasse des Pindaros," *Heidelbergische Jahrbücher der Literatur für Philologie* 3 (1810). Also in *Gesammelte Kleine Schriften* 7 (Leipzig 1872) 183-4.

BOROS, J. "Pindaros epinikionjainak metrikai Szerkezete," *EPK* 38 (1914) 679-94 and 754-84.

BOWRA, C. M. "An Alleged Anomaly in Pindar's Metric," *CQ* 24 (1930) 174-82.

BOWRA, C. M. "Metrical Correspondence in Pindar – I," *CQ* 27 (1933) 81-7.

BRENNAN, C. J. "A Peculiarity of Choric Responsion," *CR* 20 (1906) 386-92.

BREYER, B. "De positione debili," *Analecta Pindarica* (Diss. Vratislaviae 1880) 44-70.

BURY, J. B. Ἐπίτριτος, ἐπιτέταρτος, ἐπιμόριος, κ.τ.λ., *CR* 2 (1888) 42-3.

CHRIST, W. *Die metrische Ueberlieferung der pindarischen Oden, ein Beitrag zur Geschichte der Metrik* (Munich 1868).

CLAPP, E. B. "On Hiatus in Pindar," *TAPA* 33 (1902) LXXX-LXXXII.

CLAPP, E. B. "Hiatus in Greek Melic Poetry," *Univ. of California Publ. in Class. Philology* 1, 1 (Berkeley 1904) 1-34.

CLAPP, E. B. "A Quantitative Difficulty in the New Metric," *CR* 18 (1904) 339-40.

DALE, A. M. "The Metrical Units of Greek Lyric Verse, I, II, III," *CQ* 44 (1950) 138-48 and *CQ* NS 1 (1951) 20-30 and 119-29.

DRACHMANN, A. B. *Isaac Tzetzae de metris Pindaricis commentarius* (Copenhagen 1925).
    [W. J. W. Koster, *MPh* 34 (1927) 258-60; *JHS* 46 (1926) 123.]

DUNN, G. "The Dactylo-epitritic Rhythm," *CR* 7 (1893) 23-7.

FENNELL, C. A. M. "A New System of Analysing Greek Lyric Stanzas," *CR* 14 (1900) 292-5.

GARROD, H. W. "Simonidea," *CQ* 16 (1922) 65-76 and 113-23.

GENTILI, B. "Problemi di metrica. 1," *Maia* 15 (1963) 314-21.

GLEDITSCH, H. See under "Bibliography."
*GRAF, E. *De Graecorum veterum re musica quaestionum capita duo. I. De polyphonia et dialecto crumatica. II. De Pindari re musica* (Marburg 1889).
GRAF, E. *Pindars logaoedische Strophen* (Marburg 1892).
DEL GRANDE, C. *Espressione musicale dei poeti greci* (Naples 1932).
HEADLAM, W. "Greek Lyric Metre," *JHS* 22 (1902) 209-27.
HEIMER, A. "De positione apud Pindarum" and "De prosodia Pindarica annotationes," *Studia Pindarica* (Lund 1885) 89-148.
    [F. Hanssen, *PA* 16 (1886) 202-4.]
HERMANN, C. "Zu den daktylo-epitritischen Strophen bei Pindar," *JPP* 130 (1884) 481-92.
HERMANN, C. "Das daktylo-epitritische Versmasz bei Pindar und die neuere rhythmologische Theorie," *JPP* 144 (1891) 65-76.
HÖHL, H. *Responsionsfreiheiten bei Pindar* (Diss. Cologne 1950).
    [W. J. W. Koster, *Mnem* 4th S., 6 (1953) 237-8; A. M. Dale, *Gnomon* 24 (1952) 234-5.]
IRIGOIN, J. *Recherches sur les mètres de la lyrique chorale grecque: La structure du vers* (Paris 1953).
IRIGOIN, J. *Les scholies métriques de Pindare* (Paris 1958).
    [For reviews see entry under "Scholia."]
JUSATZ, H. "De irrationalitate studia rhythmica," *LSCP* 14 (1891) 173-351 (289-99).
KITTO, H. D. F. "The Rhythms of Pindar," *CR* 42 (1928) 51-3.
KITTO, H. D. F. "Rhythm, Metre, and Black Magic," *CR* 56 (1942) 99-108.
*KOLÁŘ, A. *De Dactyloepitritis* (Bratislava 1935).
KOSTER, W. J. W. "Dactylepitriti an Metra Choriambo-Ionica?" *CQ* 28 (1934) 145-55.
KOSTER, W. J. W. "Studia ad colometriam poëseos Graecae pertinentia," *Mnem* 3rd S., 9 (1941) 1-43.
KOSTER, W. J. W. "De studiis recentibus ad rem metricam pertinentibus," *Mnem* 4th S., 3 (1950) 21-53 and 127-57.
*KRÜGER, E. *Dissertatio de musicis Graecorum organis circa Pindari tempora florentibus* (Göttingen 1830).
LÖSCHHORN, K. "Die logaödischen Verse und Strophen bei den äolischen Dichtern und bei Pindar," *WKPh* 28 (1911) 1241-6.
MAAS, P. See under "*O.* 14.21."
MAAS, P. "Die neuen Responsionsfreiheiten bei Bakchylides und Pindar," *JPhV* 39 (1913) 289-320 and 47 (1921) 13-31.
    [H. Jurenka, *ZOEG* 65 (1914) 407-10; G. Fraccaroli, *RFIC* 43 (1915) 120-1; J. Sitzler, *WKPh* 32 (1915) 385-8; R. Ebeling, *Sok* 7 (1919) 117-18; C. O. Zuretti, *BFC* 24 (1918) 17-18; J. Vürtheim, *MPh* 30 (1923) 149-50.]
MOMMSEN, T. See under "Manuscripts" (Einige Bemerkungen, 34-9). On colometry.

Parker, L. P. E. "Some Recent Researches on the Versification of Pindar and Bacchylides," *BICS* 5 (1958) 13–24.

Parker, L. P. E. "Porson's Law Extended," *CQ* NS 16 (1966) 1–26 (7–9).

Perathoner, W. *Die Melodie der Sprache in den Gesängen Pindars* (Progr. Brünn 1890).

Schmidt, J. H. H. *Die Eurhythmie in den Chorgesängen der Griechen. Allgemeine Gesetze zur Fortführung und Berichtigung der Rossbach-Westphalschen Annahmen. Text und Schemata sämmtlicher Chorika des Aeschylus. Schemata sämmtlicher pindarischer Epinikien* = Vol. 1 of *Die Kunstformen der griechischen Poesie und ihre Bedeutung* (Leipzig 1868).

Schmidt, M. See under "Olympian Odes General" (I-LXXXIV).

Schmidt, M. "Die Taktmaasze einiger olympischen Oden Pindar's" *SAWM* 2 (1872) 405–53. On *O.* 2, 4, 5, 9, 14, and *P.* 2.

*Schmidt, M. *Commentatio de Caroli Lachmanni studiis metricis recte aestimandis* (Jena 1880).

Schmidt, M. *Ueber den Bau der pindarischen Strophen* (Leipzig 1882).
    [F. Vogt, *PA* 13 (1883) 656–63.]

Schroeder, O. "Die enoplischen Strophen Pindars," *Hermes* 38 (1903) 202–43.

Schroeder, O. "Pindarica V. Aeolische Strophen," *Philologus* 62 (1903) 161–81.

Schroeder, O. "Pindarica VI. Aeolische Strophen abermals," *Philologus* 63 (1904) 321–41. See also his *Enoplische und äolische Dreiheber in seinen Vorarbeiten zur griechischen Versgeschichte* (Leipzig 1908) 107–20.

Schroeder, O. "The New Metric," *CP* 7 (1912) 137–76.

Servien, P. *Les rythmes comme introduction physique à l'esthétique* (Paris 1930) 143–67.

Smyth, H. W. "Mute and Liquid in Greek Melic Poetry," *TAPA* 28 (1897) 111–43 (141–2).

Spieker, E. H. "On the Use of the Dactyl after an Initial Trochee in Greek Lyric Verse," *TAPA* 39 (1908) 5–13.

Spiro, F. "Der kyklische Dactylus und die lesbische Lyrik," *Hermes* 23 (1888) 234–58.

Theiler, W. See under "*I.* 8.70" (19–35).

Theiler, W. "Die Gliederung der griechischen Chorliedstrophe. Eine metrische Übung," *MH* 12 (1955) 181–200.

Thomson, G. "Greek Lyric Metre," *JHS* 83 (1963) 156.

Turyn, A. "Observationes Metricae," *Eos* 25 (1921–22) 91–104.

Vitelli, G. "Spicilegio fiorentino," *Museo italiano di antichità classica* 1 (1885) 159–74 (160–4). On colometry.

Vogt, F. *De metris Pindari quaestiones tres* (Diss. Argentorati 1880). Also in *Dissertationes philologicae argentoratenses selectae* 4 (1880) 203–312.
    [F. Hanssen, *PA* 12 (1882) 9–12.]

White, J. W. "The Origin and Form of Aeolic Verse," *CQ* 3 (1909) 291–309.

Williams, C. F. A. "Ancient Metre and Modern Musical Rhythm," *CR* 7 (1893) 295–300.

Young, D. "Notes on the Text of Pindar. II. Word-division at Verse-end in Pindar," *GRBS* 7 (1966) 9–15.

20. CONCEPT OF POETRY

ACCAME, S. "L'ispirazione della Musa e gli albori della critica storica nell' età arcaica," *RFIC* 92 (1964) 129–56 and 257–87 (271–87).

DAVISON, J. A. "Pindar's Conception of Poetry," *PCA* 33 (1936) 38–41.

DODDS, E. R. See under "*O.* 9.33–5" (82 and 101 nn. 121–22).

DUCHEMIN, J. "Mission sociale et pouvoirs magiques du poète comparés à ceux du roi dans le lyrisme de Pindare," *The Sacral Kingship. Contributions to the Central Theme of the VIIIth International Congress for the History of Religions (Rome, April 1955)* (Leiden 1959) 379–93.

FABBRI, G. "Gli oracoli come fonte d'ispirazione nella letteratura poetica dei Greci," *A&R* NS 11 (1930) 25–82 (34–45).

FALTER, O. *Der Dichter und sein Gott bei den Griechen und Römern* (Würzburg 1934) 20–9.

FREEMAN, K. "Pindar—The Function and Technique of Poetry," *G&R* 8 (1939) 144–59.

GUNDERT, H. *Pindar und sein Dichterberuf* (Frankfurt 1935).
  [J. Schönemann, *PhW* 58 (1938) 257–64; A. Lesky, *DLZ* 59 (1938) 10–13; Q. Cataudella, *BFC* 42 (1936) 223–5; D. S. Robertson, *CR* 49 (1935) 176.]

KRAUS, W. "Die Auffassung des Dichterberufs im frühen Griechentum," *WS* 68 (1955) 65–87 (82–7).

LANATA, G. *Poetica preplatonica. Testimonianze e frammenti. Testo, traduzione e commento* (Florence 1963) 74–97.

LASSERRE, F. "La condition du poète dans la Grèce antique," *BELL* 2nd S., 5 (1962) 3–28.

LINDSAY, J. See under "*P.* 4 General" (319–23).

MAEHLER, H. *Die Auffassung des Dichterberufs im frühen Griechentum bis zur Zeit Pindars* (Göttingen 1963).

DA ROCHA PEREIRA, M. H. "O conceito de poesia na Grécia arcaica," *Humanitas* 13–14 (1961–62) 336–57.

SNELL, B. *Poetry and Society: The Role of Poetry in Ancient Greece* (Bloomington 1961) 56–71.

SPERDUTI, A. "The Divine Nature of Poetry in Antiquity," *TAPA* 81 (1950) 209–40 (233–7).

SVOBODA, K. "Les idées de Pindare sur la poésie," *Aegyptus* 32 (1952) 108–20.

UNTERSTEINER, M. "Per una storia della poetica classica," *RSF* 1 (1946) 334–52 (340–5).

UNTERSTEINER, M. *La formazione poetica di Pindaro* (Messina 1951).
  [H. Strohm, *Gnomon* 25 (1953) 192–3; L. Pitzalis, *GIF* 6 (1953) 259–60.]

WEBSTER, T. B. L. "Greek Theories of Art and Literature down to 400 B.C.," *CQ* 33 (1939) 166–79.

21. CLASSIFICATION

See also the entries at the beginning of the various sections under "Fragments" for studies on specific classes of Pindar's poetry.

FÄRBER, A. *Die Lyrik in der Kunsttheorie der Antike* (Munich 1936).

HARVEY, A. E. "The Classification of Greek Lyric Poetry," *CQ* NS 5 (1955) 157–75.

HILLER, E. "Die antiken Verzeichnisse der pindarischen Dichtungen," *Hermes* 21 (1886) 357–71.

LÜBBERT, E. *Commentatio de Pindari carminibus dramaticis tragicis eorumque cum epiniciis cognatione* (Bonn 1884).

*WALTHER, C. H. *Commentationis de Graecae poesis melicae generibus particula* (Diss. Halle 1866 and Berlin 1867).

22. RELIGION AND MYTH

See also the following section.

✓ADAM, J. *The Religious Teachers of Greece* (Edinburgh 1908) 115-37.
AHLERT, P. *Mädchen und Frauen in Pindars Dichtung* (Leipzig 1942).
    [J. Meunier, *AC* 12 (1943) 119-21; M. F. Galiano, *Emerita* 11 (1943) 201-8; E. Kalinka, *PhW* 63 (1943) 292-3.]
*ARACRI, V. *La divinità, l'uomo e l'eliso in Pindaro* (Genoa 1896).
    [G. Fraccaroli, *BFC* 3 (1897) 25-7.]
BASSI, D. "La mitologia in Pindaro," *RIL* 74 (1940-41) 487-532.
BEAUJON, E. "Les Grâces et le Zeus Hospitalier chez Pindare," *Le dieu des suppliants* (Neuchâtel 1960) 127-45.
*BERNOCCO, S. See under "Thought."
BERRY, E. G. *The History and Development of the Concept of ΘΕΙΑ ΜΟΙΡΑ and ΘΕΙΑ ΤΥΧΗ down to and including Plato* (Diss. Chicago 1940) 14-18.
BIPPART, G. *Theologumena Pindarica* (Diss. Jena 1846).
BISCHOFF, H. See under "Thought."
DE BLOCK, R. "L'idée du destin dans Pindare," *RIB* 24 (1881) 289-300.
*BOEHME, L. See under "Thought."
BOETHKE, K. A. See under "Thought."
BORNEMANN, L. "Vom Logos spermatikos in den Siegerliedern Pindars," *Die Christliche Welt* 42 (1928) 702-5.
BRANCATO, G. "Due divinità minori della Grecia (Kairòs e Tyche)," *Quattro note di filologia classica* (Messina & Florence 1960) 67-82.
BREMOND, P. A. *Charme d'Athènes et autre essais* (Paris 1925) 74-108.
BROMMER, F. *Herakles. Die zwölf Taten des Helden in antiker Kunst und Literatur* (Münster 1953).
BURIKS, A. A. *ΠΕΡΙ ΤΥΧΗΣ. De ontwikkeling van het begrip tyche tot aan de Romeinse tijd, hoofdzakelijk in de philosophie* (Diss. Leiden 1948).
BURY, J. B. "The Graces in Pindar," *The Nemean Odes of Pindar* (London 1890) 241-4.
CANTER, H. V. "The Mythological Paradigm in Greek and Latin Poetry," *AJP* 54 (1933) 201-24.
CERRATO, L. "Gli Iperborei in Erodoto e Pindaro," *Pindaro, Le Odi. Testo, note e appendice con versione italiana* (Turin 1915, rev. ed. 1934) 595-605.
CIPOLLA, F. "Della religione di Eschilo e di Pindaro," *RFIC* 6 (1878) 366-418.
CLAUSEN, J. C. H. *Theologumena Pindari Lyrici*. Pars prior (Progr. Elberfeld 1854).
    [R. Rauchenstein, *JPh* 77 (1858) 241-3.]
COLVIN, S. "On Representations of Centaurs in Greek Vase-Painting," *JHS* 1 (1880) 107-67.
COMBELLACK, F. M. "Homer and Hector," *AJP* 65 (1944) 209-43 (214-16).

DECHARME, P. *La critique des traditions religieuses chez les Grecs, des origines au temps de Plutarque* (Paris 1904) 94–9.

DEFRADAS, J. "La religion de Pindare," *REG* 70 (1957) 224–34.

DRONKE, G. "Ueber die religiösen und ethischen Anschauungen Pindars," *ZG* 14 (1860) 68–79.

EBERZ, A. *Theologumena Pindari Lyrici* (Diss. Monachii 1839).

EICHINGER, P. F. See under "*O.* 14 General." On the Charites in Pindar.

√FARNELL, L. R. "Excursus on Pindar's Religion," *The Works of Pindar II: Critical Commentary* (London 1932, repr. Amsterdam 1961) 459–76.

FEHR, K. *Die Mythen bei Pindar* (Diss. Zürich 1936).
    [L. Illig, *Gnomon* 16 (1940) 329–31; W. Hörmann, *PhW* 59 (1939) 145–7; A. Puech, *REG* 50 (1937) 516–7; E. L. Highbarger, *CW* 31 (1937–38) 64–5.]

FERNANDES, R. M. R. *O Tema das Graças na Poesia Clássica* (Lisbon 1962) 196–225.

FONTENROSE, J. *Python. A Study of Delphic Myth and its Origins* (Berkeley & Los Angeles 1959).

FRANÇOIS, G. *Le polythéisme et l'emploi au singulier des mots θεός, δαίμων dans la littérature grecque d'Homère à Platon* (Paris 1957) 71–93.

√FRÄNKEL, H. "Pindars Religion," *Die Antike* 3 (1927) 39–63.

FRIEDLÄNDER, P. *Herakles. Sagengeschichtliche Untersuchungen=PU* 19 (1907).

GEIST, H. "Quae Corinna, Pindarus, Praxilla de Oedipo narrent?" *De fabula oedipodea* (Progr. Büdingen 1879).

GERHARDT, H.-G. *Zeus in den pindarischen Epinikien* (Diss. Frankfurt 1959).

GIGANTE, M. "Eracle in Pindaro," *ΝΟΜΟΣ ΒΑΣΙΛΕΥΣ* (Naples 1956) 56–71.

GILGUIN, J. H. *Commentatio Pindarica* (Diss. Traiecti ad Rhenum 1843).

GIRARD, J. *Le sentiment religieux en Grèce d'Homère à Eschyle étudié dans son développement moral et dans son caractère dramatique* (Paris 1869, 1879², 1887³).

*GOETSCHEL, I. C. F. *Mythologiae Pindaricae specimen* 1 (Erlangen 1790).

GOMME, A. W. "The Legend of Cadmus and the Logographi. I," *JHS* 33 (1913) 53–72 (65–6).

VAN GRONINGEN, B. A. *In the Grip of the Past. Essay on an Aspect of Greek Thought* (Leiden 1953) 4, 15, 44–5, 81.

HAAS, H. "Der Zug zum Monotheismus in den homerischen Epen und in den Dichtungen des Hesiod, Pindar und Aeschylus," *ARW* 3 (1900) 52–78 and 153–83 (153–63).

HALLSTRÖM, R. S. A. "De Diis Pindari," *Quaestiones Pindaricae* (Uppsala 1880) 17–48.

HARRISON, J. See under "*O.* 9.33" (476–7).

HELLER, L. *De pietatis et religionis sensu, quem poetarum Graecorum inprimisque Pindari carmina spirant* (Erlangen 1817).

HOEKSTRA, S. "De 'wangunst der Goden op het geluk, ook der rechtvaardigen,' naar het grieksche volksgeloof tot op het midden van de vijfde eeuw," *Verslagen en mededeelingen der kon. Akademie van Wetenschappen. Afdeeling Letterkunde* 3rd S., 1 (1884) 17–105 (77–87).

Illig, L. See under "Structure and Unity."
de Jongh, A. See under "General and Miscellaneous."
Kauer, S. *Die Geburt der Athena im altgriechischen Epos* (Würzburg 1959).
Keyssner, K. *Gottesvorstellung und Lebensauffassung im griechischen Hymnus* (Stuttgart 1932).
*King, H. R. *Myths from Pindar* (London 1904).
 [J. H. Vince, *CR* 19 (1905) 269-70.]
van der Kolf, M. C. *Quaeritur quomodo Pindarus fabulas tractaverit quidque in eis mutarit* (Diss. Rotterdam 1923).
 [M. M. Assmann, *MPh* 32 (1925) 171; O. Schroeder, *PhW* 44 (1924) 649-51.]
Krappe, A. H. "Les Charites," *REG* 45 (1932) 155-62.
Lanzani, C. "Il Dio di Pindaro," *A&R* 8 (1905) 72-84.
Lasserre, F. *La figure d'Éros dans la poésie grecque* (Diss. Lausanne 1946).
Lawson, J. C. *Modern Greek Folklore and Ancient Greek Religion: A Study in Survivals* (Cambridge 1910, repr. New York 1964) 241-2. On Centaurs.
Lesky, A. "Der Mythos im Verständnis der Antike 1. Von der Frühzeit bis Sophokles," *Gymnasium* 73 (1966) 27-44 (37-40).
Lewy, H. "Einiges über TYXH," *JPP* 145 (1892) 761-7.
Lübbert, E. *Pindaros von Kynoskephalai* (Progr. Kiel 1878).
Lübbert, E. *Diatriba in Pindari locum de Aegidis et sacris Carneis* (Progr. Bonn 1883).
Lübbert, E. *Commentatio de Pindaro theologiae Orphicae censore* (Bonn 1888).
*Menghini, V. *Ercole nei canti di Pindaro. Saggio sul valore e sulle proprietà del mito nella poesia pindarica* (Milan 1879).
Nestle, W. *Griechische Religiosität von Homer bis Pindar und Äschylos* (Berlin 1930) 107-17.
Oehler, R. *Mythologische Exempla in der älteren griechischen Dichtung* (Diss. Aarau 1925) 57-68.
Ohlert, C. *De heroologia Pindarica* (Diss. Regimonti 1870).
Onians, R. B. *The Origins of European Thought about the Body, the Mind, the Soul, the World, Time and Fate* (Cambridge 1951, 1954[2]).
*Panse, H. *Gebrauch der Mythen in den pindarischen Epinikien* (Progr. Greiffenberg 1871).
*Petri, V. F. L. *Anthologia Pindarica theologico-moralis sive locorum Pindari ad rerum divinarum officiorumque doctrinam spectantium per titulos digesta collectio* (Halle 1831).
Picard, C. "La Crète et les légendes hyperboréennes," *RA* 5th S., 25 (1927) 349-60.
Picard, C. "La religion de Pindare et l'esprit des sculptures monumentales autour du temple de Zeus à Olympie," *BAGB* No. 58 (1938) 3-24.
*Pilling, C. *Quomodo Telephi fabulam et scriptores et artifices veteres tractaverint* (Diss. Halle 1886).
de Ridder, A. *De l'idée de la mort en Grèce à l'époque classique* (Diss. Paris 1896) 108-10.

Rieder, A. "Zur pindarischen Theologie," *JPh* 141 (1890) 657–65.
Riess, E. "Studies in Superstition. Pindar and Bacchylides," *AJP* 24 (1903) 423–30.
Rivier, A. "Mythe et poésie. Leurs rapports et leur fonction dans trois épinicies de Pindare," *Lettres d'humanité*, Suppl. à *BAGB* 9 (1950) 60–96.
Rohde, E. *Psyche. Seelencult und Unsterblichkeitsglaube der Griechen*, 2 vols. (Tübingen 1890–93, 1897²). English translation of the 8th ed. in 1 vol. by W. B. Hillis, *Psyche. The Cult of Souls and Belief in Immortality among the Greeks* (London 1925).
Rossi, R. "La religiosità di Pindaro," *PP* 7 (1952) 30–40.
Rudberg, G. "Zu Pindaros' Religion," *Eranos* 43 (1945) 317–36.
*Schadewaldt, W. *Die Funktion des Mythos im pindarischen Dichten* (Meersburg 1930).
*Schadewaldt, W. "Der Gott von Delphi und die Humanitätsidee," *EEAth* 15 (1964–65) 59–75.
Schaerer, R. "L'univers spirituel de Pindare," *Mélanges de philosophie grecque offerts à Mgr Diès* (Paris 1956) 221–32.
Schroeder, O. "Die Religion Pindars," *NJA* 51 (1923) 129–52.
Schwartz, J. See under "Scholia."
Schwickert, J. J. *Kritisch-exegetische Erörterungen zu Pindar* (Progr. Trier 1882). The subtitle is "Ueber die religiös-sittliche Weltanschauung und die Theologie des Pindaros."
    [L. Cerrato, *RFIC* 13 (1885) 82–5.]
Scott, J. A. "Two Homeric Personages. Hector as a Theban Hero in the Light of Hesiod and Pindar," *AJP* 35 (1914) 309–25 (311–17).
Séchan, L. "Les noces de Thétis et de Pélée," *RCC* 32, 1 (1931) 673–88.
Seebeck, M. "Ueber den religiösen Standpunkt Pindars," *RhM* 3 (1845) 504–19.
Seippel, G. *Der Typhonmythos* (Greifswald 1939).
Sikes, E. E. "Nike and Athena Nike," *CR* 9 (1895) 280–3.
Skelnik, H. *Pindari et Aeschyli sententiae ad deos deorumque cultum et religionem pertinentes* (Diss. Regimonti 1864).
Soleri, G. "Politeismo e monoteismo nel vocabolario teologico della letteratura greca da Omero a Platone," *RSC* 8 (1960) 24–56 (28–29).
Strohm, H. *Tyche. Zur Schicksalsauffassung bei Pindar und den frühgriechischen Dichtern* (Stuttgart 1944).
    [B. Snell, *Gnomon* 23 (1951) 354–5; B. A. van Groningen, *MPh* 52 (1947) 67–8.]
Thummer, E. *Die Religiosität Pindars* (Innsbruck 1957).
    [W. J. Verdenius, *Mnem* 4th Ser., 14 (1961) 45–7; A. Kurz, *MH* 17 (1960) 42; S. Jannaccone, *GIF* 13 (1960) 79–81; P. Chantraine, *RPh* 3rd S., 34 (1960) 275–6; J. A. Davison, *JHS* 80 (1960) 203–4; É. des Places, *AC* 28 (1959) 348–9; A. Colonna, *RFIC* 87 (1959) 407–9; J. van Ooteg-

hem, *LEC* 27 (1959) 218; H. J. Rose, *CR* NS 9 (1959) 231–3; B. Snell, *AAHG* 11 (1958) 95–7.]

VILLEMAIN, M. *Essais sur le génie de Pindare et sur la poésie lyrique dans ses rapports avec l'élévation morale et religieuse des peuples* (Paris 1859).

*WINIEWSKI, F. *Ueber die Quelle von Pindars Glauben über den Zustand der Seelen nach dem Tode* (Münster 1845–46).

23. THOUGHT

ABEL, D. H. "Genealogies of Ethical Concepts from Hesiod to Bacchylides," *TAPA* 74 (1943) 92–101.

*ALLIHN, F. H. T. *De idea iusti qualis fuerit apud Homerum et Hesiodum ac quomodo a Doriensibus veteribus et a Pythagora exculta sit* (Halle 1847).

AMBROSOLI, F. "Saggio di studi letterari. Nevio-Ennio-Lucano-Pindaro," *Letteratura greca e latina. Scritti editi e inediti.* Vol. 2 (Milan 1878) 442–58 (446–58).

*BERNOCCO, S. *De Pindaro eiusque in deos et homines opinionibus* (Progr. Agrigenti 1879).
    [F. Cipolla, *RFIC* 8 (1880) 269–75.]

BISCHOFF, H. *Gnomen Pindars* (Würzburg 1938).
    [*Gnomon* 20 (1944) 107; A. Severyns, *AC* 8 (1939) 242; L. Früchtel, *PhW* 59 (1939) 673–80.]

*BOEHME, L. *Quid Pindarus tum de iure humano tum de iure divino iudicarit* (Diss. Leipzig 1872).

BOETHKE, K. A. "Pindars Ideen über das Loos der Menschen," *JPP* 80 (1859) 185–99.

BUCHHOLZ, E. *Die sittliche Weltanschauung des Pindaros und Aeschylos* (Leipzig 1869).
    [*PA* 2 (1870) 227–33.]

BULLE, C. *De Pindari sapientia* (Diss. Bonn 1866).

CANTER, H. V. "Ill Will of the Gods in Greek and Latin Poetry," *CP* 32 (1937) 131–43.

✓CLAPP, E. B. "The Mind of Pindar," *TAPA* 37 (1906) XLIII–XLIV.

*DAHL, C. *Specimen philosophiae Pindaricae* (Uppsala 1799).

EITREM, S. "The Pindaric Phthonos," *Studies Presented to D. M. Robinson on his Seventieth Birthday* 2 (Saint Louis 1953) 531–6.

FRITZSCHE, H. "Der ἀνὴρ ἀγαθός bei Pindar," *Verhandlungen der 30. Versammlung deutscher Philologen und Schulmänner in Rostock 1875* (Leipzig 1876) 30–6.

GALIANO, M. F., ADRADOS, F. R., & LASSO DE LA VEGA, J. S. *El Concepto del Hombre en la Antiqua Grecia* (Madrid 1955) 30–45.

GILGUIN, J. H. See under "Religion and Myth."

GUGLIELMINO, F. "Quel che Pindaro sentiva di sè," *A&R* NS 8 (1927) 36–46.

GUNDERT, H. See under "Concept of Poetry."

*HERTZBERG, F. *De ethicis in Pindaro monitionibus* (Diss. Helsingfors 1840).

DE JONGH, A. See under "General and Miscellaneous" (43–77).

*KOCH, L. *De hominis statu ac natura in Pindari carminibus expressa* (Gotha 1845).

LIVINGSTONE, R. W. "Two Types of Humanism: Pindar and Herodotus," *The Greek Genius and its Meaning to us* (Oxford 1915²) 139–59.

MACURDY, G. H. *The Quality of Mercy. The Gentler Virtues in Greek Literature* (New Haven 1940) 67–74.

Marg, W. *Der Charakter in der Sprache der frühgriechischen Dichtung (Semonides Homer Pindar)* (Würzburg 1938) 80–99.
    [L. A. Post, *CP* 35 (1940) 234; H. Fränkel, *AJP* 60 (1939) 475–9; A. Lesky, *DLZ* 60 (1939) 694–6; H. Diller, *Gnomon* 15 (1939) 593–9; *BAGB(SC)* 10 (1938) 18–19; J. A. Davison, *CR* 52 (1938) 120–1; L. Castiglioni, *BFC* 45 (1938) 54–5.]
Martinazzoli, F. "Pindaro," *Ethos ed Eros nella poesia greca* (Florence 1947) 337–64.
*Martino, E. *L'idea morale nei poeti lirici greci, III. Appunti per una trattazione del dovere nella morale pindarica* (Genoa 1901).
Merentitis, K. I. Αἱ ἰδεώδεις πνευματικαὶ καὶ ἠθικαὶ ἀρεταὶ τοῦ ἀνθρώπου παρὰ Πινδάρῳ (Athens 1963).
Montée, P. *Quis et qualis Pindarus moralium auctor exstiterit* (Diss. Paris 1860).
*Mortenson, E. *Pindar's Ethik* (Progr. Leutschau 1884).
de Oliviera Pulquério, M. "Evolução do conceito de justiça de Hesíodo a Píndaro," *Humanitas* 13–14 (1961–62) 305–21.
*Paranikas, M. Αἱ φιλοσοφικαὶ ἰδέαι τοῦ Πινδάρου, *Syll* 28 (1899–1902) 145–58.
Robinson, D. M. *Pindar: A Poet of Eternal Ideas* (Baltimore 1936).
    [M. Hombert, *RBPh* 20 (1941) 631–2; M. Untersteiner, *A&R* 3rd S., 7 (1939) 73–5; P. Collart, *RPh* 3rd S., 12 (1938) 182; D. S. Robertson, *AJP* 59 (1938) 119–20; A. Taccone, *MC* 8 (1938) 236; M. van der Mijnsbrugge, *PhS* 8 (1936–37) 228–9; C. Picard, *RA* 10 (1937) 305–6; C. Vellay, *L'Acropole* 10 (1935) 127; E. Kalinka, *PhW* 57 (1937) 855; A. Rostagni, *RFIC* 65 (1937) 93; *JHS* 57 (1937) 108; *G&R* 6 (1937) 125; A. Severyns, *AC* 6 (1937) 154; P. Baldini, *Religio* 13 (1937) 307; F. Charlier, *LEC* 6 (1937) 116–7; G. Mathieu, *REA* 39 (1937) 58–9; A. Puech, *REG* 50 (1937) 264; P. Treves, *Athenaeum* NS 14 (1936) 290–2; F. Guglielmino, *BFC* 43 (1936) 93–6; G. Tyler, *CW* 30 (1936) 78; H. D. F. Kitto, *CR* 50 (1936) 237.]
Sgroi, P. *I poeti del quinto secolo. Pindaro – I Tragici – Aristofane* (Messina & Florence 1963) 23–48.
*Sjöström, A. G. *De ethicis in Pindaro monitionibus* (Helsingfors 1840).
Skiadas, A. D. ' Γλυκὺς βίοτος—Μείλιχος αἰών' ("Ερευνα εἰς τοὺς πρώτους "Ελληνας λυρικοὺς ποιητὰς), Χάρις Κωνστ. Ι. Βουρβέρῃ (Athens 1964) 25–73.
Steinkopf, G. *Untersuchungen zur Geschichte des Ruhmes bei den Griechen* (Halle 1937) 53–73.
Untersteiner, M. "L'umanità in Pindaro," *RI* 27 (1924) 280–94 and 421–41.
de Vries, G. J. "Pindar's Mood," *Mnem* 4th S., 10 (1957) 8–15.
Wehrli, F. *ΛΑΘΕ ΒΙΩΣΑΣ. Studien zur ältesten Ethik bei den Griechen* (Leipzig & Berlin 1931) 67–82.
Welskopf, E. C. "Zum Inhalt der Begriffe ΜΕΓΑ ΕΡΓΟΝ und ΚΑΛΟΝ ΕΡΓΟΝ von Homer bis Pindar," *Philologische Vorträge*, edd. J. Irmscher & W. Steffen (Wroclaw 1959) 47–57.
*Zeyss, O. *Quid Homerus et Pindarus de virtute, civitate, diis statuerint et quid in his locis differat utriusque poetae sententia* (Progr. Jena 1832).

24. HISTORY AND POLITICS

Pindar's comments and views on historical and political events and his relationship with the Sicilian tyrants.

BERVE, H. "Zur Herrscherstellung der Deinomeniden," *Studies Presented to D. M. Robinson on his Seventieth Birthday* 2 (Saint Louis 1953) 537–52.

BROWN, N. O. "Pindar, Sophocles, and the Thirty Years' Peace," *TAPA* 82 (1951) 1–28.

BURY, J. B. "Pindar's Visit to Sicily," *The Nemean Odes of Pindar* (London 1890) 245–7.

BURY, J. B. "The Constitutional Position of Gelon and Hiero," *CR* 13 (1899) 98–9.

VAN COMPERNOLLE, R. See under "Chronology."

DREYKORN, J. See under "*O.* 2.56" (4–14). Lack of comments on historical and political events.

EHRENBERG, V. "Polypragmosyne: A Study in Greek Politics," *JHS* 67 (1947) 46–67 (47, 64–6).

ENGLISH, B. R. "Pindar and the Problem of Freedom," *Univ. of Toronto Quarterly* 6 (1936–37) 103–19.

ENGLISH, B. R. *The Problem of Freedom in Greece from Homer to Pindar* (Toronto 1938) 82–100.

EVEN, J.-C. "L'attitude de Pindare pendant les guerres médiques," *LEC* 26 (1958) 41–9.

FINLEY, J. H. "Pindar and the Persian Invasion," *HSCP* 63 (1958) 121–32.

FOWLER, H. N. "The Visits of Simonides, Pindar, and Bacchylides at the Court of Hiero," *TAPA* 32 (1901) xxx.

FREEMAN, E. A. *The History of Sicily from the Earliest Times*, Vol. 2 (Oxford 1891).

KIERDORF, W. *Erlebnis und Darstellung der Perserkriege. Studien zu Simonides, Pindar, Aischylos und den attischen Rednern* (Göttingen 1966) 29–47.

LLOYD, W. W. *The History of Sicily to the Athenian War, with Elucidations of the Sicilian Odes of Pindar* (London 1872).

LÜBBERT, E. *Commentatio de Pindaro Clisthenis Sicyonii institutorum censore* (Bonn 1884).

LÜBBERT, E. *Commentatio de Pindari poetae et Hieronis regis amicitiae primordiis et progressu* (Bonn 1886).

LÜBBERT, E. *Meletemata in Pindari locos de Hieronis regis sacerdotio Cereali* (Bonn 1886).
[K. Seeliger, *PA* 17 (1887) 252–4.]

MACAN, R. W. "Pindar as Historian," *PCA* 28 (1931) 44–63.

*MARCUS, J. *De argumento politico Pindari carminibus intexto* (Trieste 1856).

MOMMSEN, T. See under "General and Miscellaneous."

SCHENK VON STAUFFENBERG, A. "Pindar und Sizilien," *HJ* 74 (1955) 12–25.

WACHSMUTH, W. *De Pindaro reipublicae constituendae et gerendae praeceptore disputationes II* (Kiel 1823–24).

WADE-GERY, H. T. & BOWRA, C. M. "The Historical Background of Pythians I-III," in *Pindar, Pythian Odes* (London 1928) 156–65.
WEBSTER, T. B. L. "The Court of Hiero," *Greek Interpretations* (Manchester 1942) 32–44.
WETER, W. E. *Encouragement of Literary Production in Greece from Homer to Alexander* (Diss. Chicago 1936).
VON WILAMOWITZ-MOELLENDORFF, U. "Hieron und Pindaros," *SPAW* (1901) 1273–1318.

25. CHRONOLOGY

BEAZLEY, T. W. "Fragment d'une liste de vainqueurs aux jeux olympiques (Papyrus d'Oxyrhynchus)," *RPh* 24 (1900) 61–5.
BENNETT, H. C. See under "Pythian Odes General."
BOWRA, C. M. "Pindaric Chronology," *Pindar* (Oxford 1964) 406–13.
CHRIST, W. "Zur Chronologie pindarischer Siegesgesänge," *SAWM* (1889) 1–64.
VAN COMPERNOLLE, R. *Étude de chronologie et d'historiographie siciliotes* (Brussels 1959).
FRACCAROLI, G. "Per la cronologia delle odi di Pindaro," *Museo Italiano di Antichità Classica* 3 (1888) 125–208.
    [C. O. Zuretti, *RFIC* 17 (1889) 547–8.]
FRACCAROLI, G. "La cronologia di Pindaro," *RFIC* 29 (1901) 385–416.
GASPAR, C. *Essai de chronologie pindarique* (Brussels 1900).
    [J. H. Lipsius, *PhW* 21 (1901) 417–21; M. Croiset, *JS* NS 3 (1905) 443–4; U. von Wilamowitz-Moellendorff, *DLZ* 22 (1901) 535–7; J. De Decker, *RIB* 45 (1902) 22–6; B. L. Gildersleeve, *AJP* 21 (1900) 470–2; Ph.-E. Legrand, *REG* 14 (1901) 102–3; C. O. Zuretti, *BFC* 7 (1901) 171–3.]
*LIPSIUS, J. H. "Beiträge zur pindarischen Chronologie," *BSG* (1900) 1–22.
LÜBBERT, E. *Commentatio de Pindari studiis chronologicis* (Bonn 1887).
POHLSANDER, H. A. "The Dating of Pindaric Odes by Comparison," *GRBS* 4 (1963) 131–40.
SCHMIDT, L. "Zur Chronologie der pindarischen Gedichte," *Commentationes philologicae in honorem Theodori Mommseni* (Berlin 1877) 48–63.
SCHMIDT, L. *Supplementum quaestionis de Pindaricorum carminum chronologia* (Marburg 1880).
SCHMIDT, L. *Quaestionis de Pindaricorum carminum chronologia supplementum alterum* (Marburg 1887).
    [L. Bornemann, *PA* 17 (1887) 254–5.]
SCHROEDER, O. "Pindarica I. Jahreszahlen," *Philologus* 53 (1894) 717–28 and 762.
SEVERYNS, A. *Bacchylide. Essai biographique* (Liège 1933).
WOLOCH, M. "Athenian Trainers in the Aeginetan Odes of Pindar and Bacchylides," *CW* 56 (1963) 102–4 and 121.

26. GAMES

Included here are studies on the origin and nature of the athletic festivals, on specific contests, and on Pindar's view of the athlete and athletics.

Biliński, B. *L'agonistica sportiva nella grecia antica. Aspetti sociali e ispirazioni letterarie* (Rome 1959).

Bowra, C. M. See under δαιμόνιος.

Bury, J. B. "Origin of the Great Games," *The Nemean Odes of Pindar* (London 1890) 248–63.

Christ, W. "Schnitzel aus einer Pindarwerkstätte," *SAWM* (1895) 3–31 (3–11 and 26–8).

Curtius, E. *Olympia. Mit ausgewählten Texten von Pindar, Pausanias, Lukian* (Berlin 1935).

Drees, L. *Der Ursprung der olympischen Spiele* (Stuttgart 1962).

Dyer, L. "The Olympian Theatron and the Battle of Olympia," *JHS* 28 (1908) 250–73 (261–4).

Ebert, J. *Zum Pentathlon der Antike* (Berlin 1963).

Eitrem, S. See under "Thought."

Faber, M. "Zum Fünfkampf der Griechen. Mit Beiträgen zur Erklärung des Pindar," *Philologus* 50 (1891) 469–98.

Fedde, F. *Über den Fünfkampf der Hellenen* (Leipzig 1889).

Frost, K. T. "Greek Boxing," *JHS* 26 (1906) 213–25.

Gardiner, E. N. *Athletics of the Ancient World* (Oxford 1930; reprinted with corrections 1955).

Gardiner, E. N. "Throwing the Javelin," *JHS* 27 (1907) 249–73 (266–70).

Gardiner, E. N. "Throwing the Diskos," *JHS* 27 (1907) 1–36.

Gardiner, E. N. "The Pankration and Wrestling," *JHS* 26 (1906) 4–22.

Gardiner, E. N. "Wrestling," *JHS* 25 (1905) 14–31 and 263–93.

Gardiner, E. N. "Notes on the Greek Foot Race," *JHS* 23 (1903) 261–91.

Gardiner, E. N. "The Method of Deciding the Pentathlon," *JHS* 23 (1903) 54–70.

Gardner, P. "The Pentathlon of the Greeks," *JHS* 1 (1880) 210–23.

Harris, H. A. "Greek Javelin Throwing," *G&R* 2nd S., 10 (1963) 26–36.

Holwerda, A. E. J. "De Pythiis bipartito actis," *Sertum Nabericum* (Leiden 1908) 167–73.

*Knapp, P. "Die Traditionen über die Stiftung der olympischen Spiele," *Correspondenz-Blatt für die Gelehrten- und Realschulen Württembergs* 28 (1881) 1–16.

Krause, J. H. *Olympia, oder Darstellung der grossen olympischen Spiele und der damit verbundenen Festlichkeiten, so wie sämmtlicher kleinerer Olympien in verschiedenen Staaten, nebst einem ausführlichen Verzeichnisse der Olympischen Sieger in alphabetischer Ordnung und einigen Fragmenten des Phlegon aus Tralles περὶ τῶν Ὀλυμπίων* (Vienna 1838).

Krause, J. H. *Die Gymnastik und Agonistik der Hellenen aus den Schrift- und Bildwerken des Alterthums*, 2 vols. (Leipzig 1841).

Macurdy, G. H. "The Defeated Contestant in Pindar," *CW* 22 (1929) 208.

Mahaffy, J. P. "On the Authenticity of the Olympian Register," *JHS* 2 (1881) 164-78.

Manning, C. A. "Professionalism in Greek Athletics," *CW* 11 (1917) 74-8.

Mette, H. J. "Die 'grosse Gefahr'," *Hermes* 80 (1952) 409-19.

Mie, F. *Quaestiones agonisticae imprimis ad Olympia pertinentes* (Rostock 1888).

Mie, F. "Die Festordnung der olympischen Spiele," *Philologus* 60 (1901) 161-79.

Montgomery, H. C. "The Controversy about the Origin of the Olympic Games. Did they originate in 776 B.C.?" *CW* 29 (1936) 169-74.

Moretti, L. *Olympionikai, i vincitori negli antichi agoni olimpici* (Rome 1957).

Myers, E. "The Pentathlon," *JHS* 2 (1881) 217-21.

Pihkala, L. & Gardiner, E. N. "The System of the Pentathlon," *JHS* 45 (1925) 132-4.

Pinder, E. *Über den Fünfkampf der Hellenen* (Berlin 1867).

Robinson, R. S. *Sources for the History of Greek Athletics in English Translation* (Cincinnati 1955).

Sakellariou, P. G. Τὸ ἀθλητικὸν ἰδεῶδες κατὰ Πίνδαρον, *PAA* 28 (1953) 163-76.

Sargeaunt, G. M. "The Greek Athletic Ideal," *Classical Studies* (London 1929) 82-107.

Unger, G. F. "Der Isthmientag und die Hyakinthien," *Philologus* 37 (1877) 1-42.

Vallois, R. "Les origines des jeux olympiques. Mythes et réalités," *REA* 28 (1926) 305-22 and 31 (1929) 113-33.

Woloch, M. "Athenian Trainers in the Aeginetan Odes of Pindar and Bacchylides," *CW* 56 (1963) 102-4 and 121.

27. RELATIONSHIP TO OTHER WRITERS

General

Robinson, D. M. "Pindar and His Influence," *TAPA* 66 (1935) xxx.
Robinson, D. M. See under "Thought."

Greek

General

de Jongh, A. See under "General and Miscellaneous" (77–100).

Homer & Hesiod

Christ, W. See under "Games" (24–6). Homer.
Fitch, E. "Pindar and Homer," *CP* 19 (1924) 57–66.
Lübbert, E. *De Pindari studiis Hesiodeis et Homericis dissertatio* (Bonn 1881).
McKay, K. J. "Hesiod's Rejuvenation," *CQ* NS 9 (1959) 1–5.
Schwartz, J. See under "Scholia" (564–70). Hesiod.
Scott, J. A. *A Comparative Study of Hesiod and Pindar* (Diss. Chicago 1898).
 [W. T. Lendrum, *CR* 14 (1900) 63–4; R. Peppmüller, *WKPh* 16 (1899) 1197–1200.]
*Zeyss, O. *Quid Homerus et Pindarus de virtute, civitate, diis statuerint et quid in his locis differat utriusque poetae sententia* (Progr. Jena 1832).

Bacchylides, Corinna, Simonides

Bury, J. B. "Two Literary Compliments," *CR* 19 (1905) 10–11. Bacchylides.
Della Giovanna, I. "Bacchilide," *RFIC* 16 (1888) 465–503.
Fennell, C. A. M. "The relations between Bacchylides and Pindar," *PCPS* 76–78 (1907) 15–16.
Gentili, B. *Bacchilide. Studi* (Urbino 1958).
Goossens, R. "Pindare et Corinne," *RBPh* 14 (1935) 85–9.
Goram, O. "Zu Pindar," *Philologus* 16 (1860) 59. Bacchylides.
Guillon, P. "A propos de Corinne," *Annales de la Faculté des Lettres d'Aix* 33 (1959) 155–68.
Méautis, G. "Simonide et Bacchylide," *Pindare le Dorien* (Neuchâtel 1962) 80–97.
Michelangeli, L. A. "Della vita di Bacchilide e particolarmente delle pretese allusioni di Pindaro a lui ed a Simonide," *RSA* 2 (1897) 73–118.
 [O. Schroeder, *PhW* 19 (1899) 1603–5.]
Prentice, W. K. *De Bacchylide Pindari artis socio et imitatore* (Diss. Halle 1900).
Rose, H. J. "Pindar and Korinna," *CR* 48 (1934) 8.
Severyns, A. See under "Chronology." Bacchylides.
Von der Mühll, P. See under "*O.* 8.42–6" (55–7). Bacchylides.

Tragedy and Comedy

Brown, N. O. See under "History and Politics." Sophocles.
Finley, J. H. See under "General and Miscellaneous." Aeschylus.
Forbes, P. B. R. "Law and Politics in the Oresteia," *CR* 62 (1948) 99–104.
Kuithan, J. W. *Versuch eines Beweises, dass wir in Pindars Siegeshymnen Urkomödien übrig haben, welche auf Gastmahlen gesungen wurden; und neue Grundideen über die griechische Prosodie* (Dortmund 1808).
> [A. Boeckh, *Heidelbergische Jahrbücher der Literatur für Philologie* 2 (1809). Also in *Gesammelte Kleine Schriften* 7 (Leipzig 1872) 141–58.]

Macurdy, G. H. See under "*P*. 9.23–5." Euripides.
Schlesinger, A. C. "Indications of Parody in Aristophanes," *TAPA* 67 (1936) 296–314.
Seymour, T. D. "On the Date of the Prometheus of Aeschylus," *TAPA* 10 (1879) 111–24.

Philosophy

Bowra, C. M. See under "Style and Imagery." Parmenides.
Crusius, O. "Heraklit und Pindar," *BBG* 49 (1913) 227–31.
Duchemin, J. "Platon et l'héritage de la poésie," *REG* 68 (1955) 12–37.
Fränkel, H. "A Thought Pattern in Heraclitus," *AJP* 59 (1938) 309–37 (318 n. 18, 320 n. 24, 326 n. 38).
Friedländer, P. See under "Fr. 52h.18–20." Plato.
des Places, E. See under "General and Miscellaneous." Plato.

History and Oratory

Christ, W. See under "Games" (28–30). Herodotus.
Conrotte, E. "Pindare et Isocrate. Le lyrisme et l'éloge funèbre," *MB* 2 (1898) 168–87.
Cook, A. B. "Associated Reminiscences," *CR* 15 (1901) 338–45 (343). Thucydides.
Karydes, G. P. Ποῖοι τῶν πρὸ τοῦ Ἡροδότου γραψάντων ἐπέδρασαν ἐπ' αὐτόν, *Platon* 3 (1951) 174–87.
Livingstone, R. W. See under "Thought." Herodotus.
Smith, C. F. "Poetic Words in Thucydides," *TAPA* 23 (1892) XLVIII–LI.

Post-classical

Clapp, E. B. "Two Pindaric Poems of Theocritus," *CP* 8 (1913) 310–16.
Coleman-Norton, P. R. "St. Chrysostom's Use of the Greek Poets," *CP* 27 (1932) 213–21 (217).
Helmbold, W. C. & O'Neil, E. N. *Plutarch's Quotations* (*APA* Monograph 19, London 1959) 55–6.
Mondino, M. "Di alcune fonti di Quinto Smirneo II—Quinto Smirneo e la poesia lirica," *RSC* 5 (1957) 18–19.
Schläpfer, H. *Plutarch und die klassischen Dichter* (Zürich 1950) 38–41.

SMILEY, M. T. "Callimachus' Debt to Pindar and Others," *Hermathena* 18 (1919) 46–72.
STEFĂNESCU, N. I. "Poeţii lirici Pindar şi Bacchilyde în opera lui Clement Alexandrinul," *Ortodoxia* 12 (1960) 240–52.
ZIEGLER, K. See under "Fr. 89a." Callimachus.

LATIN

General (Except Horace)

BRAGA, D. *Catullo e i poeti greci* (Messina 1950) 17–21.
BROZEK, M. "De Prudentio-Pindaro Latino," *Eos* 49 (1957–58) 123–50.
BROZEK, M. "Pindar i pindaryzm w starożytnej literaturze lacińskiej," *Meander* 20 (1965) 83–94.
GARROD, H. W. See under "*O*. 1.115b" (133). Catullus.
GRUENEBERG, A. *De Valerio Flacco imitatore* (Diss. Berlin 1893) 20–3.
NARDI, C. "Reminiscenze Pindariche in Virgilio," *ANTIΔΩPON Hugoni Henrico Paoli oblatum* (Genoa 1956) 242–9.
STURNIOLO, L. "Affinità e differenze nelle concezioni pessimistiche di Pindaro, Lucrezio e Leopardi," *MC* NS 1 (1947) 159–66.

Horace

BLONDEL, F. *Comparaison de Pindare et d'Horace* (Paris 1673 and Amsterdam 1686). It was translated into English by J. Davies (London 1680, repr. 1696) and into Latin by J. Berkel (Leiden 1704).
BORZSÁK, I. "Descende caelo...," *AAntHung* 8 (1960) 369–86.
COSTER, R. See under "*O*. 12 General."
FONTAINE, J. "Les racines de la sagesse horatienne," *IL* 11 (1959) 113–24.
*GOTTSCHALK, A. *Vergleichung des Horaz mit Pindar* (Neuwied 1865).
HARMS, E. *Horaz in seinen Beziehungen zu Pindar* (Diss. Marburg 1936).
HIGHBARGER, E. L. "The Pindaric Style of Horace," *TAPA* 66 (1935) 222–55.
*KRAUSE, E. F. *Horaz und die griechischen Lyriker* (Hanover 1907).
MOGGIO, V. "Pindaro ed Orazio (Pindaro Ol. II – Orazio C. I)," *BSI* 6 (1893) 77–8.
NORBERG, D. *L'Olympionique, le Poète et leur renom éternel. Contribution à l'étude de l'ode I, 1 d'Horace* (Uppsala 1945).
PITZALIS, L. "Il motivo ispiratore di Horat. Carm. IV 8," *GIF* 2 (1949) 329–40.
*PUEHRINGER, A. *Horatiana, sive de ratione quae intercedit inter Horatium et poetas lyricos Graecos* (Progr. Melk 1897).
*RECHNITZ, W. "Horace's Prayer to Apollo Palatinus," *Occident and Orient. Gaster anniversary volume* (London 1936) 488–91.
*RUMMEL, E. J. P. *Horatius quid de Pindaro indicaverit et quomodo carmina eius suum in usum converterit* (Progr. Rawitsch 1892).
SMERDEL, T. "Horace sur le poète Pindare," *ŽAnt* 8 (1958) 21–5.
STEINMETZ, P. "Horaz und Pindar," *Gymnasium* 71 (1964) 1–17.

Waszink, J. H. "Horaz und Pindar," *A&A* 12 (1966) 111–24.
Whitaker, C. W. "A Note on Horace and Pindar," *CQ* NS 6 (1956) 221–4.
Wimmel, W. "Recusatio-Form und Pindarode," *Philologus* 109 (1965) 83–103.

Non-Classical

Benn, M. B. *Hölderlin and Pindar* ('s-Gravenhage 1962).
  [E. C. Mason, *AUMLA* 20 (1963) 393–5; J. Peiffer, *RBPh* 44 (1966) 297–8; V. Zernin, *Comparative Literature* 17 (1965) 177–82.]
Bergk, T. "Anecdoton Pindaricum," *ZA* 5 (1847) 1–6. Anonymous.
Campbell, L. "Milton and Pindar," *CR* 8 (1894) 349.
Galiano, F. M. See under "Fr. 110.1." Galdós.
Galiano, F. M. "Píndaro y Ben Quzmán: Coincidencia, no influencia," *EClás* 8 (1964) 210–11.
Goldstein, H. D. "Anglorum Pindarus: Model and Milieu," *Comparative Literature* 17 (1965) 299–310. Cowley.
von Hellingrath, N. *Pindarübertragungen von Hölderlin* (Jena 1911).
Highet, G. *The Classical Tradition* (Oxford 1949) 230–44 and 250–2.
*Hines, L. "Pindaric Imagery in G. M. Hopkins," *Month* 215 (1963) 294–307.
Keppeler, E. R. *Die Pindarische Ode in der deutschen Poesie des 17. und 18. Jahrhunderts* (Diss. Tübingen 1911).
von Kloch-Kornitz, P. See under "*N*. 6 General." Goethe.
La Penna, A. "De Foscolo et Pindaro adnotatiuncula," *Maia* 7 (1955) 143–4.
Lempicki, Z. "Pindare jugé par les gens de lettres du XVIIe et du XVIIIe siècle," *BAPC* (1930) 28–39.
Lendrum, W. T. "Milton and Pindar," *CR* 9 (1895) 10–11.
Marasso, A. *Píndaro en la literatura Castellana* (Buenos Aires 1930). Also in *Humanidades* 21 (1930) 69–105.
Muster, W. "Hölderlin y sus versiones de Píndaro," *EClás* 3 (1956) 359–72.
Peyre, H. *L'influence des littératures antiques sur la littérature française moderne* (New Haven 1941).
Philippson, L. "Pindar und David. Eine vergleichende Skizze," *Allgemeine Zeitung des Judenthums* 46 (1882) 201–5, 217–21, 237–42, 269–71.
Rüdiger, H. See under "*O*. 2.86–8." Dante and Robert Greene.
Schneidewin, F. W. "Anecdoton Pindaricum," *Philologus* 1 (1846) 421–42. See also G. Hermann's letter to Schneidewin, *Philologus* 1 (1846) 584–6, reprinted in *Opuscula* 8 (Leipzig 1877) 90–3. Anonymous.
Silver, I. *The Pindaric Odes of Ronsard* (Paris 1937).
  [D. S. Robertson, *CR* 54 (1940) 138–9; A. Henry, *AC* 8 (1939) 495–6; G. Tyler, *CW* 33 (1939) 41–2.]
Silver, I. "Ronsard and Du Bellay on their Pindaric Collaboration," *Romanic Review* 33 (1942) 3–25.
Smerdel, T. "Un Latinista sopre il poeta Pindaro," *ŽAnt* 8 (1958) 99–100. Josip Čobarbnić.

STURNIOLO, L. "Affinità e differenze nelle concezioni pessimistiche di Pindaro, Lucrezio e Leopardi," *MC* NS 1 (1947) 159–66.
THOMSON, J. A. K. *Classical Influences on English Poetry* (London 1951) 141–6.
TREVELYAN, H. *Goethe and the Greeks* (Cambridge 1942).
TYRRELL, R. Y. "Milton and Pindar," *CR* 9 (1895) 11–12.
VALMAGGI, L. "Pindaro e Parini," *BFC* 22 (1916) 272–8.
VÜRTHEIM, J. "Erasmianum," *CR* 30 (1916) 72–3, 128, and 175.
ZUCKER, F. "Die Bedeutung Pindars für Goethes Leben und Dichtung," *Das Altertum* 1 (1955) 171–86.
ZUNTZ, G. *Über Hölderlins Pindar-Übersetzung* (Marburg 1928).
   [W. Koch, *DLZ* 50 (1929) 1388–91; *LZB* 80 (1929) 1267.]

28. LEXICA

BINDSEIL, H. E. *Concordantiae omnium vocum carminum integrorum et fragmentorum Pindari ad modum concordantiarum biblicarum primum elaboratae* (Berlin 1875).

DAMM, C. T. *Novum lexicon Graecum; etymologicum et reale, cui pro basi substratae sunt, concordantiae et elucidationes Homericae et Pindaricae* (Berlin 1765). New ed. by J. M. Duncan (Glasgow & London 1824).

DUNCAN, J. M. *Novum lexicon Graecum ex C. D. Dammii lexico Homerico-Pindarico vocibus secundum ordinem literarum dispositis retractum emendavit et auxit* V. C. F. Rost (Leipzig 1836).

FATOUROS, G. *Index Verborum zur frühgriechischen Lyrik* (Heidelberg 1966).

GALIANO, M. F. "Lexicon Pindaricum," *Emerita* 12 (1944) 191.

*PORTUS, A. *Lexicon Pindaricum* (Hanover 1606).

RUMPEL, J. *Lexicon Pindaricum* (Leipzig 1883, repr. Hildesheim 1961).

29. BIBLIOGRAPHY

BERNARDINI, P. "Rassegna critica delle edizioni, traduzioni e studi pindarici dal 1958 al 1964 (1965)," *Quaderni Urbinati di cultura classica* 2 (1966) 136–93.

BOEHMER, E. *Verzeichniss der Pindarsammlung* (Bonn 1891).

BOGNER, H. "Bericht über die Literatur zu Pindar und Bakchylides 1928–1933 (1934)," *JAW* 251 (1936) 87–109.

BORNEMANN, L. "Jahresbericht über Pindar seit 1879, 1885–1887, 1888–1890, 1891, 1892–1896, 1897–1900, 1901–1902," *JAW* 42 (1885) 52–122, 50 (1887) 21–33, 67 (1891) 1–28, 71 (1892) 268–91, 92 (1897) 205–32, 104 (1900) 165–80, 117 (1903) 110–37.

BORNEMANN, L. "Pindar (1903–1927) und Bakchylides (1908 ff.)," *JAW* 216 (1928) 131–86.

CESSI, C. "Bollettino bibliografico: Letteratura greca (1926–1930): Poesia lirica," *Aevum* 6 (1932) 301–38 (316–19).

FOCK, G. *Catalogus Dissertationum Philologicarum Classicarum* (Leipzig 1894, 1910[2], 1937[3], repr. Hildesheim 1963).

FOSTER, F. M. K. *English Translations from the Greek. A Bibliographical Survey* (New York 1918) 87–90.

GLEDITSCH, H. "Jahresbericht über die Erscheinungen auf dem Gebiete der griechischen und römischen Metrik," *JAW* 102 (1899) 1–64 (28–30); 125 (1905) 1–85 (48–50); 144 (1909) 75–156 (106–8).

KIRKWOOD, G. M. "A Survey of Recent Publications concerning Classical Greek Lyric Poetry," *CW* 47 (1953) 33–42 and 49–54 (51–4).

VAN OOTEGHEM, J. "Bibliotheca graeca: La poésie lyrique grecque II: Pindare," *LEC* 9 (1940) 69 73 and 29 (1961) 31 3.

PEYRE, H. *Bibliographie critique de l'Hellénisme en France de 1843 à 1870* (New Haven 1932).

ROUNDS, D. *Articles on Antiquity in Festschriften. An Index* (Cambridge, Mass. 1962).

SCHNEIDEWIN, F. W. "Jahresberichte. Pindar," *Philologus* 2 (1847) 705–39.

SCHROEDER, O. "Griechische Lyriker," *JPhV* 5 (1879) 50–8 (50–6), 132; 8 (1882) 41–66 (41–56); 11 (1885) 339–69 (341–58).

THUMMER, E. "Der Forschungsbericht Pindaros 1. Bericht umfassend die Jahre 1945 bis 1957 (1958)," *AAHG* 11 (1958) 65–88.

THUMMER, E. "Der Forschungsbericht Pindaros 2. Bericht umfassend die Jahre 1959 (1958) bis 1966," *AAHG* 19 (1966) 289–322.

YOUNG, D. C. "Pindaric Criticism," *The Minnesota Review* 4 (1964) 584–641.

30. GENERAL AND MISCELLANEOUS

AMBROSOLI, F. "Pindaro (Lezione inedita)," *Letteratura greca e latina. Scritti editi e inediti*, vol. 2 (Milan 1878) 66–93.
ASOPIOS, K. Τῆς εἰς Πίνδαρον εἰσαγωγῆς, γενομένης ἐν τῷ Ὀθωνείῳ Πανεπιστημίῳ κατὰ τὴν Χειμερινὴν ἑξαμηνίαν τοῦ 1842–1843 σχολαστικοῦ ἔτους σύνοψις (Athens 1843).
*BARTELS, C. F. *Sendschreiben an Hrn. V. F. L. Petri in Braunschweig* (Potsdam 1831).
BIPPART, G. *Pindar's Leben, Weltanschauung und Kunst* (Jena 1848).
BOECKH, A. *Ueber die kritische Behandlung der Pindarischen Gedichte* (Berlin 1820–21). Also in *Gesammelte Kleine Schriften* 5 (Leipzig 1871) 248–396.
BÖHMER, W. *Bemerkungen über Pindar* (Progr. Stettin 1829).
BONNARD, A. "Pindar, Prince of Poets and Poet of Princes," *Greek Civilization from the Antigone to Socrates*, trans. by A. L. Sells (London and New York 1959) 104–24.
BORCHARDT, R. "Einleitung in das Verständnis der pindarischen Poesie," *PROSA II* (Stuttgart 1959) 131–234.
BOWRA, C. M. *Pindar* (Oxford 1964).
  [G. M. Kirkwood, *CW* 59 (1965) 51–2; W. B. Stanford, *Hermathena* 101 (1965) 63–4; A. Garzya, *P&I* 6 (1964) 309–10; M. Delaunois, *LEC* 33 (1965) 323–4; É. Janssens, *AC* 34 (1965) 576–9; J. A. Davison, *JHS* 86 (1966) 174–5; J. Lens, *Emerita* 33 (1965) 410–13; G. F. Gianotti, *RFIC* 93 (1965) 454–9; L. E. Woodbury, *Phoenix* 21 (1967) 56–63; M. Treu, *Gymnasium* 74 (1967) 149–53; É. des Places, *RPh* 3rd S., 39 (1965) 308–9; Q. Cataudella, *SicGymn* 18 (1965) 317–20.]

Table of Contents

1.	The Theory of Poetry	1–41
2.	Gods, Heroes, and Men	42–98
3.	Echoes of Politics	99–158
4.	The Athletic Ideal	159–191
5.	Manner and Mannerisms	192–238
6.	The Scope of Imagery	239–277
7.	The Treatment of Myth	278–316
8.	Unity and Variety in Structure	317–354
9.	The Poetical Personality	355–401
App. 1.	The Date of Pythian 11	402–405
App. 2.	Pindaric Chronology	406–413
App. 3.	Olympian 5	414–420

BOWRA, C. M. *Landmarks in Greek Literature* (London 1966) 106–16.
*BRIDEL, M. I. L. *Introduction à la lecture des odes de Pindare* (Lausanne 1788?).
*BROCKMÜLLER, I. I. D. *Dissertatio de ingenio Pindari* (Rostock 1807).

Brower, R. A. See under "*P.* 1 General." On the difficulty of translating Pindar.
Cadoux, T. J. "The Athenian Archons from Kreon to Hypsichides," *JHS* 68 (1948) 70–123 (112). On the date of Pindar's birth and death.
Camenz, C. W. T. *Pindari ingenium* (Misenae 1804).
Cerrato, L. See under "Structure and Unity." On the history of Pindaric criticism etc.
*Chytraeus, D. *Ex Pindari odis excerptae genealogiae principum veteris Graeciae, gnomae illustres etc.* (Rostock 1696).
Clausen, J. C. H. *Pindaros, der Lyriker. Einleitung* (Progr. Elberfeld 1834).
Cloché, P. *Thèbes de Béotie, des origines à la conquête romaine* (Namur 1952) 50–62.
Coppola, G. *Introduzione a Pindaro* (Rome 1931).

Table of Contents

1.	Antica e nuova poesia	1–21
2.	Le prime poesie	22–47
3.	La pietra di Tantalo	48–75
4.	La feconda Sicilia	76–99
5.	In medio stat virtus	100–122
6.	Ancora la Sicilia	123–139
7.	Conosci te stesso	140–154
8.	Rodi sposa del Sole	155–178
9.	Il mito di Giasone	179–192
10.	Gli eroi di Oinophyta	193–203
11.	L'uomo, sogno di un' ombra	204–216
12.	Aretá	217–228

Croiset, A. *La poésie de Pindare et les lois du lyrisme grec* (Paris 1880, 1886², 1895³).
Dedouvres, L. "La poésie lyrique dans l'antiquité I. – Pindare," *L'Instruction publique* 13 (1884) 752–3 and 768–70.
*Dedouvres, L. "De la poésie pindarique," *L'Enseignement chrétien* 13 (1894) 550–7.
Denis, J. "Pindare. – Néméennes III, IV, etc.," *Faculté des lettres de Caen. Bulletin mensuel* 2 (1890) 38–44 and 3 (1891) 67–78 (38–44). On the characteristics of the epinician.
Drachmann, A. B. *De recentiorum interpretatione pindarica. Moderne Pindarfortolkning. Kritiske og positive Bidrag. Accedit argumentum latine conscriptum* (Copenhagen 1891).
*Drachmann, A. B. *Pindar som Digter og Menneske* (Copenhagen 1910).
    [My., *RC* 2 (1911) 75.]
Duchemin, J. *Pindare poète et prophète* (Paris 1955).
    [M. de Oliveira Pulquério, *Humanitas* NS 8–9 (1959–60) xxiv–vi; P. Maon, *NRTh* 81 (1959) 556–7; Q. Cataudella, *SicGymn* 11 (1958) 125–6; P. Guillon, *Hum(RES) Lettres Class.* 35, 6 (1958–59) 22–3; J. C. Kamerbeek, *MPh* 62 (1957) 90–3; F. M. Combellack, *CP* 53 (1958) 179–81; L. Rouche, *BACILg* 6 (1958) 55–6; F. Daumas, *RHR* 154 (1958) 235–7;

E. Janssens, *RUB* 9 (1956–57) 341–3; M. F. Galiano, *EClás* 4 (1957) 46; V. Steffen, *Gnomon* 29 (1957) 145–7; J. Humbert, *RPh* 3rd S., 31 (1957) 108–10; É. des Places, *RecSR* 45 (1957) 452–4; P. Vicaire, *RA* 6th S., 50 (1957) 102–4; D. S. Robertson, *CR* NS 7 (1957) 109–11; A. Brelich, *SMSR* 28 (1957) 140–4; A. Tovar, *Emerita* 25 (1957) 537–8; L. A. Stella, *GIF* 10 (1957) 354–5; J. van Ooteghem, *LEC* 24 (1956) 398; J. Defradas, *REG* 70 (1957) 224–34; K. Marót, "Un nouveau livre sur Pindare et les recherches hongroises sur l'antiquité," *Annales Univ. Scient. Budapestinensis, Sect. Philol.* 1 (1957) 81–9.]

Table of Contents

1.	La chaîne aimantée de l'inspiration: les Muses	21–53
2.	Charis et Charites. La joie créatrice	54–94
3.	Les dieux	97–124
4.	Les allégories	125–153
5.	Les héros et les mythes	154–190
6.	La mystique de l'or, de la lumière et des couleurs	193–228
7.	Images et Symboles	229–265
8.	Poésie triomphale et symbolisme funéraire	269–296
9.	Le poète dispensateur de l'immortalité	297–334
10.	Conclusion	335–346

Eleopoulos, K. N. *Οἱ ἐπίνικοι τοῦ Πινδάρου. Εἰσαγωγή* (Athens 1935).

Table of Contents

1.	Ὁ Ἐπίνικος ὡς ποιητικὸν εἶδος	13–40
2.	Ὁ ποιητὴς Πίνδαρος	41–57
3.	Τὸ θέμα τῶν πινδαρικῶν ἐπινίκων	58–99
4.	Ἡ τεχνικὴ σύνθεσις τῶν ἐπινίκων	100–129
5.	Τὸ λεκτικὸν ὕφος τοῦ Πινδάρου	130–145
6.	Ὁ βίος τοῦ Πινδάρου	146–162

Ehrenberg, V. "Bemerkungen zu Pindar," *Polis und Imperium. Beiträge zur alten Geschichte*. Edited by K. F. Stroheker and A. J. Graham (Zürich & Stuttgart 1965) 337–45.

*Fináczy, E. "Pindaros élete és költészete," *EPK* 8 (1884) 225–37, 468–75, 668–82, 786–802.

Finley, J. H. *Pindar and Aeschylus* (Cambridge, Mass. 1955).
[E. M. Blaiklock, *CP* 53 (1958) 36–9; A. G. McKay, *Phoenix* 11 (1957) 176–8; B. A. van Groningen, *Mnem* 4th S., 10 (1957) 72–3; E. T. Vermeule, *CJ* 53 (1957) 95–6; É. des Places, *AC* 26 (1957) 188–9; J. Humbert, *RPh* 3rd S., 31 (1957) 286; F. Solmsen, *AJP* 78 (1957) 440–4; H. J. Rose, *CR* NS 7 (1957) 18–9; A. Maddalena, *RFIC* 85 (1957) 410–17; H. D. F. Kitto, *Gnomon* 29 (1957) 144–5; K. Nakamura, *JCS* 5 (1957) 197–9; W. B. Stanford, *Hermathena* 88 (1956) 105–7.]

FRÄNKEL, H. *Dichtung und Philosophie des frühen Griechentums* (New York 1951; 2nd ed. rev. Munich 1962) 483–576.

GABATHULER, M. *Hellenistische Epigramme auf Dichter* (St. Gallen 1937).

GENTILI, B. "Aspetti del rapporto poeta, committente, uditorio nella lirica corale greca," *StudUrb* 39 (1965) 70–88.

GILDERSLEEVE, B. L. "Brief Mention," *AJP* 37 (1916) 232–9. On translating Pindar.

GIRARD, J. "Pindare," *Revue des deux mondes* 44 (1881) 793–825. Also in *Études sur la poésie grecque* (Paris 1884, 1900²) 75–145.

DEL GRANDE, C. *La poesia di Pindaro* (Naples 1929). Also in *RIGI* 12 (1928) 133–42.

    [A. Puech, *REG* 43 (1930) 222; L. Previale, *BFC* 37 (1930) 28; E. Malcovati, *Athenaeum* NS 7 (1929) 283–4; N. I. Herescu, *RCl* 1 (1929) 76; E. Kalinka, *PhW* 50 (1930) 625–6.]

VAN GRONINGEN, B. A. "Pindarus en de wereld waarin hij leeft," *FL* 5 (1964) 57–66.

GUNDERT, H. "Der alte Pindar," *Mnemosynon Theodor Wiegand* (Munich 1938) 1–13.

HEDERICH, B. *De imitatione Pindarica commentatio* (Vittenbergae 1802).

HERMANN, G. *De officio interpretis* (Leipzig 1834). Also in *Opuscula* 7 (Leipzig 1839) 97–128.

*HERMANN, M. G. G. *Commentatio de conversione Pindarica* (Goerliz n.d.).

HOFFMANN, M. (ED.) *Briefwechsel zwischen August Böckh und Ludolph Dissen, Pindar und Anderes betreffend* (Leipzig 1907).

    [E. B. Clapp, *CP* 4 (1909) 329–31; U. von Wilamowitz-Moellendorff, *DLZ* 29 (1908) 592–4; O. Kern, *WKPh* 25 (1908) 1273–5.]

VON HUMBOLDT, W. "Pindar," *Sechs ungedruckte Aufsätze über das klassische Altertum*, edited by A. Leitzmann (Leipzig 1896) 34–54. Also in *Wilhelm von Humboldts Werke*, vol. 1 edited by A. Leitzmann (Berlin 1903) 411–29.

INSTINSKY, H. U. "Alexander, Pindar, Euripides," *Historia* 10 (1961) 248–55.

JAEGER, W. *Paideia: the Ideals of Greek Culture*, vol. 1 (Oxford 1939, 1945², 1946³, 1954⁴) 205–22. Translated by G. Highet from the 2nd German ed. of 1935.

JAX, K. *Die weibliche Schönheit in der griechischen Dichtung* (Innsbruck 1933) 36–58.

JEBB, R. C. "Pindar," *JHS* 3 (1882) 144–83. Also in *Essays and Addresses* (Cambridge 1907) 41–103.

JEBB, R. C. *The Growth and Influence of Classical Greek Poetry* (Boston and New York 1893) 126–56.

DE JONGH, A. *Pindarica* (Traiecti ad Rhenum 1845).

Table of Contents

1.	De Diis	7–43
2.	De rebus humanis	43–77
3.	De propria Pindari sapientiae laude	77–100
4.	Text, Latin translation and commentary of *O.* 1, 8–11	101–216

Jurenka, H. "Über die Wichtigkeit, die gegenwärtigen Richtungen und die Aufgaben der Pindar-Studien," *Verhandlungen der 42. Versammlung deutscher Philologen und Schulmänner in Wien 1893* (Leipzig 1894) 280–9.
    [B. L. Gildersleeve, *AJP* 15 (1894) 508; G. Fraccaroli, *BFC* 1 (1895) 245–6.]

*Jurenka, H. *Entwickelung des griechischen Epinikions bis auf Pindar* (Progr. Vienna 1895).

Jurenka, H. "Humor bei Pindar," *WS* 18 (1896) 91–8.

Kayser, L. "Vortrag über Pindar," *JPP* 112 (1875) 530–42.

Kemper, H. D. *Rat und Tat. Studien zur Darstellung eines antithetischen Begriffspaares in der klassischen Periode der griechischen Literatur* (Diss. Bonn 1960) 34–6.

Kowalski, J. "Pindar," *Meander* 2 (1947) 373–98. In Polish.

Laaths, E. "Die Feier des olympischen Kampfes. Pindars Siegesgesänge," *Die Neue Rundschau* 47 (1936) 791–800.

Lanciani, R. "I busti di Bacchilide e Pindaro nelle ville antiche," *RAL* 5th S., 6 (1897) 6–8.

Lattimore, R. "On Classical and English Poetry," *Phoenix* 6 (1952) 84–91.

Lefkowitz, M. R. "ΤΩ ΚΑΙ ΕΓΩ: The First Person in Pindar," *HSCP* 67 (1963) 177–253.

Lewis, D. M. "The Archon of 497/6 B.C.," *CR* NS 12 (1962) 201.

Lübbert, E. *Pindar's Leben und Dichtungen* (Bonn 1882).

Luppino, A. "Poetica Pindarica," *RAAN* 35 (1960) 165–73.

*Lutterbeck, A. B. *Die Freunde Pindar's* (Giessen 1865).

Macgregor, M. "A Professional Poet," *Leaves of Hellas. Essays on some Aspects of Greek Literature* (London 1926) 54–82.

Maddison, C. *Apollo and the Nine. A History of the Ode* (London 1960) 4–19.

Martha, C. "Pindare et le génie lyrique," *Revue Européenne* (1859) 742–70. Also in *Mélanges de littérature ancienne* (Paris 1896) 47–99.

Martinazzoli, F. "Pindaro in Pindaro," *A&R* 3rd S., 10 (1942) 153–71. See also "Pindaro," *Ethos ed Eros nella poesia greca* (Florence n.d.) 335–64.

*Maywald, J. *Pindaros gyözelmi dalairól* (Progr. Budapest 1883).

Merentitis, K. I. Ὁ ἔρως τῆς πατρίδος καὶ τῆς ἐλευθερίας παρὰ Πινδάρῳ (Athens 1967).

Merlet, G. *Etudes littéraires sur les grands classiques grecs et extraits empruntés aux meilleures traductions* (Paris 1898) 112–34.

Mitchison, N. *Black Sparta. Greek Stories* (London 1928).
    [D. S. Robertson, *CR* 42 (1928) 203.]

Mommsen, T. *Pindaros. Zur Geschichte des Dichters und der Parteikämpfe seiner Zeit* (Kiel 1845).

Mommsen, T. See under "Manuscripts" (Einige Bemerkungen, 26–33).

Morice, F. D. *Pindar* (Edinburgh and London 1879, repr. 1898).

Mueller, I. *Quomodo Pindarus chori persona usus sit* (Diss. Darmstadt 1914).
    [J. Sitzler, *BPW* 35 (1915) 993–5; *WKPh* 32 (1915) 700–1; A. Rehm, *DLZ* (1917) 419–20.]

NAUHARDT, W. *Das Bild des Herrschers in der griechischen Dichtung* (Berlin 1940) 27–42.

NEBEL, G. *Pindar und die Delphik* (Stuttgart 1961).

[W. Theiler, *Gnomon* 34 (1962) 829–31; E. Janssens, *RUB* 14 (1961–62) 343–4; F. Jouan, *RBPh* 40 (1962) 1339–43; J. A. Davison, *Erasmus* 16 (1964) 114–17.]

NORWOOD, G. *Pindar* (Berkeley 1945, repr. 1956).

[W. Marg, *Gnomon* 21 (1949) 334–9; E. S. Forster, *JHS* 65 (1945) 127–8; *G&R* 16 (1947) 43; W. C. Greene, *CW* 40 (1946) 4–6; D. M. Robinson, *AJP* 68 (1947) 332–4; T. S. Duncan, *CJ* 42 (1947) 511–3; H. J. Rose, *CR* 61 (1947) 12–3; É. des Places, *REG* 59–60 (1946–47) 456–60; P. Chantraine, *RPh* 3rd S., 21 (1947) 170–2; A. Severyns, *AC* 14 (1945) 381–3; G. Smith, *CP* 41 (1946) 239–41.]

Table of Contents

1. The Approach to Pindar	1–21
2. His Subjects; His Vision of the World	22–43
3. Views on the Life of Man	44–71
4. Technique in Construction and Narrative	72–93
5. Diction, Symbolism	94–116
6–7. Symbolism	117–164
8. Pindar on the Art of Poetry; Conclusion	165–186
App. A. Symbolism in the Second Pythian	187–190
App. B. The Fifth Isthmian	191–196
App. C. Metre and Rhythm	197–210
Notes	213–271

NORWOOD, G. *Pindaro*. Traduzione di S. Croce (Bari 1952).

[D. Pieraccioni, *GIF* 6 (1953) 180; A. Rostagni, *RFIC* 80 (1952) 354–7.]

OLLIER, F. *Le mirage spartiate* (Paris 1933) 132–8. Pindar's idealization of Sparta.

*PAPAKONSTANTINOS, P. Πίνδαρος ὁ κορυφαῖος τῶν λυρικῶν, κατὰ τὰς ἀρχαίας πηγὰς καὶ τὰ νεώτερα τῆς ἐπιστήμης πορίσματα (Constantinople 1894).

PARODI, E. G. *Poeti antichi e moderni. Studi critici* (Florence 1923) 3–15.

PERREAU, A. *Pindare* (Paris 1817).

PERROTTA, G. *Saffo e Pindaro* (Bari 1935).

[O. Tescari, *Convivium* 7 (1935) 473–5; P. Collart, *RPh* 3rd S., 11 (1937) 171–2; E. Turolla, *ICS* 19 (1936) 47; A. Puech, *REG* 49 (1936) 320–1; A. Ronconi, *BFC* 42 (1935) 1–5; F. De Ruyt, *BIBR* 17 (1936) 244–5; W. Ferrari & G. M. Lattanzi, *MC* 6 (1936) 1–5; E. Kalinka, *PhW* 55 (1935) 913–15; C. M. Bowra, *CR* 49 (1935) 61–2; C. del Grande, *RIGI* 19 (1935) 105–7; A. Perosa, *A&R* 3rd S., 6 (1938) 38–49.]

PERROTTA, G. *Pindaro* (Rome 1958).

Table of Contents

1.	Pindaro nel giudizio degli antichi e dei moderni	5–31
2.	Il problema dell' unità dell' epinicio	32–66
3.	La poesia di Pindaro	67–141
4.	Translation and commentary of *O*. 1–13	142–303

PHLOROS, A. ʻΗ ποίησις καὶ τὰ σύνθετα τοῦ Πινδάρου, *Platon* 18 (1966) 289–99.

PICARD, C. "Les originaux retrouvés des statues grecques du Sérapeion de Memphis," *CRAI* (1951) 71–81.

PICARD, C. "Le Pindare de l'exèdre des poètes et des sages au Sérapeion de Memphis," *MMAI* 46 (1952) 5–24.

PITMAN, A. M. "A Study of Pindar," *Classical Studies in honour of C. F. Smith* (Madison 1919) 149–57.

DES PLACES, É. *Pindare et Platon* (Paris 1949).

[Q. Cataudella, *Paideia* 7 (1952) 310–12; H. Gerstinger, *AAHG* 6 (1953) 76–9; P. Louis, *RPh* 3rd S., 26 (1952) 238–9; J. Moreau, *RPhilos* 141 (1951) 136–7; D. Amand, *RB* 62 (1952) 185; V. Goldschmidt, *RHR* 138 (1950) 120–3; J. Tate, *CR* NS 1 (1951) 17–18; H. N. Porter, *AJP* 72 (1951) 448–50; A. Diès, *REG* 64 (1951) 519–22; J. C. Kamerbeek, *Mnem* 4th S., 4 (1951) 185–7; R. Mouterde, *MUB* 28 (1949–50) 307–8; L. A. Post, *CW* 44 (1950) 21–2; D. Tarrant, *JHS* 70 (1950) 79; É. de Strycker, *AC* 19 (1950) 252–4; M. Diez Presa, *Helmantica* 1 (1950) 269–70; P. Von der Mühll, *MH* 7 (1950) 242; B. Snell, *Gnomon* 23 (1951) 455.]

Table of Contents

1.	Les apologies de Pindare	21–30
2.	Patriotisme	31–40
3.	L'idéal dorien	41–49
4.	Respect de la divinité et religion personnelle	51–61
5.	Génie et talent	63–69
6.	Lignes et couleurs	71–78
7–13.	Platon	81–168
14.	Pindare chez Platon. Les citations expresses	169–179
15.	Conclusion – Affinités	181–185

RAUCHENSTEIN, R. *Zur Einleitung in Pindar's Siegeslieder* (Aarau 1843).

Table of Contents

1.	Ob und wie Pindar auf Gymnasien zu lesen sei	1–16
2.	Das Epinikion	17–46
3.	Pindar's Persönlichkeit	47–82
4.	Eigenthümlichkeiten der Pindarischen Kunst	83–127
5.	Ueber die Composition	128–151

RAUCHENSTEIN, R. *Zwei Abschnitte aus einer Einleitung zu Pindar's Siegesliedern* (Aarau 1843). Chapters 1 and 2 only of preceding entry.

REINHOLD, H. *Griechische Oertlichkeiten bei Pindaros* (Progr. Quedlinburg 1894).
  [J. Sitzler, *NPR* (1896) 17–19.]
ROMAGNOLI, E. *Pindaro* (Florence 1910).

Table of Contents

1.	Pindaro	9–99
2.	Polemiche Pindariche	100–127
3.	I contributi del Wilamowitz	128–181

ROME, A. "L'humour chez Pindare," *BCH* 70 (1946) 524–32.
ROSE, H. J. "The Epigram on Pindar's Death," *CQ* 25 (1931) 121–2.
SCHEFOLD, K. "Grabrelief eines Dichters," *AK* 1 (1958) 69–74.
SCHMIDT, L. *Pindar's Leben und Dichtung* (Bonn 1862).
  [F. Mezger (see under *P.* 10 General); L. Kayser, *Eos(S)* 1 (1864) 577–92.]
SCHMIDT, L. *Commentatio de iusta ratione interpretationis Pindaricae* (Marburg 1864–65).
*SCHNEIDER, J. G. *Versuch über Pindars Leben und Schriften* (Strassburg 1774).
SCHWARTZ, E. "Hesiod und Pindar," *Charakterköpfe aus der antiken Literatur* (Leipzig 1956[4]) 13–33.
SCHWENN, F. *Der junge Pindar* (Berlin 1940).
  [B. Snell, *DLZ* 61 (1940) 900–1; E. Kalinka, *PhW* 61 (1941) 436–7.]
SCHWENN, F. "Pindaros," *RE*, Erste Reihe 20, 2 (1950) 1606–97.
*SCHWICKERT, J. J. *De l'Allemagne littéraire et philologique et des travaux de critique et d'interprétation des Anciens, en particulier de Pindare. Pour servir de prolégomènes à une restauration complète des poésies conservées de cet auteur* (Luxembourg 1879).
SEIDENADEL, C. *De Pindaro non immodesto sui ipsius laudatore* (Progr. Karlsruhe 1855).
*SIMEONI, G. "L'arte greca ai tempi di Pindaro," *Pennellate letterarie* (Conegliano 1893) 19–24.
*SOMMER, C. *Du caractère et du génie de Pindare* (Diss. Paris 1847).
SYMONDS, J. A. *Studies of the Greek Poets*, vol. 1 (London 1873, 1879[2], 1893[3], repr. 1902) 322–52.
TREZZA, G. "Pindaro ed il lirismo greco," *Nuovi studi critici* (Verona-Padua 1881) 9–20.
*TURYN, A. "Sylwety greckie," *Wiedza i Życie* 9 (1934) 623–41.
TURYN, A. ΠΙΝΔΑΡΟΣ, *Νέα Ἑστία* 21 (1937) 436–41.
UNTERSTEINER, M. *Pindaro* (Milan n.d.).
  [C. Cessi, *Aevum* 6 (1932) 408.]

Table of Contents

1.	Evoluzione del lirismo greco	9–21
2.	La vita	23–50
3.	Le idee	51–80
4.	L'artista	81–146

*Valaori, J. "Pindare," *RCl* 1 (1929) 202–9.
*Vaszary, D. *Pindarus* (Progr. Raab 1873).
Vitet, L. "Pindare et l'art grec," *RDM* 25 (1860) 711–26.
Von der Mühll, P. "Weitere pindarische Notizen," *MH* 21 (1964) 168–72. ("Persönliche Verliebtheit des Dichters?")
Welcker, F. G. "Ueber den Plan einzelner Gesänge des Pindar," *RhM* 2 (1834) 364–90 (364–72). Also in *Kleine Schriften* 2 (Bonn 1845) 191–214 (191–8).
Winter, F. "Parallelerscheinungen in der griechischen Dichtkunst und bildenden Kunst," *NJA* 23 (1909) 681–712 (693–99).
Woodhead, W. D. "Fragment of a Pindaric Ode: Celebrating a Californian Heifer," *Phoenix* 5 (1951) 86.
Young, D. C. "Pindaric Criticism," *The Minnesota Review* 4 (1964) 584–641.
Yourcenar, M. *Pindare* (Paris 1932).
 [S. Lyonnet, *Études* 261 (1933) 364–5; J. van Ooteghem, *LEC* 2 (1933) 270.]